Teaching College-Level Disciplinary Literacy

Juanita C. But
Editor

Teaching College-Level Disciplinary Literacy

Strategies and Practices in STEM and Professional Studies

palgrave
macmillan

Editor
Juanita C. But
New York City College of Technology
City University of New York
Brooklyn, NY, USA

ISBN 978-3-030-39806-4   ISBN 978-3-030-39804-0   (eBook)
https://doi.org/10.1007/978-3-030-39804-0

This Palgrave Macmillan imprint is published by the registered company Springer Nature Switzerland AG.
The registered company address is: Gewerbestrasse 11, 6330 Cham, Switzerland

PREFACE

Each year, many students entering college lack the academic skills to succeed in content area courses. Research indicates that over 40% of students in their final year of high school lack proficiency in reading (Institute of Education Sciences, 2014). This means that a large number of beginning college students will encounter difficulties in reading college-level texts. This challenge is especially evident in introductory Science, Technology, Engineering and Mathematics (STEM) and professional studies courses. In these disciplines, not only are the literacy requirements particularly complex, the languages and concepts are also highly specialized. Therefore, content area instructors need to be equipped with pedagogical approaches to develop students' active reading and discipline-specific literacy skills to support their engagement in disciplinary discourse, thinking, and practices (Fang, 2012; Moje, 2008; Shanahan & Shanahan, 2008, 2012).

To address students' lack of college readiness in reading and to foster their learning in various disciplines, Reading Effectively Across the Disciplines (READ) was established at New York City College of Technology in 2013. READ takes a literacy instructional approach that is directed by disciplinary perspectives. The program's success relies on its model that allows literacy and content experts to work together to identify literate practices that are unique to each discipline and to embed them in content area instruction.

Teaching College-Level Disciplinary Literacy: Strategies and Practices in STEM and Professional Studies features the extensive work of literacy and content specialists in the READ program. It foregrounds the disciplinary literacy approach to college teaching and learning with in-depth discussions of theory and research, as well as broad illustrations and practices in various content areas. It discusses the program's design, professional development, assessment, and discipline-specific strategies and practices in five content areas, including Accounting, Architecture, Biology, Electromechanical Engineering, and Mathematics. With specific focus and design built on empirical evidence and actual instructional practices by content specialists, it is the first edited volume that addresses college-level disciplinary literacy in STEM and professional studies.

In this book, administrators, literacy specialists, and faculty from various content areas who participated in READ discuss:

- the structure and design of the program;
- the program's professional development cycle;
- the role, design, and implementation of READ assessments in improving disciplinary literacy;
- in-depth analysis of the specific literacy needs by experts in the disciplines;
- discipline-specific literacy approaches used to improve student learning in professional and STEM disciplines, including Accounting, Architecture, Biology, Electromechanical Engineering, and Mathematics;
- meeting the content literacy needs of a diverse student population;
- the development of both general and discipline-specific literacy strategies in student learning;
- the connection between reading and writing in fostering disciplinary literacy;
- the use of instructional technology to improve disciplinary literacy;
- the use of strategies in reading multimodal texts;
- the syntheses of strategies and practices to scaffold disciplinary learning;
- the integration of active learning and reading in different classroom settings;
- specially designed approaches to disciplinary learning in online and hybrid courses; and
- the research on students' academic reading with affective, self-efficacy, and metacognitive measures to inform our strategy design.

Part I, Teaching College-Level Disciplinary Literacy, offers an overview of the READ program and its components, with special focus on professional development and assessment.

Chapter 1, "READ: A Strategy-Based Approach to Developing Disciplinary Literacy Development," introduces the program's innovative approach to learning, particularly its structure and implementation to serve a diverse student population. It describes the program's objectives and how its components, which include professional development, discipline-specific assessments, peer-led team learning, and an online platform, work together to achieve our goals. Chapter 2, "Professional Development: Disciplinary Literacy Instruction," outlines the stages of the READ professional development cycles, from analyzing and decoding the disciplines and designing and developing discipline-specific strategies and practices to implementing them and evaluating their effectiveness. Chapter 3, "Assessment: A Tool for Improving Disciplinary Literacy," describes the design and implementation of discipline-specific assessments, which are instrumental in identifying students' literacy needs, informing the design of strategies, and improving disciplinary literacy learning.

Part II, Strategies and Practices in STEM and Professional Studies, focuses on disciplinary literacy instruction in five content areas.

Chapter 4, "Literacy Strategies and Instructional Modalities in Introductory Accounting," discusses ways to optimize student learning in introductory accounting courses in different instructional settings, including online, hybrid, and traditional classrooms. It also describes the implementation of varying approaches and strategies to develop students' disciplinary literacy in these settings. Chapter 5, "Teaching a Broad Discipline: The Critical Role of Text-Based Learning to Building Disciplinary Literacy in Architectural Education," offers an in-depth discussion of text-based teaching and learning in Architectural Technology, which has not been a well-established practice in this broad discipline, to cultivate students' disciplinary thinking and multimodal literacy. The focus of Chap. 6, "Poetry in Biology: Enhancing Science Education with Creative Writing," turns to creative writing, specifically the use of figurative language and poetry to engage students in learning key concepts and content knowledge in College Biology.

The final two chapters cover disciplinary literacy practices in Engineering and Mathematics respectively. Chapter 7, "Engineering Technology: Engaging Disciplinary Thinking and Doing," focuses its discussion on a sequence of electromechanical engineering courses, including a hands-on manufacturing lab, a foundational Electromechanical Engineering course, and an advanced Electronic Circuits course. It describes specific approaches used to enhance student learning in acquiring content knowledge and developing disciplinary thinking in each course in the sequence. Chapter 8, "Mathematical Literacy and Critical Thinking," discusses the development of beginning college students' mathematical literacy and overcoming math anxiety through observation, inquiries, communication, listening skills, vocabulary strategies, metacognitive skills, cooperative learning, and emotional engagement.

KEY FEATURES

The expertise represented in this edited volume covers a wide range of educational needs that include program design, classroom practices, and auxiliary educational supports in strengthening disciplinary literacy. This book includes key features and resources to foster disciplinary literacy practices in various ways.

1. It features the works and perspectives from administrators, faculty from various content areas, and literacy researchers and specialists that offer a comprehensive overview of the structure and components of a *successful disciplinary literacy program*, as well as detailed discipline-specific practices that enhance students' learning experience and performance.
2. It includes original disciplinary literacy research, practices, and examples in specific *professional and STEM disciplines.*
3. The design and formal use of *discipline-specific reading assessments* based on the City University of New York reading requirements serves as a tool to improve disciplinary literacy.
4. It introduces peer-led team learning in a disciplinary literacy model.
5. It highlights the use of different modes of writing, including formal, informal, and creative writing, to enhance disciplinary learning.
6. In addition to instruction in the traditional classroom, it provides examples of disciplinary literacy approach to lab, online, and hybrid learning.
7. It covers strategies for reading multimodal texts.
8. It highlights the diverse literacy needs of students in acquiring content knowledge.
9. It synthesizes learning theories and approaches.

10. Featured research tools and assessment rubrics can provide practical frameworks for planning disciplinary literacy programs.
11. It includes specially designed survey tools to evaluate students' academic reading activities, reading attitudes and habits to inform strategy designs and target problem areas.

Brooklyn, NY, USA   Juanita C. But
                                                      Pamela Brown

REFERENCES

Fang, Z. (2012). Language correlates of disciplinary literacy. *Topics in Language Disorders, 32*(1), 19–34.
Institute of Education Sciences. (2014). The nation's report card: Reading (NCES 2014-087). Washington, DC: Author, U.S. Department of Education. Retrieved from http://nationsreportcard.gov/reading_math_g12_2013/#/
Moje, E. B. (2008). Foregrounding the disciplines in secondary literacy teaching and learning: A call for change. *Journal of Adolescent & Adult Literacy, 52*(2), 96–107.
Shanahan, T., & Shanahan, C. (2008). Teaching disciplinary literacy to adolescents: Rethinking content-area literacy. *Harvard Educational Review, 78*(1), 40–59.
Shanahan, T., & Shanahan, C. (2012). What is disciplinary literacy and why does it matter? *Topics in Language Disorders, 32*(1), 7–18.

ACKNOWLEDGMENTS

This volume represents the efforts and expertise of colleagues who are current and past participants of Reading Effectively Across the Disciplines (READ) at City Tech. Since its inception in 2013, the program's continuous growth lends itself to the countless hours of their collaborations and contributions inside and outside of numerous content area classrooms. As educators and forerunners, despite the limited resources, competing priorities, and in some cases, no established models to follow, they have inspired readers and learners and have turned their work into transforming learning experiences.

We are grateful to our current faculty team and our colleagues Henry Laboy, Michael Loo, Jeremy Seto, Anna Matthews, Paul Salisbury, Melissa Yee, and Davida Smyth for their participation and contributions to piloting the READ initiative. We would also like to thank Nina Bannett, Sunghoon Jang, Andleeb Zameer, Sanjve Vaidya, Sandie Han, and Lucas Bernard for their support as department chairs, Julia Jordan and her staff in the Faculty Commons, Reneta Lansiquot for her very helpful suggestions, Carlos Estremera for designing the READ logo and Katherine Figueroa (Borough of Manhattan Community College) for generously sharing her wisdom and expertise. Finally, we would like to express our appreciation to Provost Bonne August for her continuous support.

Support for this project was provided by a PSC-CUNY Award, jointly funded by The Professional Staff Congress and The City University of New York.

CONTENTS

Notes on Contributors

Nadia Benakli is Associate Professor of Mathematics and Quantitative Reasoning Course Coordinator at New York City College of Technology, City University of New York. She holds a doctorate in Geometric Group Theory from Paris-Sud University in France. Before coming to City Tech, she taught at Princeton University and Columbia University. Her research interests are in geometric group theory, graph theory, and pedagogy in mathematics.

Pamela Brown is Associate Provost at New York City College of Technology (City Tech), the City University of New York. Prior to this position, she served for six years as Dean of the School of Arts & Sciences. She holds a PhD in Chemical Engineering from the Polytechnic University (now NYU Polytechnic University). She also served as program director in the Division of Undergraduate Education at the National Science Foundation (NSF).

Juanita C. But is Associate Professor of English and Reading Coordinator at New York City College of Technology, City University of New York. She is the principal developer of the Reading Effectively Across the Disciplines (READ) program and co-leads the college's Integrated Reading and Writing Co-requisite pilot program. She has co-edited a book on the literature of New York and published articles on college reading, disciplinary literacy, and literary studies.

A. E. Dreyfuss is a learning specialist in the field of Adult Learning and Leadership. She contributed to the development of the Peer-Led Team Learning model, which has been implemented in STEM disciplines as well as social sciences and humanities at over 200 colleges and universities. She trained peer leaders at the City University of New York (CUNY) campuses for 15 years. She co-founded the Peer-Led Team Learning International Society (www.pltlis.org) and has extensive experience designing materials, conducting training sessions for faculty, administrators, and staff, and evaluating programs. Her articles have appeared in peer-reviewed journals and conference proceedings. She holds doctorate degrees from Teachers College, Columbia University.

Michael Gotesman teaches Biology at New York City College of Technology, City University of New York. He specializes in Molecular Biology, Biotechnology, Cell Culture, and Polymerase Chain Reaction (PCR). He holds a PhD in Biology from the CUNY Graduate Center and was a post-doctoral fellow at the University of Veterinary Medicine, Vienna, Austria. He has published numerous research articles on virology and cytoskeleton.

Ohbong Kwon is Assistant Professor of Electromechanical Engineering Technology at New York City College of Technology, City University of New York. He holds a PhD in Electrical and Computer Engineering Technology from University of Florida. His areas of research include digital signal processing, digital design, and control systems.

Kenneth Markowitz is Professor Emeritus of Computer Engineering Technology at New York City College of Technology, City University of New York. For many years, he served as a program evaluator for *Accreditation Board for Engineering and Technology* (ABET), reviewing academic and curricular materials, key facilities, and institutional self-study reports of engineering programs across the nation. He was a project engineer before he joined the engineering faculty at City Tech.

Jason A. Montgomery is an architect, urban designer, and educator. He has worked in international practices where he led design projects in many parts of the world, including Costa Rica, Morocco, United Arab Emirates, England, and Egypt as well as many parts in the United States, including New York, California, West Virginia, and Montana. His work focuses on the nature of place, building tectonics, rural and urban space. He taught at University of Notre Dame's Rome Program, Yale University, and Andrews

University. He holds an MA in Architecture from the University of Wales and is Assistant Professor of Architectural Technology at New York City College of Technology, City University of New York.

Robert Ostrom is Associate Professor of English at New York City College of Technology, City University of New York. He has published three books of poetry. He co-leads the READ program.

Rachel Raskin is Assistant Professor of Accounting at New York City College of Technology, City University of New York. She holds an MS degree in Accounting from Brooklyn College. Before beginning her career in teaching, she worked as a financial analyst in the private sector. While at PricewaterhouseCoopers, she served clients in the banking and capital markets industry.

Estela Rojas is Professor of Mathematics at New York City College of Technology (City Tech), City University of New York. She holds a doctorate in Mathematics Education from Teachers College at Columbia University. She was the director of the Learning Communities Title V Program at City Tech. For the last 23 years, she has given national and international professional development and workshops on pedagogy and created learning communities at high school and university levels and has served as a consultant in education at several educational institutions. She is one of the leaders of the Strong Start to Finish (SSTF) Mathematics Initiative Team (MIT) at CUNY. She has received several awards and grants.

Chen Xu is Assistant Professor of Electromechanical Engineering Technology at New York City College of Technology, City University of New York. She holds a PhD in Biomedical Engineering from University of Connecticut. Her research interests are engineering education and biomedical optics.

LIST OF FIGURES

LIST OF TABLES

PART I

Teaching College-Level Disciplinary Literacy

CHAPTER 1

READ: A Strategy-Based Approach to Disciplinary Literacy Development

Juanita C. But and Pamela Brown

As college readiness is continuously in decline (ACT, 2019), more first-year college students nationwide are underprepared for the academic tasks required in foundational courses across the curriculum. This can be attributed to their lack of academic skills, prior knowledge (Fisher, 2004; Hewson & Hewson, 1983), and active learning strategies to succeed in college (Freeman et al., 2014; Walczyk & Ramsey, 2003). Among others, "A major risk factor of academic preparedness is low reading ability" (Perin, 2018, p.183), and this deficit is compounded by the increasing reading requirements in higher education (Bowen & Berry, 2017), which makes learning in the disciplines challenging, especially in introductory college courses. First-year students often find college readings demanding, due to the use of specialized language, high readability levels (Armstrong, Stahl, & Kantner, 2015), complex concepts, a high density of technical vocabulary, and the requirements of prior knowledge in the subject areas. Students need more advanced thinking, reading, and literacy skills to navigate the texts, process the specialized language, and organize the discipline-based

J. C. But (✉) • P. Brown
New York City College of Technology, City University of New York, Brooklyn, NY, USA
e-mail: jbut@citytech.cuny.edu; pbrown@citytech.cuny.edu

© The Author(s) 2020   3
J. C. But (ed.), *Teaching College-Level Disciplinary Literacy*,
https://doi.org/10.1007/978-3-030-39804-0_1

knowledge. They also have to redirect their focus from understanding surface features to mastering implicit conceptual discourses. This cannot be achieved without having a set of sound strategies. When approaching difficult texts, the difference between a novice and a content expert is that the latter can deploy a range of strategies to generate meaning, analyze and evaluate arguments, and make connections while reading. Students cannot develop these strategies if they are not given models to follow or opportunities to learn, apply, and practice.

Conventional teacher-centered instructional approaches that focus on delivering content knowledge and skills are insufficient to address students' literacy needs in disciplinary learning. A study showed that the lack of appropriate active learning strategies is the main contributing factor to attrition in Science, Technology, Engineering and Mathematics (STEM) majors (Cannon, 1997). Among the active learning and instructional approaches that prepare students for academic success is an emphasis on literacy instruction in the content areas. Though STEM and literacy skills are often perceived as two different spheres of learning, they are intricately linked. As in the other content areas, literacy skills are essential to student success in the STEM disciplines, which "require the interpretation of technical texts, a vast knowledge of content specific vocabulary, critical thinking, and the ability to clearly communicate these complex concepts to others verbally and in writing" (Kaczmarek, 2016).

Historically, numerous studies showed the benefits of embedding literacy instruction in content area classes (Anders & Guizzetti, 1996; Bond, Bond, & Wagner, 1941; Herber, 1970; Huey, 1968; Moore, Readence, & Rickelman, 1983), with results warranting a call for all teachers to be reading teachers. These studies were based on the assumption that literacy skills are universally applicable to all content areas, and general reading and writing strategies can find expressions in a variety of content area classrooms (Herber, 1970).

While general literacy strategies are foundational to learning, they have limitations, mainly because the varying disciplinary literacy demands cannot be adequately met with general strategies. In some cases, the strategies students use may not be suitable or sufficient for the literacy and thinking tasks required by specific content areas. Overall, college-level texts are diverse in function and purpose, and "College academic discourse varies in terms of technical vocabulary, rhetorical structures, symbolic systems, and metadiscursive properties" (Bean, Gregory, & Dunkerly-Bean, 2018, p. 91).

In the past two decades, there has been a gradual shift in emphasis from general to discipline-specific instruction in content area learning. Expansive calls to engage students in disciplinary literate practices (Moje, 2008; Shanahan & Shanahan, 2012) are based on the observations that individual disciplines demand specific sets of goals and conventions in thinking, reasoning, and communication. These practices also require particular attention to the role of language in presenting knowledge, construing values, and creating discipline-specific texts (Fang, 2012). The design and implementation of disciplinary literacy approaches are therefore rooted in the specialized knowledge and cognitive processes. In order to develop deep conceptual knowledge in a discipline, students are required to adopt the habits of thinking and practices valued and used by the discipline (McConachie and Petrosky, 2009). With the help of literacy specialists, content area experts and instructors can effectively identify these tools and practices (Moje, 2008).

1.1   COLLEGE-LEVEL LEARNING AND DISCIPLINARY LITERACY

Though disciplinary literacy practices are at the forefront of secondary education (grades 6 to 12) as they are necessitated by curricular reforms and education policies, they have not been widely adopted in college-level courses, where disciplinary literacy is critical to effective and lifelong learning. In addition to the literacy demands, cognitive processes and text materials in college content area courses are far more complex than that in high school courses (Conley, 2007, 2008). However, college content area instructors seldom actively engage students in discipline-specific literate practices (Armstrong et al., 2015) to encourage active reading and specialized habits of thinking. The deficit in literacy engagement in the disciplines can be attributed to:

- *The lack of exposure to and utilization of disciplinary literacy practices among college instructors*
  Though college-level content area faculty are experts in their disciplines and have in-depth knowledge in research and scholarship, many of them have limited perception of their roles as literacy educator (Bean, Gregory, & Dunkerly-Bean, 2018) and are not equipped with pedagogical approaches to teach and model the thinking processes and strategies they use in ways that enable novices to participate in the disciplinary discourses and perform disciplinary tasks effectively.

- *The lack of institutional support to offer incentives and train faculty to redesign courses and employ teaching practices to meet students' literacy needs in individual disciplines*

  Higher educational institutions are often confronted with competing needs and priorities, such as student support, research, and infrastructure updates. When selecting to support various initiatives, college administrators do not always prioritize professional and curricular development, especially when there is no external funding to cover adjunct faculty compensation and course release time for point faculty to oversee training and strategy implementation. While there are other established pedagogical support programs such as Writing Across the Curriculum and Quantitative Reasoning that are enjoying central roles in higher education and institutionalized resources, disciplinary literacy programs that fortify these existing programs are not as widely supported (Armstrong & Stahl, 2017).

- *Content area faculty members do not receive sufficient institutional rewards for their efforts in fostering teaching and learning*

  With increasing demands to engage in more research and scholarship, faculty members are left with devoting limited time and resources to develop teaching approaches, including disciplinary literacy practices, which often involve extra work in course redesign and efforts to experiment with strategies and evaluate their effectiveness. The perception of privileging the rewards of engaging in research over improving teaching practices adversely affects faculty involvement in pedagogical reforms (Fairweather, 2005). Without systematic policy changes and re-prioritization, institutions tend not to allocate resources to support disciplinary literacy training and practices, and, as a result, faculty members lack incentives for participating in pedagogical reforms that promote deeper learning and motivation among students.

- *The lack of an efficient way to balance between the time allocated for content coverage and disciplinary literacy practices*

  One way in which college courses differ from high school courses is that the instructional pacing for college courses is significantly accelerated (Conley, 2007). In STEM courses, instructors often express that the amount of material needed to be covered and the rapid pacing of classroom instruction often leave them with no time to assess if students can readily grasp the concepts and topics taught. Some instructors tend to feel that literacy activities infringe on subject matter time (McKenna & Robinson, 2014). Though embedding disciplinary literacy practices in the content area classroom can effectively foster and assess student learning, instructors are less likely to prepare and apply such practices.

- *The importance of reading and writing are undermined in content area learning*

Reading to learn is not commonly practiced in many content area courses for various reasons. Research indicates that many students do not complete assigned readings, and a significant number of them are neither buying nor reading textbooks (Sappington, Kinsey, & Munsayer, 2002). Some students simply lack the necessary reading skills and strategies to comprehend and navigate complex college texts (National Center on Education and the Economy [NCEE], 2013). Outside of English and some science courses, most reading assignments for lower-level content area courses are intended for straightforward knowledge retrieval, with little expectation of analysis of what was read (NCEE, 2013). In some cases, there are also discrepancies between student and faculty perceptions of whether completing the assigned readings is actually essential for success in a course, while students viewing course texts as less important than lectures and/or PowerPoint slides (Schnee, 2018). Furthermore, faculty may not know effective evidence-based strategies or may be reluctant to address non-reading for fear of negatively impacting their teaching evaluations (Lei, Bartlett, Gorney, & Herschbach, 2010). Thus, the documented decline in reading compliance (Clump, Bauer & Bradley, 2004) can be attributed not only to students' lack of motivation or the required academic skills, but also to faculty's failure to convey the importance of reading for academic success, and thereby to apply active learning approaches to promote disciplinary reading (Freeman et al., 2014; Schnee, 2018; Walczyk & Ramsey, 2003).

In some content area courses, instructors often make no deliberate effort in developing students' discipline-specific reading and writing techniques. Some even eliminate this need by reducing literacy requirements in their courses, leaving no room for reading and writing activities. They may simply try to solve the problem by substituting the texts with lecture slides and explaining the reading to the students. Alger (2009) labels this instructional sidestep as workarounds, which preclude content area learning from literacy activities. Some instructors also assume that most of their students are capable of handling the material assigned (McKenna & Robinson, 2014) and perceive no need to scaffold the assignments with guided literacy supports. There are still other instructors who believe there is no need to support reading in their courses, which should only be done in pre-college settings. No matter what the reasons are, "literacy avoidance" in the content area classroom is "at odds with student learning needs and the reality of the subject matters" (Shanahan, Shanahan, & Misischia, 2011).

- *The lack of a systematic program to contextualize disciplinary literacy approaches that are based on collaborative efforts of content and literacy experts*

  Knowledge of teaching and learning strategies does not always translate into their implementation. Therefore, disciplinary literacy professional development cannot be limited to strategy introduction. Instead of asking content area faculty to apply literacy strategies, a preferred measure is to establish a disciplinary literacy program (Moje, 2008), in which literacy specialists and content area faculty work together to develop, implement, and evaluate discipline-specific strategies and practices. However, currently, there is a perceivable lack of such programs in higher education institutions.

- *The lack of transformative forces to cultivate teaching conceptions that promote active learning and reading*

  College teaching is deeply rooted in didactic lecture instruction; therefore, content knowledge is often delivered and imparted by the teachers rather than built and developed by the students. Until teaching practices of faculty move from a teacher-centered to a learner-centered approach, which allows the development of active learning and literacy strategies, and caters to the diverse needs of students, discipline-specific literacy practices cannot be broadly established in the content area classrooms.

1.2   Meeting the Challenges in Disciplinary Learning in a College of Technology

Although the needs for establishing disciplinary literacy practices are common in higher education across the disciplines, they are especially critical in STEM disciplines, which have seen a decline in students choosing to major in the fields and in the percentages of undergraduates continuing to graduate school (National Science Foundation, 1996; National Research Council, 1999). One of the contributing factors to these problems is poor teaching practices in college STEM courses (Seymour & Hewett, 1997), as instructional approaches play a crucial role in improving student learning in STEM (Smith, Jones, Gilbert, & Wieman, 2013).

Despite continuous discussion on pedagogical reforms in STEM education that address the urgent need for student-centered teaching, the predominant mode of learning in STEM courses is still traditional lecture with limited student engagement (Stains et al., 2018). It is no exception at New York City College of Technology (City Tech), the only college that primarily focuses on STEM education and professional studies in the City University of New York system. City Tech is one of the most diverse colleges in the nation, with an open admission policy and a student body that consists of predominantly first-generation college students. They come from diverse sociocultural and academic backgrounds, including a large number of English as Foreign Language learners and entering students who are underprepared for college courses.

The pedagogical challenges in STEM education at City Tech, like many colleges, are not limited to the lack of active learning approaches in the content area classrooms. More critical is that every semester a significant number of students who take STEM and professional studies courses lack the academic skills to succeed. As a result, the failure and attrition rates in some of these courses at the beginning levels are consistently high. Some faculty perceived the problems as direct results of students' inadequate quantitative reasoning and related cognitive skills or their lack of incentive to study. However, their lack of literacy skills and strategies was rarely considered as obstacles to their learning. In 2012, the results of a college-wide general education reading assessment revealed that around 70% of City Tech students were underprepared in reading in various content areas (But, Brown, & Smyth, 2017). Their lack of comprehension, vocabulary, and analytical skills were identified as major hindrances to their success in these courses. In response to the findings, Reading Effectively Across the Disciplines (READ), a college-wide program to improve student learning and disciplinary literacy was established at City Tech in 2013. The initial launch of the program was funded by a grant from the CUNY Office of Academic Affairs.

The primary mission of READ is to implement effective evidence-based literacy strategies and approaches to improve teaching and learning in content area courses. To achieve this, READ establishes a model that is based on the collaboration between literacy specialists and content area faculty. Together they identify discipline-specific practices, develop and implement strategies to support disciplinary learning, evaluate the strategies, and disseminate those that are effective. The core components of the program include:

1. *Professional Development.*
   The READ professional development activities are divided into stages and take various formats. Each stage caters to different audiences and meets specific needs. The initial stage consists of outreach workshops that offer introduction to general literacy approaches. These introductory workshops are open to faculty across the disciplines, with some specifically catered to new hires. The main purpose of the outreach workshops is to expose faculty to practices in literacy instruction, with specific examples to demonstrate how they are relevant, and can be applied to teaching and learning in their disciplines. READ literacy specialists lead these workshops, which are also held at the request of department chairs as departmental professional development.

   After going through the introductory stage, the faculty can choose to participate in subsequent READ training and collaborative team activities. At this stage, content area faculty work with literacy specialists to develop discipline-specific strategies and approaches and apply them in selected courses. To identify students' literacy needs and to evaluate the effectiveness of strategies used to improve teaching and learning, pre and post-READ assessments are administered, with specific focus on students' abilities to comprehend, analyze, apply, and evaluate text-based content knowledge. The assessment results are examined to inform modifications of existing strategies and the design and implementation of new ones. The READ team also discusses challenges in strategy implementation and troubleshoots problem areas.

   Twice a year, content area faculty participate in READ faculty workshops where they receive more in-depth training, engage in discipline-specific conversations on literacy instruction, share their practices, and compare results. The goals of these workshops are to exchange ideas, discuss challenges, reflect on the approaches they use, and disseminate best practices. Content area faculty who are new to the program, especially those who teach in the same disciplines as the existing READ faculty, are invited to participate. It is crucial for them to see the relevance of their colleagues' disciplinary literacy practices in the context of their content areas.

2. *Pre- and Post-READ Assessment*

Assessment plays a central role in the READ program. The pre- and post-READ assessments are designed according to the following guidelines:

- The assessments are discipline-specific and are relevant to assigned course work.
- The assessments are text-based, including multimodal formats.
- Texts used in the pre- and post-READ assessments have matching readability.
- Questions are written by content area faculty and literacy specialists.
- A standardized READ rubric based on the CUNY Reading Outcomes is used to guide the assessment design.
- Content area faculty and literacy specialists develop a scoring guide for each assessment.
- Content area faculty and literacy specialists collaborate on grading the assessments to ensure reliability.

The primary objective of the pre-READ assessments is to acquire a clear picture of students' specific literacy needs and challenges in each content area course. The results inform faculty on the type of interventions required, the design of instructional strategies, and their implementation. The post-READ assessments are designed to evaluate students' disciplinary literacy gains and the effectiveness of the strategies used.

3. *Peer-led Team Learning*

Peer-led team learning (PLTL) was introduced to City Tech in the mid-1990s to support STEM education by Chemistry Professor Victor Strozak. The philosophy and practices of PLTL are different from other cognitive support such as tutoring and recitation. Peer leaders are advanced undergraduate students who performed well in the courses they serve. PLTL emphasizes small group learning with special focus on the learning environment as a social context in which a diverse set of skills of interpersonal techniques intersects with academic skills to facilitate learning.

The implementation of PLTL in READ meaningfully synthesizes the techniques in traditional peer-led team learning contexts with disciplinary literacy approaches. An education specialist, using typical peer-training approaches (Gosser et al., 2001), trains peer leaders. Peer leaders also work closely with content area faculty who familiarize the peer leaders with the literacy strategies they are using in their courses and prepared materials, so that peer leaders can employ the same READ strategies in peer mentor sessions.

4. *READ OpenLab*

OpenLab at City Tech is an open-access teaching and learning platform with an array of applications. The READ OpenLab site consists of a main site and content area sites, in which faculty share strategies, practices, and research that promote disciplinary literacy. This resource is available for both READ faculty and those who are interested in literacy instruction.

Discipline-specific research by READ faculty, worked examples, and content area literacy survey results are some of the resources that help promote and develop disciplinary literacy approaches. The main READ OpenLab site and the linked READ content sites document the efforts and results and inform future works in the disciplines within and outside the program.

5. *READ Student Workshops*

Student workshops are held in collaboration with the First-Year Program to prepare incoming students for active reading in college learning. They open to students who are enrolled in courses that are not taught by READ faculty. With no specific input of content area expertise, these workshops aim mainly at teaching students general literacy strategies. However, the use of content area sample texts can serve as an entry point to expose students to discipline-specific practices and the foundation to develop strategies that support their learning in content area courses. Though the impacts of these workshops are not formally assessed, students self-report the strategies they plan to use in post-workshop surveys. Instead of prescribing discipline-specific strategies, these workshops introduce students to literacy tools and allow them to reflect on their applications in content area learning.

1.3   Getting Started: Literacy in the Content Areas

The READ program was launched in response to two institutional challenges at City Tech (But, Brown, & Smyth, 2017). The first was poor student learning outcomes in reading comprehension and analysis, that was part of the college's general education assessment—over 70% of students evaluated were found to struggle with college-level reading, and the second was gatekeeper discipline courses where over a hundred students had failed (Fall 2011). A City University grant was acquired to start an initiative to foster students' reading and literacy skills in content courses. It was used to provide course release time to two faculty members, a reading specialist and a faculty member in the disciplines (biology) to form a READ development team, which was later joined by faculty from several disciplines who served as content area liaisons. The initial charge of the team was to provide professional development, support course redesigns, and oversee discipline-specific READ assessments. Funding was also used to provide stipends to support peer mentors, in order to promote students' reading and literacy in the disciplines. Three content area courses were initially selected to participate: Biology I (BIO 1101), Essentials of Marketing (MK 1100), and Electromechanical Manufacturing Laboratory (EMT 1130).

Based on a review of 191 published report or organizational reform efforts, Henderson et al. demonstrated that in order for new institutional initiatives to likely be successful, they must: (1) align with institutional culture and beliefs and (2) include long-term (more than one semester) interventions. The main pitfalls of unsuccessful efforts were reliance on disseminating specific pedagogical materials and top-down directives for change (Henderson, Beach, & Finkelstein, 2011). It was thus recognized that in order to be successful this effort would require ongoing institutional support, faculty "champions" within each course, alignment with the goals and culture of the institution and participating departments, and effective assessment to demonstrate impact, in order to sustain funding and expand adoption. Ongoing support was recognized as critical, because, in order for instructors to implement READ strategies, they must modify their teaching practices to focus more on incorporating strategies to promote reading and embed disciplinary literacy into classroom discussions, quizzes, and so forth, and convincing students of the value of assigned readings.

The program was also designed to tie into the college's faculty evaluation system. Traditionally, college faculty in many disciplines view teaching and research as two separate spheres of their careers. As a result, many of them perceive that the more time they devote to teaching and improving their teaching means the less time they can spend on doing research and scholarship, which in many cases, carries more weight in their tenure and promotion evaluations. The design of READ is to knit teaching and research together to generate scholarship of teaching and learning (SoTL). One of the main tenets of SoTL is that "faculty ought to treat their teaching in the same way as they treat their research, and that teaching should not be an isolated, individual activity, but rather, should be grounded in the work of others" (Airey, 2011, p. 2). Therefore, knowledge of teaching and learning should be publicly shared and critiqued in the way that research is published and peer reviewed (Airey, 2011). Due to the expectation of rigorous assessment, participation in READ could contribute to teaching, service, and scholarship via educational publications and presentations, the activities needed for tenure and promotion.

The READ program began in the spring of 2013 by inviting all instructors of these courses to an introductory reading and literacy strategies workshop offered by an outside reading/literacy expert. The goal was to introduce faculty to the program and the various strategies that can be employed to promote reading and literacy practices in the disciplines. This was followed up by another workshop in the summer for those who committed to participate, in order to help them implement strategies and design meaningful pre/post assessments.

The immediate tasks for the READ faculty were to identify the literacy practices that students need the most to succeed in their disciplines. Content area faculty collaborated with literacy specialists to review learning outcomes, syllabi, and text materials to inform course restructuring and assignment redesign to facilitate teaching and learning. Subsequently, a set of faculty learning outcomes was designed for professional development that included understanding language functions and disciplinary text productions, setting purposes for assigned reading, scaffolding reading and writing assignments, active reading and vocabulary strategies, identifying appropriate strategies and approaches, and embedding them in the disciplinary instruction.

Professional development took place throughout the academic year. After the initial workshop, content area and literacy specialists collaborated to develop assignments and literacy approaches to be applied in the content area courses. Peer leaders were also recruited that summer in biology and electromechanical engineering technology, and they too were provided training on pedagogical theories, literacy strategies, and leading group discussions and peer workshops. The training emphasized that even though they are advanced students, they do not provide answers but instead ask leading questions to help the students discover knowledge themselves (Gosser et al., 2001). This approach worked to promote growth among students as active readers and independent learners.

Beginning in fall 2013, the READ development leaders started working individually with participating faculty, who were encouraged to select and customize research-based strategies and embed them in assignments and instructional routines. The development leaders visited classrooms to observe faculty implementation of discipline-specific strategies. They read the disciplinary texts and assisted with the design of pre/post assessments and provided guidance on the effective use of peer mentors to facilitate the use of literacy strategies in student workshops. This approach has continued each subsequent semester, with continuing faculty receiving sustained support as they hone their approaches and new recruits are introduced into the program.

1.4   Peer-Led Team Disciplinary Literacy Learning Model

One of the innovations of this program was the application of peer mentoring not only to promote content area learning but also to encourage active reading, vocabulary building, and higher-order thinking within the disciplines. This was accomplished by exposing the peer mentors to the READ strategies, in addition to the typical peer mentoring training. This aligns with broad initiatives to promote college-readiness and self-regulation, particularly among underprepared students.

Evaluation of peer mentoring across multiple campuses suggested that there were six critical components of successful peer mentoring programs (Gafney, 2001):

1. The peer-led team learning workshop is integral to the course and coordinated with other course components;
2. Course instructors are closely involved with organizing the workshops and training of peer leaders;

3. Peer leaders are trained and closely supervised, with knowledge of workshop problems and content, teaching and learning strategies, and small group leadership skills;
4. Workshop materials are challenging at an appropriate level, integrated with other course components, and designed to encourage active and collaborative learning;
5. Organizational arrangements promote learning, through factors including size of group (preferably six–eight students), space, time, and low noise level; and
6. At administrative and departmental levels, the institution encourages innovative teaching and provides logistical and financial support.

1.5   Program Effectiveness and Sustainability

As reflected by the feedback of participating faculty and students and the outcomes of the discipline-specific assessments, READ has been effective in improving students' disciplinary literacy in all participating courses. The program does not aim at any instant fix-up strategies which usually do not have lasting effects on improving teaching, as short standalone workshops often do not have an impact on teacher practice and student achievement (Bush, 1984; Yoon, Duncan, Lee, Scarloss, & Shapley, 2007). From the introduction of a new approach to its effectual implementation, a process of experimentations, repeated practices, and modifications is required. The strategies and practices that READ faculty developed and applied have evolved over time, as more research, classroom applications, and multi-modal assessments continuously help to identify areas that need development.

Most of the content area instructors in the program were new to the disciplinary literacy approach. They had to familiarize themselves with the concepts and purposes behind the learning outcomes before they could apply the strategies fluently and meaningfully to achieve their teaching goals. Even though it appears that a given disciplinary language is like a native language to the content experts in that field, it is not granted that they can make explicit the underlying structure and cognitive processes that the specialized language entails. As teachers in their disciplines, their primary mission is not just to deliver content knowledge proficiently but to promote students' discipline-based habits of thinking. A clear understanding of how the disciplinary language is produced and performed can facilitate faculty's instruction of novice students to access and use it to engage in the discipline-specific cognitive processes. READ provides the pedagogical opportunities for content area faculty to explore, negotiate, and develop the space for disciplinary literacy teaching and learning. As evidence-based strategies are learned and applied, READ faculty and their students make it possible to personalize them and enhance their implementations through creative discipline-specific practices.

Assessment is a critical component for sustaining the READ program, as it provides direct evidence of improved student learning and success (increased pass rates in READ sections), which is necessary for both recruitment of participating faculty and continued institutional support. More importantly, assessment in READ has been an important tool to inform the direction of professional development design and improvement of strategies and practices. However, maintaining a robust assessment schedule can be a challenging task for any disciplinary literacy program, especially when faculty members are already facing all sorts of increasing assessment demands. To achieve this, READ sustains its efforts and alleviates the burden of assessment by embedding discipline-specific assessments in the curriculum as tools to support disciplinary literacy learning. To prevent assessment fatigue, learning outcomes are assessed over a period of years.

Since its inception, READ has evolved into a multidisciplinary program with a faculty team that represents all of the three schools in the college, and a widening circle of faculty. In electromechanical engineering technology, READ has been expanded into multiple courses. Factors contributing to this success included demonstrable and sustained improvement in student learning and grade distributions, as well as incorporation of READ assessment into their existing assessment requirements for their accrediting agency (Accrediting Board for Engineering and technology, ABET). In architectural technology, READ has been implemented in all sections of the Building Technology course. READ also plays an important role in reorienting the architecture faculty's teaching conception to a text-based approach that is essential to building students' literacy in this broad discipline.

An ongoing challenge to sustained involvement has been that the teaching assignments of participating adjunct faculty may not consistently include the READ sections every semester. Adjunct faculty, whose teaching assignments depend on the vagaries of enrollment and departmental need, teaches over 50% of the sections at our campus. While upper administration does encourage chairs to guarantee assignments to READ faculty, and indeed this encouragement is used as a tool for recruitment of adjunct faculty, it is not always possible.

1.6   CONCLUSION

Each new READ course presents a set of new challenges and opportunities. With the accumulation of experiences and resources among the READ team members, the program has increased its capacity to expand to more disciplines. Trained practitioners of disciplinary literacy instruction can help build a repository of resources that inform future participants. The READ content area faculty team also plays an important role in promoting disciplinary literacy practices and advocating pedagogical changes in their discipline to support student learning.

As a program of pedagogical practices and research, READ also operates as a collegial community in which faculty collaborate and share resources, ideas, and best practices within and across the disciplines. The interdisciplinary connections among content areas can productively inform disciplinary teaching and learning while bringing in perspectives and creative approaches that could not have been developed otherwise. The program emphasizes the growth of both the affective and cognitive domains in student learning. It is equally important to strengthen these two domains in disciplinary teaching. This is achieved through professional development, institutional support, and most importantly, extended collaboration between literacy and reading specialists and faculty from various disciplines.

REFERENCES

ACT (2019), The condition of college and career readiness 2019. Retrieved from: https://www.act.org/content/dam/act/secured/documents/cccr-2019/National-CCCR-2019.pdf

Airey, J. (2011, October 8). The disciplinary literacy discussion matrix: A heuristic tool for initiating collaboration in higher education. *Across the Disciplines, 8*(3). Retrieved from https://wac.colostate.edu/docs/atd/clil/airey.cfm

Alger, C. L. (2009). Secondary teachers' conceptual metaphors of teaching and learning: Changes over the career span. *Teaching and Teacher Education, 25*(5), 743–751.

Anders, P., & Guizzetti, B. (1996). *Literacy instruction in the content areas.* New York: Harcourt.

Armstrong, S. L., & Stahl, N. A. (2017). Communication across the silos and borders: The culture of reading in a community college. *Journal of College Reading and Learning, 47*(2), 99–122.

Armstrong, S. L., Stahl, N. A., & Kantner, M. J. (2015). *What constitutes 'college-ready' for reading? An investigation of academic text readiness at one community college* (Technical report number 1). DeKalb, IL: Center for the Interdisciplinary Study of Literacy and Language, Northern Illinois University.

Bean, T. W., Gregory, K., & Dunkerly-Bean, J. (2018). Disciplinary reading. In *Handbook of college reading and study strategy research* (p. 89). Oxon, UK: Routledge.

Bond, G. L., Bond, E., & Wagner, E. B. (1941). *Developmental reading in high school.* New York: Macmillan.

Bowen, L. S., & Berry, E. (2017). Reading with understanding: What do college students say? In E. Berry, B.J. Huber, & C. Rawitch (Eds.), *Reading with understanding. Learning from the learners: Successful college students share their effective learning habits.* London: Rowman and Littlefield.

Bush, M. M. (1984). The complexity of institutionalizing a program: Acquisition of training, observing, and computing capability. *Journal of Classroom Interaction, 20*(1), 6–15.

But, J. C., Brown, P., & Smyth, D. S. (2017). Reading effectively across the disciplines (READ): A strategy to improve student success. *Insight: A Journal of Scholarly Teaching, 12*, 30–50.

Cannon, J. (1997). *Influence of an extended elementary science teaching practicum experience upon pre-service elementary teachers' science self-efficacy.* In Proceedings of the 1997 Annual International Conference of the Association for the education of teachers in science (pp. 247–260). Cincinnati, OH, January 9–12, 1997.

Clump, M. A., Bauer, H., & Bradley, C. (2004). The extent to which psychology students read textbooks. A multiple class analysis of reading across the psychology curriculum. *Journal of Instructional Psychology, 31*(3), 227–232.

Conley, D. T. (2007). *Redefining college readiness.* Eugene, OR: Educational Policy Improvement Center.

Conley, D. T. (2008). *College knowledge: What it really takes for students to succeed and what we can do to get them ready.* San Francisco: Wiley.

Fairweather, J. S. (2005). Beyond the rhetoric: Trends in the relative value of teaching and research in faculty salaries. *The Journal of Higher Education, 76*(4), 401–422.

Fang, Z. (2012). Language correlates of disciplinary literacy. *Topics in Language Disorders, 32*(1), 19–34.

Fisher, A. (2004). *The logic of real arguments.* Cambridge: Cambridge University Press.

Freeman, S., Eddy, S. L., McDonough, M., Smith, M. K., Okoroafor, N., Jordt, H., et al. (2014). Active learning increases student performance in science, engineering, and mathematics. *Proceedings of the National Academy of Sciences, 111*(23), 8410–8415.

Gafney, L. (2001). Chapter 6: Workshop evaluation. In D. Gosser, M. Cracolice, J. Kampmeier, V. Roth, V. Strozak, & P. Varma-Nelson (Eds.), *Peer-led team learning: A guidebook*. Upper Saddle River, NJ: Prentice Hall.

Gosser, D. K., Cracolice, M. S., Kampmeier, J. A., Roth, V., Strozak, V., & Varma-Nelson, P. (2001). *Peer-led team learning: A guidebook*. Upper Saddle River, NJ: Prentice Hall.

Henderson, C., Beach, A., & Finkelstein, N. (2011). Facilitating change in undergraduate STEM practices: An analytic review of the literature. *Journal of Research in Science Teaching, 48*(8), 952–984. https://doi.org/10.1002/tea.20439

Herber, H. (1970). *Teaching reading in the content areas*. Englewood Cliffs, NJ: Prentice-Hall. Inc.

Hewson, M. G., & Hewson, P. W. (1983). Effect of instruction using students' prior knowledge and conceptual change strategies on science learning. *Journal of Research in Science Teaching, 20*(8), 731–743.

Huey, N. A. (1968). The lead dioxide estimation of sulfur dioxide pollution. *Journal of the Air Pollution Control Association, 18*(9), 610–611.

Kaczmarek, S. (2016). Why STEM and reading go hand in hand. Retrieved from https://readingpartners.org/blog/why-stem-and-reading-go-hand-in-hand/

Lei, S., Bartlett, K. A., Gorney, S. B., & Herschbach, T. (2010). Resistance to reading compliance among college students: Instructor perspectives. *College Student Journal, 44*(2A), 219–229.

McConachie, S. M., & Petrosky, A. R. (2009). Content matters: A disciplinary literacy approach to improving student learning. John Wiley & Sons.

McKenna, M. C., & Robinson, R. D. (2014). *Teaching through text: Reading and writing in the content areas* (2nd ed.). Boston: Pearson.

Moje, E. B. (2008). Foregrounding the disciplines in secondary literacy teaching and learning: A call for change. *Journal of Adolescent & Adult Literacy, 52*(2), 96–107.

Moore, D. W., Readence, J. E., & Rickelman, R. J. (1983). An historical exploration of content area reading instruction. *Reading Research Quarterly, 18*(4), 419–438.

National Center on Education and the Economy [NCEE]. (2013). *What does it really mean to be college and work ready? The English literacy required of community college students*. Washington, DC. Retrieved from http://nces.org/college-and-work-ready/

National Research Council. (1999). *Transforming undergraduate education in science, mathematics, engineering, and technology*. Washington, DC: The National Academies Press. https://doi.org/10.17226/6453

National Science Foundation (US). Directorate for Education, & Human Resources. (1996). *Shaping the future: New expectations for undergraduate education in science, mathematics, engineering, and technology* (Vol. 1). Alexandria, VA: National Science Foundation, Division of Undergraduate Education.

Perin, D. (2018). Teaching academically underprepared students in community colleges. In *Understanding community colleges* (pp. 135–158). Abingdon, UK: Routledge.

Sappington, J., Kinsey, K., & Munsayer, K. (2002). Two studies of reading compliance among college students. *Teaching of Psychology, 29*(4), 272–274. https://doi.org/10.1207/S15328023TOP2904_02

Schnee, E. (2018). Reading across the curriculum at an Urban Community College: Students and faculty perspectives on reading. *Community College Journal of Research and Practice, 42*(12), 825–847.

Seymour, E. H., & Hewett, N. M. N. (1997). *Talking about leaving: Why undergraduates leave the sciences.* Boulder, CO: Westview Press.

Shanahan, T., & Shanahan, C. (2012). What is disciplinary literacy and why does it matter? *Topics in Language Disorders, 32*(1), 7–18.

Shanahan, C., Shanahan, T., & Misischia, C. (2011). Analysis of expert readers in three disciplines: History, mathematics, and chemistry. *Journal of Literacy Research, 43*(4), 393–429.

Smith, M. K., Jones, F. H., Gilbert, S. L., & Wieman, C. E. (2013). The Classroom Observation Protocol for Undergraduate STEM (COPUS): A new instrument to characterize university STEM classroom practices. *CBE—Life Sciences Education, 12*(4), 618–627.

Stains, M., Harshman, J., Barker, M. K., Chasteen, S. V., Cole, R., DeChenne-Peters, S. E., et al. (2018). Anatomy of STEM teaching in North American universities. *Science, 359*(6383), 1468–1470.

Walczyk, J. J., & Ramsey, L. L. (2003). Use of learner-centered instruction in college science and mathematics classrooms. *Journal of Research in Science Teaching: The Official Journal of the National Association for Research in Science Teaching, 40*(6), 566–584.

Yoon, K. S., Duncan, T., Lee, S. W. Y., Scarloss, B., & Shapley, K. L. (2007). Reviewing the evidence on how teacher professional development affects student achievement. Issues & answers. REL 2007-No. 033. *Regional Educational Laboratory Southwest (NJ1).*

CHAPTER 2

Professional Development: Disciplinary Literacy Instruction

Juanita C. But

2.1 Introduction

Over the past few decades, there have been expansive calls for reform in content area pedagogy from a teacher-centered approach, which relies mainly on the teacher's delivery of content knowledge, to a student-centered approach, which focuses on students' active acquisition and construction of knowledge (e.g., Barr & Tagg, 1995; National Science Foundation [NSF], 1996; National Research Council [NRC], 1999, 2003; Stokstad, 2001; Wood, 2009). In line with these calls, more recently, there has been growing interest in foregrounding disciplinary literacy instruction, which focuses on developing students' ability to engage in discipline-specific discourses, cognitive processes, and practices (Fang & Schleppegrell, 2010; Moje, 2007; Shanahan & Shanahan, 2008, 2012). The need for this pedagogical engagement is especially pronounced at the college level, where the literacy demands are highly specialized, and reading college texts requires multi-literacies and advanced cognitive skills. However, there have been consistent barriers to

J. C. But (✉)
New York City College of Technology, City University of New York, Brooklyn, NY, USA
e-mail: jbut@citytech.cuny.edu

© The Author(s) 2020
J. C. But (ed.), *Teaching College-Level Disciplinary Literacy*,
https://doi.org/10.1007/978-3-030-39804-0_2

pedagogical change, and the most commonly cited obstacles are insufficient training, time, and incentives among the faculty (Anderson, Banerjee, Drennan, & Elgin, 2011; Brownell & Tanner, 2012; Henderson, Beach, & Finkelstein, 2011; Henderson, Finkelstein, & Beach, 2010).

As content specialists and scholars in their fields, college faculty often do not have formal training in teaching and pedagogy to engage novice students by scaffolding course material effectively to facilitate disciplinary learning (Armstrong & Stahl, 2017). Though it might seem that this is more evident among new instructors who lack classroom experience, research suggests that increased teaching experience does not necessarily improve instructors' teaching approaches or teaching-related perceptions (e.g., Norton, Richardson, Hartley, Newstead, & Mayes, 2005; Richardson, 2005). Therefore, there is a perceivable need for higher education institutions to offer instructors opportunities to develop teaching skills and approaches at different stages of their careers. Equally important is for instructors to recognize such opportunities as necessary and fruitful to improve their teaching.

Achieving the goal of enhancing teaching through professional development does not start with introducing faculty to new strategies and approaches and asking them to implement them in their courses. Effective teaching approaches that facilitate learning and knowledge transmission rely on the alignment between learning objectives and teaching conceptions, which defines how educators perceive and understand teaching and learning (Gunersel & Etienne, 2014). Successful professional development, among other criteria, must also address the faculty's core teaching conceptions (Lotter, Harwood, & Bonner, 2007).

2.2   UNDERSTANDING TEACHING CONCEPTIONS OF DISCIPLINARY LITERACY

Teaching approaches are determined by teaching conceptions, which prescribe the choice of strategies, teaching styles, and instructional practices (Donche & Van Petegem, 2011; Kember & Kwan, 2000; Prosser & Trigwell, 1999). Instructors who adopt teacher-centered conceptions tend to prefer extensive lecturing and didactic classroom routines that emphasize the agency of the teacher in delivering content knowledge (Eley, 2006; Kember & Kwan, 2000). On the other hand, instructors who assume a student-centered orientation tend to use strategies and activities that engage students in active learning that motivate them to reflect on their activities (Bonwell & Eison, 1991) and in turn enhance their learning (Benek-Rivera & Mathews, 2004; Blanchard et al., 2010; Derting & Ebert-May, 2010; Sarason & Banbury, 2004; Watkins, 2005).

A recent report has revealed that teacher-centered didactic practices have been prevalent throughout the undergraduate STEM curriculum nationwide despite ample evidence that has shown the limited impact of these practices and a shared interest in education reform among institutions and national organizations (Stains et al., 2018). As a result, many students leave STEM disciplines before they can realize their potentials (Petrillo, 2016). Compared to traditional lecturing, active learning activities engage STEM students better in critical thinking, retaining information, and motivating them to learn with interest and persistence (Olson & Riordan, 2012).

What motivates instructors to change their teaching approaches relies not only on institutional policies but also on transforming individual teaching conceptions. This is not limited to a general shift from a teacher-centered to a student-centered approach. To develop students' disciplinary literacy in STEM and other content areas, instructors need to adopt a new approach that incorporates literacy strategies into the content classrooms. However, many college instructors are either not exposed to literacy instructional practices or are reluctant to adopt them in their courses (Hall, 2005; Stewart & O'Brien, 1989).

Though there is a general consensus among college faculty that academic literacy and the ability to navigate content area texts are important to college success, most faculty do not purposely develop students' disciplinary literacy in their classrooms. Content area instructors often consider literacy practices as relevant only in English courses, and their efforts are mostly devoted to fostering quantitative reasoning and other skills in STEM and professional studies. Instructors tend to prioritize content knowledge instruction over cultivating students' capacity to think, read, and communicate in ways that are consistent with those of content experts. Therefore, the initial step of professional development in Reading Effectively Across the Disciplines (READ) at City Tech is to afford a change in the conception of teaching disciplinary literacy among content area faculty.

To make our goals clear, we had to identify the pedagogical needs and make them explicit. In a preliminary faculty survey, we asked STEM faculty to rate the importance of the academic skills (writing, reading, quantitative reasoning, and presentation skills) required for student success in their disciplines. Among the respondents (N = 35) from seven STEM disciplines, most (71%) considered reading as the most important set of skills, followed by quantitative reasoning (45%), writing (37%), and presentation skills (34%). Despite that, only 17% and 40% of the respondents described their students as "competent" and "somewhat competent" readers, respectively. The results revealed that faculty perceived a gap between students' competence and the skills required in academic and disciplinary reading. Irrespective of this awareness, there was a general perception that reading and literacy instruction should occur only in English courses. Some of our respondents also thought that reading skills and strategies should be taught only at the pre-college level.

Instructors who do not acknowledge the complexity of the reading and writing processes tend to be less inclusive and use reading and writing only as assessment measures, rather than as instructional tools (Colombo & Prior, 2016). The division between teacher-centered and student-centered approaches in content area instruction is apparent. Those who take a student-centered approach are more likely to move beyond the delivery of content knowledge and focus their goals on fostering students' disciplinary literacy (Linder, Airey, Mayaba, & Webb, 2014). A key conclusion that arose in our findings was the need to conceptualize how content knowledge is generated and delivered in specific disciplines at the undergraduate level and how they can be contextualized in a disciplinary literacy professional development framework.

In a college of technology, the challenges of READ, therefore, involve more than just changing the faculty's teaching conception from teacher-centered to student-centered. Equally important is to expand their teaching conceptions to include disciplinary literacy instruction. To achieve this, initially, the READ development team did not set a general college-wide agenda, but it started with several selected content areas. Our goal was to develop a pilot that was targeted at the local academic environment, which is predominantly STEM-oriented. This pilot later served as our model for other participating disciplines. The benefit of this approach is to allow content area faculty to learn from their peers, rather than only from reading and literacy specialists, so that the faculty can readily perceive the necessity and relevance of the disciplinary literacy instruction process. It can also help redirect their teaching conceptions toward this pedagogical framework.

2.3   The Groundworks

City Tech is a comprehensive college of technology that offers 27 two-year Associate and 26 four-year Baccalaureate degree programs in the Schools of Arts and Sciences, Technology and Design, and Professional Studies. Given the particular academic context and student population, the READ development team selects courses from programs that offer both Associate and Baccalaureate degrees in each of the three schools. As READ is designed as an intervention mainly for incoming freshmen, we specifically target first-year gateway courses.

In the first year of the program, we selected Biology from the School of Arts and Sciences, Business from the School of Professional Studies, and Electromechanical Engineering from the School of Technology and Design. In each program, we appointed one faculty liaison who participated in the planning and recruitment of instructors teaching the same course. In the semester before the official roll-out of the READ professional development activities, the faculty liaisons attended an orientation session on the overview of literacy instruction in the content areas, including theories and practices. Subsequently, they met with the READ development team to review the learning outcomes, course materials, textbooks, assessments, and other requirements of each course. Members of the development team also scheduled class visits with the faculty liaisons to gain deeper knowledge of how the courses were taught. After evaluating the course requirements, classroom routines, instructional environments, and the literacy challenges students faced in the courses, the development team and content area faculty collaborated to redesign the selected courses to incorporate discipline-specific literacy approaches.

2.4   READ Professional Development Cycle

The READ professional development cycle runs in a full academic year. Before the beginning of the first semester, faculty members attend a READ workshop to receive training in disciplinary literacy pedagogy. In this workshop led by the development team of literacy and content experts, instructors teaching the same courses collaborate to develop teaching units and assignments integrating the disciplinary literacy approach. Throughout the semester, the development team leaders schedule class visits and meet with content area faculty to review strategy implementation, challenges, and outcomes.

The READ development leaders also collaborate with content area faculty to design discipline-specific assessments based on four areas of cognitive competence: comprehension, analysis, application, and evaluation. The assessments are administered twice in the semester in each discipline. The results of the initial assessment serve to inform the literacy needs of the students and areas that need intervention. This set of results also help shape and revise the design and implementation of literacy instructional strategies in each discipline. Literacy specialists and content area faculty evaluate the results together and adjust teaching approaches according to the needs demonstrated in the assessments. A final assessment is administered at the end of the semester to measure the level of success of strategy implementation in each course.

The professional development of the program corresponds with an improvement cycle that starts and ends with student learning. Based on the needs and goals of the program, the READ professional development cycle follows the principles of the strategic multi-stage course design model that consists of analysis, design, development, implementation, and evaluation (ADDIE), which is relatively dynamic and offers a flexible guide for developing learning materials (Melanie, 2008; Ozdileka & Robeckb, 2009). This is both a cyclical and a sequential model in which the formative evaluation of each stage informs its effectiveness and modifications for improvement (Kurt, 2017). In the professional development process, content area instructors are also guided through the structured stages as they redesign their courses to integrate disciplinary literacy practices.

2.5   Disciplinary Reading Analysis

The first stage of the READ professional development cycle involves the analysis of obstacles and needs in the stages of disciplinary learning. Among all components in the ADDIE model, analysis is the most important step in the instructional design process (Sugie, 2012), as it sets the overall direction. Before the actual faculty training, we analyze qualitative and quantitative evidence to identify learning issues and determine the discipline-specific learning goals. The sources of evidence we examine include input from content area faculty, content classroom visit, course learning outcomes, and student assessment.

As a starting point, content area instructors responded to a set of questions in which they self-assess their reading assignments. They were asked to evaluate in general the amount of reading their students were able to complete, and if they have any specific policies to assess the completion of the assigned readings. They also estimated their students' competence in meaningful reading and identified the challenges they face in navigating and engaging the texts. The responses from the faculty depended mostly on their impression, rather than on empirical evidence. Therefore, the purpose of this questionnaire was not to emphasize accuracy but to gain insight into the faculty's perception of reading in the content area courses. When responding to the questions, faculty also reflected on their instructional practices and whether they actively engaged students in active reading and disciplinary literacy development.

To gauge if the faculty's perceptions yield an accurate picture of student engagement in disciplinary reading, the READ team designed another set of questions for students to report their content area reading practices. The purpose of these questions is to examine the students' perceptions of the text materials, their abilities to complete and learn from course readings, the main challenges they face in content area reading, and their capacities to use strategies to unpack challenging texts. When putting together the responses from faculty and students, we can identify disparities between faculty's perceptions and students' actual reading and literacy practices. The juxtaposition of both sets of responses can thereby familiarize faculty with the real challenges students encounter in literacy practices and help them focus on areas that require intervention.

In the initial meetings with content area faculty, literacy specialists review syllabi and course material, including textbooks, lab manuals, lecture slides, and other resources. Learning outcomes are also reviewed to match the instructional material with the course requirements. At this stage, the readability, text structures, conceptual complexity, and specialized expressions and vocabulary of course materials in each content area are examined. This helps identify the literacy requirements and align them with the approaches that meet the discipline-specific instructional needs.

To make the learning, thinking, and literacy practices in the disciplines explicit, content area faculty are also asked to decode their disciplines. Middendorf and Pace (2004) proposed seven steps to decoding the disciplines: (1) what the bottlenecks to learning are in their courses, (2) how experts deal with the problems, (3) how the tasks can be modeled, (4) how students can practice those skills and receive feedback, (5) what will motivate students, (6) how well do students master the learning tasks, and (7) how to share the resulting knowledge about learning. In our program, we contextualize these steps with a specific literacy focus and apply them in different stages of our professional development cycle.

The first two steps of decoding the disciplines are essential for the analysis stage of the professional development cycle. First, READ content area faculty identify the common and specific obstacles students experience in accessing and mastering the material. These varying challenges may range from cognitive and intellectual to affective and experiential. For instance, faculty often report that students lack interest in the assigned readings or have difficulties in retaining complex information, while others perceive that students lack prior knowledge to understand the topics or fail to match the appropriate skills to the problems.

After understanding the main challenges students face, content area instructors proceed to reflect on the practices they use and the thinking processes that are involved in their disciplines. As experts who are used to embedding the distinct thinking and practices in their disciplines, they very often are not conscious of their discipline-specific tasks and thinking processes. To make their practices visible is the initial step for them to understand how to prepare their students, as novices to the disciplines, to learn effectively.

This awareness requires the faculty to reflect actively on the way they analyze ideas and concepts, the decisions they make in problem-solving, and the specific languages and cognitive processes they employ in the contexts of their disciplines. To facilitate this stage of decoding, literacy specialists hold class visits and interviews with content area faculty. Through inquiry and observation, literacy specialists help faculty map their thinking, reasoning, and presentation as they approach disciplinary texts and deliver knowledge in the content area classroom. This process also helps faculty identify the gaps between their instructional approaches and the student learning objectives. They have to be cognizant of how deeply they examine their students' thinking, as both experts and educators (Middendorf & Pace, 2004).

As the instructors become aware of the strategies they use and are required to enable students to partake in their disciplines successfully, they can begin to develop ways to teach the students how to learn these tasks.

2.6   Professional Development Design

Beginning college students often do not have the required skills and strategies to succeed in content area courses. Even if they have the general literacy skills for college learning, they still need to be equipped with specific strategies to be active learners and players who can understand and apply the sets of specialized knowledge, as well as engage in discipline-specific communication.

Informed by the particular challenges that students face in content area courses and what has yet been done to support their disciplinary literacy development, literacy specialists in READ identify what content area faculty need to learn and know to achieve their instruction goals. Subsequently, a set of overall learning outcomes are created for the READ professional development sessions for content area faculty across the disciplines. The preliminary outcomes include:

1. To understand the principles of readability and assess the level of complexity of texts used in their courses
2. To contextualize the instructional design to engage students effectively in the cognitive and reading processes specific to the disciplines
3. To be familiar with research-based active reading and literacy strategies and practices in individual and collaborative learning
4. To be able to identify discipline-specific language functions and literacy practices
5. To identify the main challenges that students encounter in developing disciplinary literacy
6. To apply disciplinary literacy pedagogy to promote deeper knowledge and motivation among students
7. To facilitate the use of both general and discipline-specific literacy strategies among students to promote text-based learning
8. To select and customize research-based literacy tools and strategies to enhance content area learning
9. To use formative disciplinary literacy assessments to improve instruction

In order to tackle the problems in student learning, faculty have to identify common and specific challenges students have when handling the required material for content area learning. These challenges are frequently found in the cognitive and affective domains. At times, the roots of these problems are not related solely to students' academic abilities and aptitudes. Very often, text complexities, requirements of prior knowledge, instructional routines, and other factors can generate obstacles to learning.

Even though in some content area classrooms the role of reading and text-based learning is somewhat undermined (see, e.g., Chap. 5), it does not diminish the importance of reading in content area learning. In STEM and professional studies, students often feel intimidated by the sheer volume of the texts they have to read. Their difficulties in reading can be further multiplied by their unfamiliarity with the text structures or the disciplinary conventions of reading and writing, as well as the variations in text readability and complexity in certain disciplines. Instead of asking students to read or delivering course material in lectures, faculty have to reacquaint with the material and identify difficult spots in the texts and possible obstacles students encounter in content area reading. Activities that introduce text features and organizations such as textbook previews at the beginning of the course are ways to invite students to purposeful reading and defray their anxiety in reading.

Content area faculty have different levels of familiarity with disciplinary literacy instruction. Most of the READ faculty started in the program with very limited exposure to the research and practices in the area. One of the common misconceptions that faculty have about student learning is that they can independently handle assigned tasks without formal introduction, thorough explanation, or enough scaffoldings, even for novices and underprepared students (McKenna & Robinson, 2002). As most of the faculty members who participate in the READ professional development are new to disciplinary literacy instruction, we do not assume they have enough background knowledge in the area. However, we also keep in mind that they have extensive experience as teachers and learners, which can offer an entry point to connecting disciplinary literacy instruction and their teaching practices.

A literacy teaching inventory is useful in documenting, evaluating, and improving teaching, as it allows faculty to reflect on the approaches they use to achieve learning goals and support students with different academic and literacy needs at each stage of the reading process. Prior to professional development sessions, we ask our faculty to take inventory of their teaching in the form of guided discussion among colleagues across the disciplines. It also helps them see the connections between their teaching and discipline-specific practices when compared to those in other content areas. This also develops a schema for disciplinary literacy instructional practices and facilitates the adoption of strategies.

In planned professional development activities, literacy teaching practices are introduced, modeled, and discussed. Based on the specific contents and requirements in the disciplines, faculty are guided to develop assignments and activities to support learning goals and engage students in reading and cognitive processes in content knowledge acquisition, with emphases on teaching students how language and the evolving cultural practices and learning work in the disciplines (Moje, 2007). This includes addressing the use of classroom technology, online tools, and supporting active reading of electronic textbooks and open access resources. Faculty feedback on the professional development sessions is collected and reviewed to identify aspects that need further attention.

2.7   DEVELOPMENT AND IMPLEMENTATION OF DISCIPLINARY LITERACY PEDAGOGY

The READ team that consists of literacy specialists and content area faculty continues to collaborate to create or redesign instructional materials and assignments after the professional development workshops. Syllabi are revised to embed strategies and routines that are based on discipline-specific designs to achieve the learning objectives. The materials can be found in the following areas:

1. In-class materials and lesson plans
   Lecture slides are edited and revised to actively engage students in active reading, writing, listening, and thinking during lectures. They can promote disciplinary learning in various ways, including enhancing retention of information, enabling meaningful connections between concepts and ideas, fostering understanding of specialized vocabulary, modeling of disciplinary thinking and language, and assessing understanding of the material. Chunking, fill-in-the-blanks, and embedded short review/discussion questions and responses are some examples that effectively turn a teacher-centered didactic lecture into an active learning environment where students are constantly engaged.
   Some of the course syllabi include a day-to-day breakdown of course coverage, which mainly focus on the topics and contents

covered. In some courses, the syllabi are standardized documents that are pre-designed by academic departments and course coordinators. There is a need for more detailed lesson plans that include not only the topics but also the strategies and activities that enable students to learn the material actively. The developments of detailed lesson plans are highly specialized, to be supported by relevant assignments, instructional and pre-lab materials for individual and collaborative learning.

2. Reading guides and reading companions

Reading guides can be used effectively to support student reading in and outside of class. They help motivate students to read and set specific purposes for reading. Varying in structures and purposes, reading guides can range from pre-reading questions that develop and activate prior knowledge to graphic organizers that map and define the relationships between key concepts and ideas in disciplinary texts.

In STEM courses, reading companions can be used to support didactic and lab teaching and learning. The reading companions can take the form of a simple list of selected texts and related resources organized to match the course schedule. The list can include textbook sections and literature related to the topics covered. Some also include multimodal texts such as curated repertoires of videos, websites, and online resources that facilitate student learning of content knowledge.

3. Literacy strategy guides and models

While reading guides are designed with specific contents, reading strategies are tools and techniques that help students navigate and engage the texts and read effectively for better retention, comprehension, analysis of concepts and ideas, and evaluate scenarios and arguments. These can be used in different modes of text-based instruction, including lecture-based classes, collaborative learning, online class discussion, pre-lab activities, and problem-based learning. Students do not necessarily use identical strategies to perform literacy tasks in the content areas. Instead of prescribing and requiring students to apply given strategies, a more effective way is to allow them to develop those they prefer to use. Strategy guides and models are instrumental in achieving active reading goals. They can also increase students' concentration and ability to retain information when they read both print and electronic texts. With guided focus, students can read more effectively in an online and interactive environment, especially when hyperlinks with varying modes of information are embedded in the texts. Step by step, modeling of strategies for reading graphs and charts can ensure coherent understanding and analysis of the information presented by the data sets.

4. Companion lessons and assignments for disciplinary language support

   Embedded assignments and activities are often used to enhance student learning in and out of class. In some courses, companion lessons with specific interdisciplinary input and special consideration of implementation settings are designed to achieve specific disciplinary literacy goals. They require close collaboration between literacy or language arts specialists and content area faculty in the development, design, and implementation stages. An example of companion assignments involves the use of creative writing in STEM classrooms to foster deep reading, understanding of key ideas and vocabulary, and application of concepts. Lesson plans are parallel to the curriculum with supplemental instructions on creative writing principles, such as the use of metaphors and similes. Content concepts and vocabulary are carefully selected by STEM and creative writing faculty to be included in the assignments. They are embedded in a sequence that integrates the instruction of literary devices, close reading, modeling of figurative language to describe scientific concepts, and the application of content knowledge in creative expressions (see, e.g., Chap. 6). Students are also asked to reflect on their thinking processes and contributions to the assignments/lessons to reinforce their learning.

   Another important aspect of supporting students in accessing disciplinary knowledge is to center the instruction around the syntax and discourse that underline the process of knowledge production. For example, in a mathematics course, students are asked to go through multiple stages of examining the cognitive and linguistic processes of mathematical writing before they begin to solve the word problems (see Chap. 8). The observation of the use of language and vocabulary to produce meaning in an algebra word problem is just as essential as the proficiency in using mathematical formulas and methods. Rather than passive reception and artificial repetition, active discussion of the instructor's problem-solving models is a more productive way for students to discover and build knowledge, as well as to explore and participate in the core practices and literacy in the discipline. The development of mathematical thinking and the ability to master the mathematical language is key to success, especially for beginning college students.

5. Disciplinary Literacy Assessments

In STEM and professional studies, quizzes and exams are tools frequently used to assess students' content knowledge. However, they are designed not specifically for assessing their disciplinary literacy and the cognitive processes involved. In READ, with the support of literacy specialists, content area faculty design pre-READ or baseline and post-READ or final discipline-specific reading assessments based on the READ assessment rubric. The rubric is used to measure students' abilities to comprehend, analyze, apply, and evaluate content knowledge and engagement in disciplinary thinking processes. These assessments are designed for both formative and summative purposes (see Chap. 3).

6. Metacognition of content learning and use of strategies

Metacognition is widely applied as an instructional approach for self-assessments of learning and thinking processes. Metacognitive thinking is deliberate, planful, intentional, goal-directed, and future-oriented mental behaviors (Flavell, 1971) that can be used to accomplish discipline-specific cognitive tasks. Instructors cannot operate under the assumption that students automatically benefit from the learning tasks and the tools they are taught to use in learning and content area reading. Effective readers use a wide variety of comprehension monitoring and literacy strategies and use them with more efficacy than less successful readers (Paris, Lipson, & Wixon, 1994).

READ faculty employ instructional tools to enable students' metacognitive thinking in discipline-specific literacy practices. These include post-reading questions, responses, student-generated questions, exit slips, and learning logs. Exit slips and learning logs are used to help students assess their mastery of class material. They can be used at the end of each class to offer instructors a clearer picture of how students learn, and if learning has occurred. The main advantage of these activities is to make students' learning and reading processes visible. They are especially useful in the content area classrooms where instructors prioritize content coverage and leave limited time for assessing teaching and learning to inform appropriate interventions. Based on student responses, instructors can adjust their lessons and instructional pacing accordingly.

2.8   Implementation of Disciplinary Literacy Instructional Practices

Many instructors have gained knowledge of new teaching approaches in professional development but stop short at applying them to their classrooms and incorporating them into their teaching practices (McConachie & Petrosky, 2010). The reason traditional professional development does not have lasting impacts is that it does not support faculty during the stages of learning, especially the pivotal stage of implementation. Without ongoing support in the initial stage of implementation when the results of adopting the new approaches are not optimal, faculty may not be able to persevere. Studies have shown that it takes multiple trials and instances of practice before an instructor can master a new skill (Joyce & Showers, 2002).

Apart from ongoing support, the effectiveness of professional development relies on the faculty's perceived coherence of their professional development experiences to their teaching and program implementation (Penuel et al., 2007). Therefore, the professional development design of disciplinary literacy pedagogy needs to be contextualized with discipline-specific considerations to achieve the learning goals. Between the initial delivery of strategies and practices in professional development and the actual classroom applications, what is required is the time for planning and the provision of technical and pedagogical support. Understanding the nature, contexts, and tools of disciplinary literacy practices is essential to their effective application.

Disciplinary Language and Text Production

The language of a given discipline is specific and is framed by the cognitive processes used by the experts in the field. As these same processes are central to the discipline-specific text productions, it is necessary to make them explicit as content area faculty instruct novice students the language of the discipline. To facilitate the implementation of disciplinary literacy strategies, instructors have to foreground language production, knowledge organization patterns, the encoding and decoding expressions and presentations (these include written, symbolic, numerical, and graphic), and specialized concepts and vocabulary.

Disciplinary texts are a logical entry point for students to learn the disciplinary language. Textbooks, primary literature, and articles in the field all demonstrate different and complementary aspects of specialized languages in the content areas. Reading these texts can foster students' engagement in learning and critiquing new knowledge and disciplinary practices (Moje, 2007). The ability to think and perform as practitioners in a specific discipline begins with the knowledge of how language works in that particular field. Therefore, to be able to unpack and utilize disciplinary language is just as important as extracting meaning from content area texts. For instance, "in scientific discourse, nouns are key grammatical components and agents for compacting meaning and information, creating technical objects, developing logical reasoning, facilitating discursive flow, and achieving precision," and its "technicality, density and abstraction very often produce complex and abstract texts that conceal agency and referential information, making comprehension and critique more difficult" (Fang, 2012, p. 25). When these texts are used in the content areas to achieve the instructional and learning goals, instructors need to be aware of their specific structures and purposes. As these texts present content knowledge and model disciplinary thinking and problem-solving processes, students have to be taught how the disciplinary language is used in order to read actively, purposefully, and effectively.

Technical and specialized vocabulary is not the only challenge in reading disciplinary texts, language patterns and discourse grammar also make these texts difficult to navigate (Fang, 2012) and require students to develop the ability to handle in new ways by applying discipline-specific strategies. To be proficient in reading disciplinary texts, students have to engage in deep and meaningful reading through active interaction with the texts, which "demands readers to stop and talk with the texts" (Wineburg, 1991, p. 503) in the process of producing meaning. To support reading in the disciplines, READ content area faculty pay special attention to text structure and language production and model the cognitive processes of reading based on functional language analysis that focuses on the content, organization, and style/voice of the texts (Fang & Schleppegrell, 2010). Reading sample texts aloud and interrogating and interacting with texts in think-aloud sessions can help model the thinking and analyze the discursive structures and patterns in the disciplines. Readers need to "pause periodically to analyze the language patterns in the text, sort out potential linguistic issues, and carry out deliberate conversations with the author" (Fang, 2012, p. 31) in order to achieve full comprehension.

To be able to apply the cognitive and literacy strategies they have already developed effectively, students need knowledge of both disciplinary language and disciplinary content (Hirsch, 2005). In the READ content area classrooms, strategies such as annotation, note-taking, and responses are not used solely to record and assess what students already understand, but are also used with specific purposes for students to dissect the structure of the language and to identify challenging comprehension issues through interacting with the texts.

Understanding the Structures of Disciplinary Texts

Understanding the text structures is the basis of understanding the language and convention of disciplinary thinking and communication. Research shows that college students have difficulty in identifying text features and sorting patterns of organization (Cook & Mayer, 1988), which help support cognitive processes in reading a variety of academic texts. The ability to decipher how information, concepts, and arguments are organized promotes disciplinary literacy, as it improves retention of high conceptual information and application of content knowledge rather than retention and literal comprehension of low conceptual information (Cook & Mayer, 1988).

Despite that familiarity with text structures plays an important role in facilitating active reading and modeling disciplinary thinking, most instructors do not explicitly focus on text structures in content area instruction. Content and textual information rather than formal elements, such as information organization and language function, remains the focus in most content area classrooms. Effective implementation of reading guides and practices that are informed by and reinforce the learning of disciplinary-specific text structure and conceptual organization can help engage students in disciplinary reading. Text structures are examples of implicit features that are already embedded in the course material but are not often used to enhance disciplinary learning. The role of the READ literacy specialists is to make explicit such tools, so that content area faculty can apply them effectively.

In the world of STEM textbooks, there is a variety of embedded tools and resources to promote learning, with some more user-friendly than others. However, when focusing on delivering content knowledge, many instructors condense textbook contents or topics into comprehensive and well-designed lecture slides, with which some students tend to replace reading to learn by passive listening and visual intake of information. Students also tend to neglect the assigned readings if instructors do not make the readings necessary and relevant. Therefore, instructors have to establish a purpose for assigned reading, motivate students to read by making reading assignments part of the course requirements and assessments, and support active reading with the development of disciplinary literacy strategies. Previewing, predicting, and modeling the way discipline-specific language makes sense at a syntactic level with special focus on symbols, words, and sequences are some of the ways to develop the students' disciplinary literacy. For some STEM courses, reading for the lectures should be connected to the laboratory sections. Pre-lab reading guides also help prepare students to follow the instructions in the lab manuals to conduct experiments safely and with precision.

Beginning college students are often intimidated by the density and complexity of some textbooks, especially in STEM and professional studies. Fang and Pace (2013) have identified five factors that make a text complex: high frequency of content-specific vocabulary words, lack of text cohesion, grammatical metaphors, lexical density, and grammatical intricacy. These factors characterize most college textbooks and render content area reading challenging for students who do not have sufficient strategies to navigate the texts. In STEM and professional studies texts, in particular, students often encounter difficulties in understanding specialized vocabulary and densely packed concepts and complex formula. Some STEM textbooks are filled with long and complex sentences formed by multiple clauses, which make it even more difficult for students to dissect the relationships between concepts and retain information. These factors often discourage students from reading content area texts.

Instructors need to gain a good understanding of how content area texts are produced and to evaluate their complexity when they engage students in disciplinary learning through reading. Many instructors assign readings without considering their levels of complexity and if their students can handle them independently. Some of the content area texts are more considerate than others (Anderson & Ambruster, 1984). Considerate texts are written to support readers to navigate the information. They typically have well-defined structures, clear headings, vocabulary support, and graphic and visual aids to make the texts easier to understand. On the contrary, inconsiderate texts often do not have these supporting features (Armbruster & Anderson, 1985). To be able to identify considerate texts can help faculty make appropriate choices.

As instructors choose to use considerate texts, they can lead students to actively utilize some of these tools and text features, such as chapter overview, keywords preview, the glossary, and review questions. However, in some cases, content area texts are assigned by the departments rather than selected by individual instructors. If the assigned texts are inconsiderate, instructors can develop reading guides and other resources to help scaffold student reading. More support is required to process difficult texts.

An understanding of textbook components and structure helps students overcome barriers to disciplinary reading. To achieve this, READ instructors preview course textbooks with students to help familiarize them with the structure, chapter organization, textual elements, and embedded tools that support content area reading and vocabulary development. An active reading checklist that is tailored to the needs in specific content areas also helps students monitor their use or lack of strategies throughout the reading process. Based on the discipline-specific reading needs and the areas that require reinforcement, instructors apply pre-designed strategies accordingly. They can be modified based on the results and information from formal and informal assessments.

Implementation Settings
As disciplinary texts and cognitive processes vary considerably, disciplinary literacy instruction also takes multiple forms and is applied in different contexts with specific purposes. Various classroom settings, instructional modes, and learning objectives are contributing factors to the design and implementation of practices and strategies. The READ courses consist of lectures, lab, studio, and online and hybrid courses. Given the specific purposes of teaching and learning and disciplinary conventions, literacy and content area faculty collaborate in ways that afford both flexibility and specificity.

Embedded Peer-Led Team Learning

Student support in the forms of recitation and tutoring are common in many content area courses. Instead of depending on these traditional models, some STEM faculty in READ choose to implement peer-led team learning (PLTL) to create a more open and student-centered learning environment. PLTL is an innovative model of STEM education in which student leaders (peers) guide small-group activities in weekly student workshops. This model typically uses group activities where students are directed to work together cooperatively to solve challenging problems. The peer leaders, who are experienced students in the content area courses, are trained to ensure that the students are actively and productively engaged with the material and with each other (Gosser & Gosser, 2001). With the goal of developing students' disciplinary literacy, faculty embed peer-led team learning into their courses to deepen students' conceptual understanding and strengthen strategy development—content area faculty guide peer leaders, who have been trained by literacy and educational specialists, to model the literacy strategies in disciplinary reading and problem-solving activities. This format is especially productive because faculty can focus on content instruction and ensure coherence in the application of disciplinary literacy strategies, which are further reinforced and practiced by students in the peer-led team learning workshops. To align content with strategy implementation, content area faculty meet with peer leaders before each PLTL workshop to go through workshop material. In addition to the use of material/activities provided by the faculty and literacy specialists, peer leaders also review post-lecture learning logs and exit slips to help troubleshoot problems students face in learning.

Peer-led team learning can also be used effectively to enhance students' disciplinary literacy in laboratory classes. To a large extent, the success of lab assignments relies on students' comprehension and accurate organization and interpretation of written instructions. Lab manuals offer step-by-step instructions, but students do not always understand the procedures or interpret the information correctly in the manual. Therefore, they cannot follow the instructions and apply the information precisely. These issues are more complex when lab projects are not carried out in a well-defined sequence and pre-determined procedures. In these cases, students are required to plan a workable sequence to complete the project or experiment. For instance, in the Electromechanical Manufacturing Lab course, before outlining a sequence of procedures, students need a holistic understanding of the entire project and the interconnectedness of components. They are also required to troubleshoot and resolve problems. To ensure accurate application of principles and procedures, READ faculty develop flowcharts, concept maps, and feature analysis organizers to support lab activities (see Chap. 7). These prelab activities and student reflections are guided by peer leaders who are embedded in the lab classroom.

Feedback and Portfolios

There is an array of strategies that can be integrated into the content area curriculum. They are associated with active reading and learning that can be used to develop students' disciplinary literacy. However, "Learning to think and work within the culture of a particular discipline is more complex than generally appears to be the case to professionals in the field, and students must be given a chance to perfect these skills and to receive feedback that clarifies where they are and are not succeeding" (Middendorf & Pace, 2004, p. 7). Throughout the process of learning disciplinary thinking and practices, students need to be given feedback and enough time to develop, practice, and utilize a set of tools that match their learning needs. Therefore, faculty feedback should not be limited to students' content knowledge proficiency; it should also address students' competence in mastering the targeted strategies. For this reason, it is not uncommon for READ faculty to focus on a single strategy or routine until their students can utilize it productively.

Once a particular set of strategies has been mastered by most of the students, the instructor can move on to more complex applications that incorporate other components. For students who have low reading ability, general strategies are used as foundational tools for students to extract meaning and build knowledge from disciplinary texts. For instance, visual note-taking in a foundational architecture course is used as a central strategy to consolidate text-based learning in the discipline. This strategy can be applied to reading a range of texts, as it incrementally incorporates visual elements such as drawings, graphs, and sketches, to reinforce the learning of essential topics in the discipline. This routine can be connected to other activities such as observations and discussions in field seminars to further students' fluency in more advanced disciplinary practices. In addition, low-stakes writing assignments drawn from readings can also help students actively engage the texts, identify important points, and connect textual information to their prior knowledge (Felder & Brent, 1996).

A portfolio of assignments and revisions that are based on instructors' feedback can also ensure coherence in strategy implementations and development of disciplinary literacy through reinforcing and connecting content learning to the application of literacy strategies. The portfolio can contain selected formal and low-stakes assignments, including summaries, lecture notes, learning logs, reading guides, concept maps, vocabulary banks, and pre-lab assignments. Students can also evaluate their learning and growth as learners in the disciplines by including a reflection documenting their learning experience.

Online and Hybrid Classrooms

Online and hybrid classes may be similar to traditional classes in content and pedagogy, but because of the use of technology, reduced time for face-to-face instruction, and blended learning, these courses often require different instructional strategies. In online and hybrid courses, the responsibility of learning is placed mainly on the students, and the primary role of the teacher is to create opportunities and foster environments for student learning (Caulfield & Leahy, 2011). Independent reading plays an essential role in online learning. READ faculty teaching online and hybrid content area courses pay special attention to practices that develop active reading strategies and scaffold challenging parts of the texts. Pre-reading activities and reading guides are used to ensure the completion of reading assignments. They are especially effective when used with online platforms such as Blackboard and the web-based Openlab at City Tech, on which students can post web blogs and responses to assigned readings. These platforms can be used to create purposes for reading and guide students to preview content material to support reading to learn.

In recent years, the flipped classroom approach is becoming more common in STEM and other content area instruction. Flipping the classroom is considered to be more student-centered and afford instructors more time to engage students in learning activities and working through problems during class time as they make lecture materials and lessons available beforehand. The general consensus among instructors who flipped their classes is that what makes the difference is not the accessibility of class materials themselves, but how they are integrated into an overall approach (Tucker, 2012). Instructors can also query individual students more readily and assess their understanding of key concepts and identify where misconceptions or errors occur. In using the flipped classroom delivery of literacy strategies, content area faculty can develop students' prior knowledge on topics and engage them in discipline-specific cognitive processes by setting objectives as they read and preview the lessons. To build class activities that forge a virtual discourse community they can also ask students to generate questions for discussion. Flipping the classroom can enhance disciplinary literacy instruction in online and hybrid courses. Online platforms and computers can serve as mediational means and tools (Vgotsky, 1987) to achieve learning goals.

When the flipped classroom is applied in hybrid or blended learning environments, instructors can freely use the face-to-face class time to engage students with literacy instruction and practices. For instance, in accounting courses, students can create concept maps or scenarios in the industry based on assigned readings and lecture materials they have previewed before class (see Chap. 4). These activities enable active and deep learning, and the literacy practices facilitate higher-order cognitive processes in which they can synthesize information and concepts, apply content knowledge, connect existing and prior knowledge, evaluate arguments and make judgments based on evidence, and generate new hypotheses or models that require practicing their use of disciplinary language and thinking.

Collaborative Learning

Lecture-based and teacher-centered instruction still dominates the college instructional landscape despite constant calls for more active learning and student-centered approaches. It creates a classroom environment where students are consistently passively receiving knowledge and feeling isolated in their learning experience. While some instructors include group works, many do not use them systematically, effectively, or with variations to achieve intended learning goals. In READ professional development, faculty are engaged in integrating discipline-specific literacy strategies into collaborative activities to foster disciplinary learning. It requires a new mindset of prioritizing literacy engagement when designing collaborative learning units. The primary objective is to use various group settings to facilitate discipline-specific literacy development and ensure more extensive student participation in active learning.

Knowledge is not simply handed down from the teacher to the student. The process of knowledge appropriation is reciprocal, and cognitive change occurs within this mutually constructive process (Newman, Griffin, & Cole, 1989). Meaning, therefore, is constructed through joint activities rather than being transferred from teacher to learner (Lee & Smagorinsky, 2000). In the content area classrooms, this principle applies not only to knowledge acquisition but also to students' literacy development in given disciplines. Reciprocity can rarely be achieved in a teacher-centered learning environment where students are put in a passive mode of knowledge reception. In addition to teachers' feedback, collaborative learning can facilitate disciplinary literacy practices, both interactively and constructively.

Disciplinary competencies in the twenty-first century are no longer limited to an individual's appropriation of specialized knowledge and practices. Knowledge distribution and negotiation are essential to achieving common goals and carrying out collective tasks within small groups. They are also crucial to the problem-solving process and disciplinary literacy development, which can yield enhanced results in collaborative learning. READ content area faculty configure disciplinary literacy instruction in various group settings to optimize results and achieve fuller student engagement. Therefore, instead of asking a student to hand in a checklist of active reading strategies they use, instructors can ask students to share in groups to reflect and evaluate the effectiveness of strategies they apply or do not apply. When students practice annotating disciplinary texts, they can compare their annotations in groups and learn about diverse ways of interacting with the texts. When pre-reading activities are conducted in small groups, students are encouraged to discuss their answers and predictions before reading. They can also note any opposing or contradictory points of view. This can generate conversations about content knowledge and examine reasoning and arguments at the different stages of the reading process and disciplinary literacy development.

Student-Centered Team Teaching and Guest Lectures

Guest lectures are commonly used to enrich students' learning experience and broaden their perspectives on specific topics. These include lectures by experts in the field or speakers who have in-depth knowledge of the given topics or professions that are directly related to the disciplines. As content area faculty in READ are trained to apply disciplinary literacy approaches in their classroom, we also plan lectures and presentations co-taught by English/reading and content area faculty to introduce and model strategies that support disciplinary learning.

Team teaching and guest lectures are effective when the approaches introduced require specialized literacy expertise. For instance, as described earlier, a biology professor and a poetry professor collaborate to use creative writing as teaching and learning tools to engage students in disciplinary thinking and content knowledge acquisition. They work together through various stages, from planning and selection of material to developing lesson plans and class implementation. The primary goal of the poetry professor is not to teach poetry in the content area classroom, but to introduce background knowledge, provide literacy tools for student assignments and class activities, demonstrate the process, and offer guidance and feedback. These lessons offer an alternative vision of biology and enable students to re-conceptualize the production of disciplinary knowledge through the creative writing process. Because of the detailed lesson plans, some of these assignments and activities are replicable without subsequent participation of the poetry professor, once the routines have been established.

Interdisciplinary team teaching and guest lectures are valuable supports for disciplinary literacy instruction. They broaden students' and faculty's ways of thinking and approaching disciplinary teaching and learning. As a biology student remarked, creative writing allowed her to perceive knowledge differently. Diverse perspectives and new experiences of learning in the content areas can positively impact students both cognitively and emotionally.

2.9   Professional Development Evaluation

Professional development efforts habitually focus mainly on planning, implementation, and follow-up support, while leaving evaluation on the sideline. Evaluation's marginal role, when compared to other professional development activities, can be attributed to its lack of perceivable value or the lack of the skills and expertise to undertake it effectively (Guskey, 2002). Despite that professional development evaluation is generally understated, it plays a central role in READ by providing meaningful information to enable thoughtful and responsible decisions in the professional development cycle, in the areas of program design, content, focus, implementation, organization, and format.

Professional Development Evaluation

The evaluation of READ professional development takes various forms with specific purposes at different stages of the professional development cycle. The first level of evaluation focuses on participants' feedback and reactions to the faculty training workshops. In a simple post-workshop survey developed by the college's Office of Assessment and Institutional Research, participants are asked to rate their satisfaction level and reflect on general details such as the organization, presentation, content, and quality of the workshop to specific questions such as their favorite and least favorite parts of the workshop. Suggestions for improvement and potential workshop topics are also collected to provide information for future planning.

The satisfaction survey provides general information and opinions that address the overall organization and structure of professional development workshops. The participants' responses can help improve the design and delivery of activities in certain ways. However, the feedback collected in this context does not provide a full picture of the extent to which the participants have attained new knowledge and strategies and are able to apply them. Therefore, in addition to the post-workshop survey, we also engage in the ongoing evaluations of the implementation of new knowledge and teaching strategies in the content area classrooms. They are done through regular communications between content area faculty and literacy specialists on classroom practices, challenges, and course results. These evaluations also inform our modifications of lesson plans and implementation formats to enhance student learning throughout the process.

At the end of each READ professional development evaluation cycle, faculty participate in a workshop in which they reflect on their practices and provide examples they applied to enhance students' disciplinary literacy. Sample assignments and student works are discussed with faculty across the disciplines. The interdisciplinary discussion is especially productive when content area faculty are not only able to see divergence but also find common ground in their works. For instance, engineering and math faculty share common concerns when teaching students disciplinary language. Very often, prior knowledge in specific math topics is required for engineering students to learn effectively in their discipline. The presentations and observations among faculty, as well as peer feedback, help elucidate the required changes in the process of achieving their instructional goals.

Student learning outcomes are also evaluation tools for measuring the success of professional development. Apart from student grades, READ implements discipline-specific assessments to gauge students' literacy competencies. The pre-READ assessments, which are conducted before the implementation of disciplinary literacy practices, are given at the beginning of each semester. They serve as baseline assessments to inform faculty areas in which students need support and development. Instructional strategies are then applied to strengthen students' disciplinary literacy throughout the semester. The effectiveness of these strategies is reflected in the post-READ assessment, which is conducted at the end of the semester. The READ assessment results are analyzed and recorded to provide evidence-based information about the program's overall impact. They are used to guide our planning in the diverse aspects of professional development.

2.10   Dissemination of Practices

READ uses several platforms to disseminate knowledge and practices on disciplinary learning and instruction. In addition to best practices workshops where faculty share their strategies and student outcomes, examples of disciplinary literacy applications are shared internally and externally in different settings. The READ OpenLab site is an online platform that features the practices and research of content area faculty. It aims at showcasing best practices and outreaching faculty who are not participating in the program. A main READ site that provides general research and resources is linked to content area sites that appeal to the discipline-specific audience.

READ content area faculty also present their works in departmental and college-wide workshops, as well as national and international conferences to reach a wider audience and promote disciplinary practices in the college community and beyond. Scholarship of Teaching and Learning is a key component of the program. The success of READ greatly depends on the collaborative efforts of a core team of faculty members who are both researchers and practitioners of disciplinary literacy instruction. As we acknowledge that professional development is an ongoing endeavor, participating faculty typically remain in the READ community for multiple semesters to perfect their skills, experiment with new approaches, and share their experiences and resources with new participants.

References

Anderson, T. H., & Ambruster, B. B. (1984). Studying. In P. D. Person (Ed.), *Handbook of reading research.* New York: Longma.

Anderson, W. A., Banerjee, U., Drennan, C. L., & Elgin, S. C. R. (2011). Changing the culture of science education at research universities. *Science, 331,* 152–153.

Armbruster, B. B., & Anderson, T. H. (1985). Producing 'considerate' expository text: Or easy reading is damned hard writing. *Journal of Curriculum Studies, 17*(3), 247–274.

Armstrong, S. L., & Stahl, N. A. (2017). Communication across the silos and borders: The culture of reading in a community college. *Journal of College Reading and Learning, 47*(2), 99–122.

Barr, R. B., & Tagg, J. (1995). From teaching to learning—A new paradigm for undergraduate education. *Change: The Magazine of Higher Learning, 27*(6), 12–26.

Benek-Rivera, J., & Mathews, V. E. (2004). Active learning with jeopardy: Students ask the questions———. *Journal of Management Education,* *28*(1), 104–118.

Blanchard, M. R., Southerland, S. A., Osborne, J. W., Sampson, V. D., Annetta, L. A., & Granger, E. M. (2010). Is inquiry possible in light of accountability?: A quantitative comparison of the relative effectiveness of guided inquiry and verification laboratory instruction. *Science Education, 94*(4), 577–616.

Bonwell, C. C., & Eison, J. A. (1991). *Active learning: Creating excitement in the classroom.* 1991 ASHE-ERIC higher education reports. ERIC Clearinghouse on Higher Education, The George Washington University, One Dupont Circle, Suite 630, Washington, DC 20036-1183.

Brewer, C. A., & Smith, D. (2011). *Vision and change in undergraduate biology education: A call to action.* Washington, DC: American Association for the Advancement of Science.

Brownell, S. E., & Tanner, K. D. (2012). Barriers to faculty pedagogical change: Lack of training, time, incentives, and… tensions with professional identity? *CBE—Life Sciences Education, 11*(4), 339–346.

Caulfield, B., & Leahy, J. (2011). Learning to cycle again: Examining the benefits of providing tax-free loans to purchase new bicycles. *Research in Transportation Business & Management, 2,* 42–47.

Colombo, L., & Prior, M. (2016). How do faculty conceptions on reading, writing and their role in the teaching of academic literacies influence their inclusive attitude. *Ilha do Desterro, 69*(3), 115–124.

Cook, L. K., & Mayer, R. E. (1988). Teaching readers about the structure of scientific text. *Journal of Educational Psychology, 80*(4), 448.

Derting, T. L., & Ebert-May, D. (2010). Learner-centered inquiry in undergraduate biology: Positive relationships with long-term student achievement. *CBE—Life Sciences Education, 9*(4), 462–472.

Donche, V., & Van Petegem, P. (2011). Teacher educators' conceptions of learning to teach and related teaching strategies. *Research Papers in Education, 26*(2), 207–222.

Eley, M. G. (2006). Teachers' conceptions of teaching, and the making of specific decisions in planning to teach. *Higher Education, 51*(2), 191–214.

Fang, Z. (2012). Language correlates of disciplinary literacy. *Topics in Language Disorders, 32*(1), 19–34.

Fang, Z., & Pace, B. G. (2013). Teaching with challenging texts in the disciplines: Text complexity and close reading. *Journal of Adolescent & Adult Literacy, 57*(2), 104–108.

Fang, Z., & Schleppegrell, M. J. (2010). Disciplinary literacies across content areas: Supporting secondary reading through functional language analysis. *Journal of Adolescent & Adult Literacy, 53*(7), 587–597.

Felder, R. M., & Brent, R. (1996). Navigating the bumpy road to student-centered instruction. *College Teaching, 44*(2), 43–47.

Flavell, J. H. (1971). First discussant's comments: What is memory development the development of? *Human Development, 14,* 272–278.

Gosser, D. K., & Gosser, D. K. (2001). *Peer-led team learning: A guidebook.* Upper Saddle River, NJ: Prentice Hall.

Gunersel, A. B., & Etienne, M. (2014). The impact of a faculty training program on teaching conceptions and strategies. *International Journal of Teaching and Learning in Higher Education, 26*(3), 404–413.

Guskey, T. R. (2002). Does it make a difference? Evaluating professional development. *Educational Leadership, 59*(6), 45.

Hall, P. (2005). Interprofessional teamwork: Professional cultures as barriers. *Journal of Interprofessional Care, 19*(sup1), 188–196.

Henderson, C., Beach, A., & Finkelstein, N. (2011). Facilitating change in undergraduate STEM instructional practices: An analytic review of the literature. *Journal of Research in Science Teaching, 48,* 952–984.

Henderson, C., Finkelstein, N., & Beach, A. (2010). Beyond dissemination in college science teaching: An introduction to four core change strategies. *Journal of College Science Teaching, 39,* 18–25.

Hirsch Jr., E. D. (2005). Reading comprehension requires knowledge—Of words and the world. In Z. Fang (Ed.), *Literacy teaching and learning: Current issues and trends* (pp. 121–130). Columbus, OH: Merrill.

Joyce, B. R., & Showers, B. (2002). *Student achievement through staff development.* National College for School Leadership. Danvers. MA: ASCD.

Kember, D., & Kwan, K. P. (2000). Lecturers' approaches to teaching and their relationship to conceptions of good teaching. *Instructional Science, 28*(5), 469–490.

Kurt, S. (2017, August 29). ADDIE model: Instructional design. In *Educational Technology* [Online]. Retrieved from educationaltechnology.net: https://educationaltechnology.net/the-addie-model-instructional-design/

Lee, C. D., & Smagorinsky, P. (Eds.). (2000). *Vygotskian perspectives on literacy research: Constructing meaning through collaborative inquiry.* Cambridge: Cambridge University Press.

Linder, A., Airey, J., Mayaba, N., & Webb, P. (2014). Fostering disciplinary literacy? South African physics lecturers' educational responses to their students' lack of representational competence. *African Journal of Research in Mathematics, Science and Technology Education, 18*(3), 242–252.

Lotter, C., Harwood, W. S., & Bonner, J. J. (2007). The influence of core teaching conceptions on teachers' use of inquiry teaching practices. *Journal of research inscience teaching, 44*(9), 1318–1347.

McConachie, S. M., & Petrosky, A. R. (2010). Engaging content teachers in literacy development. In *Content matters: A disciplinary literacy approach to improving students learning* (pp. 1–14). San Francisco, CA: Jossey-Bass.

McKenna, M. C., & Robinson, R. D. (2002). *Teaching through text: Reading and writing in the content areas.* Boston: Allyn & Bacon.

Melanie, M. (2008). Improving the flow of materials in a Cataloging Department: Using ADDIE for a project in the Ohio State University Libraries. *Library Resources and Technical Services, 52*(2), 54–60.

Middendorf, J., & Pace, D. (2004). Decoding the disciplines: A model for helping students learn disciplinary ways of thinking. *New Directions for Teaching and Learning, 2004*(98), 1–12.

Moje, E. B. (2007). Chapter 1 developing socially just subject-matter instruction: A review of the literature on disciplinary literacy teaching. *Review of Research in Education, 31*(1), 1–44.

National Research Council (NRC). (1999). *Transforming undergraduate education in science, mathematics, engineering, and technology.* Washington, DC: National Academies Press.

National Research Council (NRC). (2003). *BIO2010: Transforming undergraduate education for future research biologists.* Washington, DC: National Academies Press.

National Science Foundation. (1996). *Shaping the future: New expectations for undergraduate education in science, mathematics, engineering, and technology.* Washington, DC: NSF Division of Undergraduate Education.

Newman, D., Griffin, P., & Cole, M. (1989). *The construction zone: Working for cognitive change in school.* Cambridge: Cambridge University Press.

Norton, L., Richardson, T. E., Hartley, J., Newstead, S., & Mayes, J. (2005). Teachers' beliefs and intentions concerning teaching in higher education. *Higher Education, 50*(4), 537–571.

Olson, S., & Riordan, D. G. (2012). *Engage to excel: Producing one million additional college graduates with degrees in science, technology, engineering, and mathematics.* Report to the President. Executive Office of the President.

Ozdileka, Z., & Robeckb, E. (2009). Operational priorities of instructional designers analyzed within the steps of the Addie instructional design model. *Procedia Social and Behavioral Sciences, 1*(1), 2046–2050.

Paris, S. G., Lipson, M. Y., & Wixon, K. K. (1994). Becoming a strategic reader. In R. B. Ruddell, M. R. Ruddell, & H. Singer (Eds.), *Theoretical models and processes of reading* (4th ed.). Newark, DE: International Reading Association.

Penuel, W. R., Fishman, B. J., Yamaguchi, R., & Gallagher, L. P. (2007). What makes professional development effective? Strategies that foster curriculum implementation. *American Educational Research Journal, 44*(4), 921–958.

Petrillo, J. (2016). On flipping first-semester calculus: a case study. *International Journal of Mathematical Education in Science and Technology, 47*(4), 573–582.

Prosser, M., & Trigwell, K. (1999). *Understanding learning and teaching: The experience in higher education*. Buckingham: The Society of Research into Higher Education & Open University Press.

Richardson, J. T. E. (2005). Instruments for obtaining student feedback: A review of the literature. *Assessment & Evaluation in Higher Education, 30*(4), 387–415.

Sarason, Y., & Banbury, C. (2004). Active learning facilitated by using a game-show format or who doesn't want to be a millionaire? *Journal of Management Education, 28*(4), 509–518.

Shanahan, T., & Shanahan, C. (2008). Teaching disciplinary literacy to adolescents: Rethinking content-area literacy. *Harvard Educational Review, 78*(1), 40–59.

Shanahan, T., & Shanahan, C. (2012). What is disciplinary literacy and why does it matter? *Topics in Language Disorders, 32*(1), 7–18.

Stains, M., Harshman, J., Barker, M. K., Chasteen, S. V., Cole, R., DeChenne-Peters, S. E., et al. (2018). Anatomy of STEM teaching in North American universities. *Science, 359*(6383), 1468–1470.

Stewart, R. A., & O'Brien, D. G. (1989). Resistance to content area reading: A focus on preservice teachers. *Journal of Reading, 32*(5), 396–401.

Stokstad, E. (2001). Reintroducing the intro course. *Science, 293*, 1608–1610.

Sugie, S. (2012, June). Instructional design of the communicative blended learning for Chinese as a foreign language. Paper presented at *The Second International Conference on Advanced Collaborative Networks, Systems and Applications* COLLA 2012 June 24–29, 2012 - Venice, Italy. Retrieved from Hokkaido University Collection of Scholarly and Academic Papers HUSCAP. https://eprints.lib.hokudai.ac.jp/dspace/bitstream/2115/54553/1/BLforCFL%28sugie%2920120427resend.pdf

Tucker, B. (2012). The flipped classroom. *Education Next, 12*(1), 82–83.

Vgotsky, L. S. (1987). *The collected works of LS Vygotsky: Volume 1: Problems of general psychology*. New York: Plenum Press.

Watkins, R. (2005). Developing interactive e-learning activities. *Performance Improvement, 44*(5), 5.

Wineburg, S. (1991). On the reading of historical texts: Notes on the breach between school and academy. *American Educational Research Journal, 28*(3), 495–519.

Wood, W. B. (2009). Innovations in teaching undergraduate biology and why we need them. *Annual Review of Cell and Developmental, 25*, 93–112.

CHAPTER 3

Assessment: A Tool for Improving Disciplinary Literacy

Juanita C. But

3.1 INTRODUCTION

In gateway college content area courses, student learning is mainly measured by tests, exams, and other summative assessments that evaluate content knowledge. Because of demanding instructional pacing and the vast amount of material need to be covered in their courses (Conley, 2007), college instructors may not have sufficient time to identify areas individual students are struggling with, and thereby provide timely interventions throughout the instructional/learning process. While content assessment dominates college courses across the disciplines, little has been done in disciplinary literacy assessment, especially for formative purposes, which represents a critical aspect of student learning. This vacuum is palpable as "assessment of discipline-appropriate literacy is an all but ignored topic in the professional literature" (Gillis & Van Wig, 2015, p. 455). This omission has inevitably created a deficit in college learning assessment, particularly in disciplinary learning.

J. C. But (✉)
New York City College of Technology, City University of New York,
Brooklyn, NY, USA
e-mail: jbut@citytech.cuny.edu

© The Author(s) 2020
J. C. But (ed.), *Teaching College-Level Disciplinary Literacy*,
https://doi.org/10.1007/978-3-030-39804-0_3

Disciplinary literacy requires not just one single skill but a set of skills, abilities, and cognitive processes that enable participants to engage actively in the practices and discourse of a specific discipline. To achieve this, various discipline-specific components and skill requirements have to be adequately addressed. As much as summative assessments can measure students' content knowledge, what they lack is the mechanism that allows students and instructors to determine where and when effective learning fails to take place, and how to modify instruction and apply strategies to close the gap.

In college-level courses, knowledge acquisition and literacy requirements are highly specialized and discipline specific; therefore, identifying students' literacy needs and the areas that require development will enable appropriate and effective instruction. In developing students' disciplinary literacy, assessments are not merely a summative tool to measure course outcomes; they need to be contextualized with a formative purpose to drive and support teaching and learning. Therefore, formative assessments have to be embedded in individual content area classrooms to be effective (Gillis & Van Wig, 2015).

3.2   READ Assessment Method

In college-level reading and general literacy assessments, standardized tests have been widely used to assess students' reading abilities. However, these tests hardly cover the literacy requirements in individual disciplines and are therefore not effective in assessing students' readiness for content area learning. At City Tech, Reading Effectively Across the Disciplines (READ) assessments are developed to serve this purpose; they are designed to be strategic, discipline-specific, and vary from one content area to another.

As a vehicle for fostering disciplinary learning and instruction, READ emphasizes the significance and impact of literacy assessments in the content areas. Instructors use specially designed formal and informal assessments in the content area classrooms for both formative and summative purposes. Each set of assessments measures students' general literacy, technical vocabulary knowledge, and discipline-specific cognitive and literacy skills. The primary focus of READ is to empower students to be active learners through reading effectively to access the knowledge and language in the disciplines. In Science, Technology, Engineering and Mathematics (STEM) courses, this approach also fosters students' abilities to make connections between knowledge acquired in lectures/texts and its application in the lab. Therefore, the use of appropriate text materials, including textbooks, lab manuals, and other discipline-specific texts is essential to the design of READ assessments.

Assessments in READ take both formal and informal formats and follow a planned timeline. Discipline-specific formal assessments consist of pre-READ and post-READ assessments, which are administered at the beginning and toward the end of each semester respectively. The pre-READ assessments are also used to identify students' areas of strength and weakness in reading and in accessing and processing disciplinary language. The results of pre-READ assessments provide information for instructors to modify approaches and select strategies to improve student learning. The post-READ assessments, though mainly summative, help evaluate the effectiveness of strategies and their implementations to guide future modifications.

Since the materials and procedures of reading assessments are most effective when they are carefully matched to specific purposes (Afflerbach & Cho, 2011), the selection of appropriate texts for assessment is an important process. Literacy specialists and content area faculty work together to select texts in the pre-READ and post-READ assessments. The length of assessment, text features, and readability are among the factors to be considered in text selection. Typically, an assessment takes approximately 30 minutes and is administered within one class period. For this reason, passage length needs to be appropriate. Also important are text features, which should correspond to the outcomes to be assessed in the scoring rubric. Another consideration is text readability. The reading level of the texts of the pre-READ should be similar to that of the post-READ assessment. In addition to using the readability formulas, text complexity and conceptual density are also factors to determine text choices.

Assessment texts are also discipline-specific. For instance, in the introductory accounting courses, articles addressing existing practices in the industry are selected to assess students' cognitive skills and accounting literacy. In Architecture, drawings, images together with written texts are used to assess students' literal and inferential comprehension, higher-order thinking skills, as well as their corresponding visual literacy. For STEM and engineering lab courses, the lab manual is used to assess students' ability to understand processes and technical components, troubleshoot problems, and engage in reading to apply knowledge and information. In Biology, textbook excerpts or articles of related topics are used to assess students' understanding of core concepts and key terms and their relationships to other elements in the system. In a course that emphasizes problem solving such as College Algebra, word problems are created to assess students' comprehension, reasoning, and problem-solving skills, as well as metacognitive skills.

3.3   READ Assessment Standards and Criteria

Creating a standard for evaluating the READ assessments requires an apparatus that measures both the general and specific literacy needs in the disciplines. The general READ rubric (Table 3.1) was partially based on the CUNY reading requirements, with additional criteria that cover the literacy requirements in most content areas. The main assessment categories include comprehension, analysis, application, and evaluation. Scoring is based on four levels of competencies: full proficiency (4), adequate proficiency (3), approaching proficiency (2), and low proficiency (1).

Comprehension skills are essential and fundamental to all levels and disciplines of learning. They cover literal and inferential comprehension, as well as vocabulary knowledge. Higher-order thinking skills are essentially built upon comprehension, which is the precursor to applying, analyzing, and evaluating concepts and knowledge. Students' comprehension competency in the READ assessment is demonstrated by their understanding of the main idea, major details, and specialized vocabulary in the text, as well as their abilities to make logical inferences.

The application of knowledge plays a vital role in many STEM and professional studies courses. It is a transaction from *reading to learn* to *reading to do* while using the knowledge learned in reading and lectures to a new or real-life context. This competency is especially central to preparing students for their future careers. The curriculum of many STEM and health science studies carries a heavy component of practice and application. To demonstrate this competency in the assessment, students have to be able to use concepts and ideas in the text to solve problems proficiently or make connections and/or apply them to a new context accurately and in a meaningful and relevant way.

Another set of essential disciplinary literacy skills is analysis. When students are asked to analyze a text, a problem, an experiment, or a set of data, they often cannot grasp the full extent of their tasks. The application of analytical skills is a crucial step before reaching a meaningful conclusion and is essential to success in every content area. They are required to identify the relationships among ideas and concepts, as well as connecting parts to the overall entity to demonstrate this competency in the assessment. The development of analytical skills becomes increasingly essential to learning in today's classrooms where information is presented in diverse and multimodal formats and media.

Table 3.1 READ assessment rubric

Performance criteria	4	3	2	1
Comprehension	Understands the main idea, major details, and specialized vocabulary in the text and is able to make logical inferences	Understands most of the information and specialized vocabulary in the text and is able to make some logical inferences	Understands some ideas and specialized vocabulary in the text, but struggles to make logical inferences	Mostly unable to understand the main points and specialized vocabulary in the text and make logical inferences
Analysis	Able to identify text structure, fully understand and analyze the relationships among ideas, and interpret information presented in diverse formats and media	Able to identify text structure, understand and analyze some of the relationships among ideas, and interpret some information presented in diverse formats and media	Has some difficulties in identifying text structure, understand and analyze the relationships among ideas, and interpret information presented in diverse formats and media	Mostly unable to identify text structure, understand and analyze the relationships among ideas, and interpret information presented in diverse formats and media
Context/application	Able to use concepts and ideas in the text to solve problems proficiently or make connections/apply them to a new context accurately and in a meaningful and relevant way	Able to use concepts and ideas in the text to solve problems or make connection/apply them to a new context accurately, but has some limitations	Able to use some concepts and ideas in the text to solve problems partially or make connections/apply them in a new context with minor mismatching of information and limitations	Mostly unable to use concepts and ideas in the text to solve problems or make connection/apply them in a new context
Evaluation	Able to make informed judgment about/assess ideas, situations, or arguments with adequate support, including valid reasoning, relevant and sufficient evidence based on the text	Able to make informed judgment about/assessment of ideas, situations, or arguments with some support, including valid reasoning, relevant and sufficient evidence based on the text	Able to make judgment about/assess ideas, situations, or arguments but with limited or no support, including valid reasoning, relevant and sufficient evidence based on the text	Mostly unable to make judgment about/assessment of ideas, situations, or arguments with support, including valid reasoning, relevant and sufficient evidence based on the text

4 = Full proficiency; 3 = Adequate proficiency; 2 = Approaching proficiency; 1 = Low proficiency

Critical thinking is inseparable from the ability to judge and assess ideas, situations, and arguments. Therefore, evaluation is a crucial component in the READ assessments. Evaluation is the ability to make informed judgment, assess ideas, and make arguments that are based on evidence. This includes the judgment or assessment of ideas and situations, or if arguments have adequate support, including valid reasoning, and relevant evidence based on the text.

3.4   Assessment Design

It is common that higher education programs depend on standardized tests or general assessment tools to evaluate students' academic literacy. The main advantages of this practice are its efficiency and uniformity. However, these assessment results only demonstrate students' general literacy and very often do not offer a full picture of students' proficiency in specific areas of disciplinary learning. Discipline-specific READ assessments aim to fill this gap. In the design process, not only content area texts are used, but the development of the READ assessment rubric is also aligned with the learning outcomes in the disciplines. To ensure reliability and content validity, literacy specialists and content area faculty work together to design and review assessment items and questions in each category. The questions are carefully matched with the outcomes in the rubric.

The texts used in the assessments include textbook passages and discipline-based articles. They are selected based on their content relevance, readability level, length, textual complexity, text features, and the amount of prior knowledge required. In the initial round of assessment design, both content area faculty and literacy specialists collaborate to create several sets of assessments for each course. The assessment development team coordinates to select texts, create, and then revise the questions. After the questions are created, the development team works on the answers and generates a scoring guide for each question. Team members and other participating instructors of the assessed course then carefully review the scoring guide to ensure that it is accurate and properly aligned with the READ assessment rubric. Among the sets of assessments developed, one set will be used as the pre-READ assessment in the participating sections of the same course. Later in the semester, after the implementation of disciplinary literacy pedagogy, a second set will be given as the post-READ assessment.

The most important process in creating the assessment is the design of the questions based on specific learning objectives. If assessments are misaligned with learning objectives or instructional strategies, it can undermine the assessment efforts. The READ assessments employ an integrative design that is guided by the discipline-specific assessment criteria. The assessment questions represent a wide variety of cognitive inquiries in various modes. Depending on the disciplines, they include multiple-choice questions, constructed-response questions, cloze questions, true/false questions, ranking, matching, and, in some cases, drawing (see, e.g., Table 3.1).

The main benefit of including different types of questions is to balance between the uniformity of scoring standards and the flexibility of measuring complex and varying skills. Often dominating standardized tests, multiple-choice questions are effective in assessing a broad range of knowledge and can be scored efficiently and with objectiveness. What multiple-choice questions cannot achieve, however, is to measure complex skills that are often required in college content area courses. For instance, a biology multiple-choice assessment can test a students' factual knowledge and can determine if they can differentiate between correct and incorrect statements of the relationships between concepts, entities, and procedures. However, it cannot evaluate, among other tasks, students' reasoning process in making judgments and drawing conclusions.

Compared to multiple-choice questions, constructive-response questions have much more versatility in both design and assessment goals, and more often they evoke complex thinking (Martinez, 1999). Constructive-response questions can take many forms, with responses ranging from simple short answers that contain a single word or complex analysis of a scientific hypothesis (Livingston, 2009). There is a plethora of advantages in using constructive-response questions in the READ assessments for the purposes of gauging students' ability in disciplinary thinking, particularly in describing, analyzing, and evaluating content ideas, information, and problem-solving procedures. Constructive-response questions are highly effective in discipline-specific assessments because the tasks required in these questions are as varied as the skills to be measured. Other types of questions such as cloze, ranking, and matching questions can dynamically measure students' ability to contextualize knowledge and comprehend the hierarchical and relational network of concepts and information. Figure 3.1 shows some examples of READ assessment questions in different disciplines.

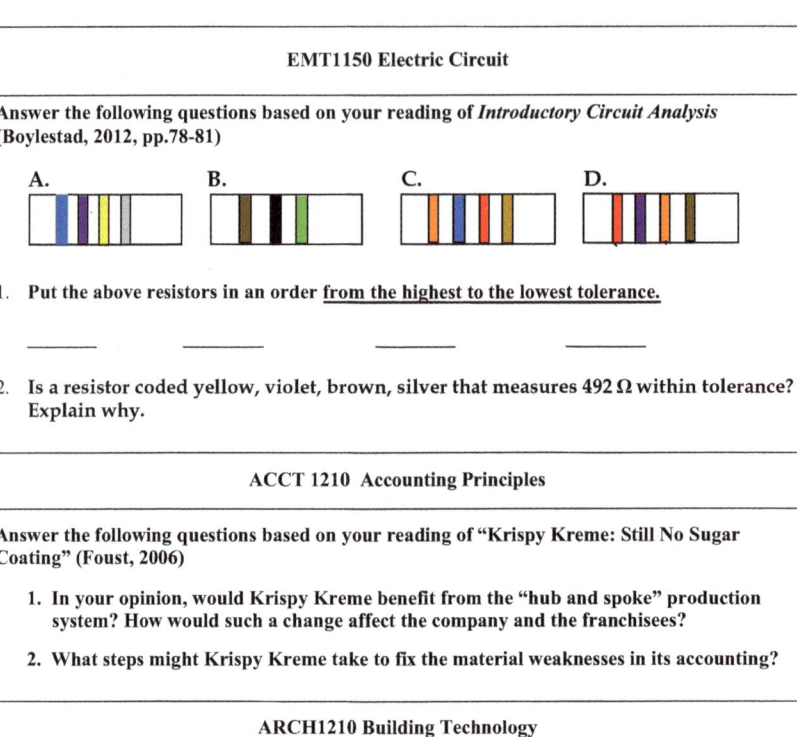

EMT1150 Electric Circuit

Answer the following questions based on your reading of *Introductory Circuit Analysis* (Boylestad, 2012, pp.78-81)

A.   B.   C.   D.

1. Put the above resistors in an order <u>from the highest to the lowest tolerance.</u>

    _____   _____   _____   _____

2. Is a resistor coded yellow, violet, brown, silver that measures 492 Ω within tolerance? Explain why.

ACCT 1210 Accounting Principles

Answer the following questions based on your reading of "Krispy Kreme: Still No Sugar Coating" (Foust, 2006)

1. In your opinion, would Krispy Kreme benefit from the "hub and spoke" production system? How would such a change affect the company and the franchisees?

2. What steps might Krispy Kreme take to fix the material weaknesses in its accounting?

ARCH1210 Building Technology

Answer the following questions based on your reading of "The Expansion of Modernism" in *Understanding Architecture* (Roth & Clark, 2013, pp. 609-611).

1. Based on the passage, <u>when</u> and <u>why</u> did the architectural style in Figure 20.1 become popular in the United States?

2. Which of the critics of Modernist architecture mentioned in the passage would most likely share Mario Botta's opinion? On what subject would they agree with each other? Support your answers with textual evidence.

BIO1201 Biology II

Answer the following questions based on your reading of "Antibiotic resistance: World on cusp of 'post-antibiotic era'" (Gallagher, 2015).

1. According to the passage, what is a "post-antibiotic era?"

2. Specifically, how does antibiotic resistance spread?

Fig. 3.1   Sample assessment questions by discipline/course

3.5   ASSESSMENT EVALUATION

Since some constructive-response questions have no standardized answers, it is important for the responses to be rated reliably, especially when the assessments are administered in multiple sections of the same course that involve different instructors. To achieve uniformity and consensus, in addition to an answer key, the faculty team creates scoring guides that correspond to the READ assessment rubric, with a well-defined and detailed point system for each item. Content area faculty and literacy specialists also collaborate to implement the scoring guide in the scoring process to establish accuracy and consistency. The faculty team then collects student works that exemplify each level. These samples help set up benchmarks for future scoring.

The pre-READ assessment is used to establish a baseline and to inform faculty of any learning gaps and areas of instruction that need changes or special attention to close the gap. Therefore, reviewing the assessment is an important process that can provide information for identifying and implementing strategies in the classrooms to reinforce learning and help students meet the learning objectives. In the review process, the faculty team also examines the validity of the assessment questions and revises them as needed.

The goals of the READ assessments are not limited to measuring student learning. By involving students in the assessment process and motivating them to grow as learners, they do not simply receive their assessment results to mark their levels and performance. In post-assessment discussions, instructors go through each assignment with students to identify any problematic topics, misconceptions, and specific areas that need development and reinforcement. This is to make sure that students, as stakeholders of their own learning, are aware that assessment is also an essential part of effective teaching and learning (Chappuis & Stiggins, 2002). At the same time, READ faculty members use assessment as a tool to promote greater student achievement (Shepard, 2000). When students become involved in the process, assessment for learning appears to be a part of the instructional routine rather than testing that is isolated from teaching (Davies, 2000). In addition, keeping students connected to a vision of quality as the course progresses helps them self-assess and close the gap by formulating their next steps in learning (Sadler, 1989).

The post-READ assessments are scored in a similar process as the pre-READ. They are administered at the end of the semester to evaluate the effectiveness of the disciplinary literacy strategies and approaches used.

The pre- and post-READ assessment results are then compared across sections to show the areas of improvements and those that fall short of our goals. This evaluation can guide future instructional design and implementation to develop disciplinary learning.

The READ assessments are conducted in class where students are given ample time for reading a disciplinary text from which assessment questions are generated. Instructors communicate the purpose of the assessments clearly to the students, which is not used as a test, but a measure of how well they practice disciplinary literacy. As the results do not affect their course grades, students' assessment anxiety is kept at a very low level. Because the assessments do not deliberately require students to recall information they have learned previously, they can focus on engaging the present tasks of answering questions and solving problems by reading the assigned texts. Moreover, students seldom feel constrained by the lack of time, as the assessments are relatively short, to the point that its length is sufficient to assess the rubric outcomes. Instructors can also choose to assess selected categories from the READ rubric to optimize the use of time and afford flexibility.

Specialized Rubric Outcomes

The READ assessment is designed to include outcomes that generally apply to courses across the disciplines. To customize some of the READ assessments, discipline-specific analytic rubrics are also developed to align with professional and institutional standards. For example, the American Board of Engineering Technology (ABET), an accreditation body for engineering education, publishes required student outcomes that meet the latest standards of college engineering programs. The READ development team observed that some of the cognitive processes required in engineering correspond to the reading and literacy production processes. To integrate both sets of standards, the READ literacy specialists and engineering faculty collaboratively designed a new set of student outcomes that match the ABET criteria and the READ assessment requirements.

The customized rubric (Integrated READ-ABET assessment rubric) incorporated five ABET (2019) student outcomes:

- An ability to identify, formulate, and solve complex engineering problems by applying principles of engineering, science, and mathematics
- An ability to develop and conduct appropriate experimentation, analyze and interpret data, and use engineering judgment to draw conclusions

When aligned with the READ rubric outcomes, the ABET-READ rubric (see Chap. 7) provides a set of comprehensive and discipline-relevant assessment guidelines that cover both lab and lecture learning. The design of these assessments is embedded in the engineering curriculum for disciplinary literacy development and specialized learning objectives.

3.6   The READ Survey

In the realm of academic assessments, self-assessments and surveys can provide valuable information for instructional planning and design. To establish an understanding of how faculty perceive students' literacy skills in their disciplines, READ conducted a pilot faculty survey in which content area instructors were asked to rate the importance of reading, writing, and presentation skills of the students. In addition, they also estimated the amount of assigned reading students completed and the obstacles students encounter in reading to learn content area texts. After collecting and analyzing the faculty survey results, a large-scale student survey was developed to collect information on student reading in various disciplines. When evaluating the results of both sets of surveys, READ administrators were able to identify mismatched areas between faculty perceptions and students' self-assessments. In general, faculty members across the disciplines perceive students as more able to complete the assigned readings independently than what students have reported.

To acquire a more detailed picture of how students engage in disciplinary reading, the READ student survey (see Fig. 3.2) poses both general and discipline-specific questions to identify the cognitive, intellectual, and affective challenges students face in reading in the disciplines and the extent to which they apply literacy strategies to enable deeper learning.

The READ survey is conducted in an ongoing basis in a range of content area courses, particularly in STEM and professional studies, to examine aspects of student reading and literacy practices. Students respond anonymously to the online survey. They are asked to reflect on their perceptions of academic reading, reading habits, use of their textbooks, completion of assigned readings, difficulties in reading disciplinary texts, and strategies they use or do not use while reading. This set of information gives content area faculty important insight into how well their students learn, the challenges they face in learning through reading, and the literacy strategies they need to develop to read disciplinary texts effectively.

General Information

How many college credits have you taken?

- Less than 20
- 30 to 60
- 60 to 90
- More than 120

What is the current course being surveyed?

What is your major?

Perception of College Reading

Reading is important to your college success.

(Strongly agree/Agree/Not sure/Disagree/Strongly Disagree)

Textbook Usage and Assigned Readings

How do you access your textbook(s)?

- Purchase
- Rent
- Borrow from the library
- BitTorrent or related methods
- Online
- I don't use a textbook

If you don't use a textbook, state the reason(s):

- Cannot afford to buy
- Don't think they are necessary
- Read lecture notes instead
- No time to read
- Texts are too hard
- No interest
- Not a required course
- Not required

Fig. 3.2 READ student survey

How often do you use your textbook(s)?

- Almost everyday
- A few times per week
- Once a week
- Only before tests
- Seldom
- Never

If you don't use your textbook(s), check the following reasons:

- Cannot afford to buy/rent
- Read lecture notes instead
- Read class material/text posted online
- No time to read
- Texts are too hard
- No interest
- Not a required course
- Textbook not required by instructors
- Other (please specify)

How much of the assigned readings do you complete in your current course?

- Almost none
- Around 20%
- Around 50%
- Around 75%
- Almost all

The completion of assigned readings in the current course counts towards your final grade.

(Yes/No)

While reading to assigned texts, I am able to:

- Understand and summarize the main points
- Interpret meaning by using evidence in the text and personal experience
- Analyze the details/ideas and their relationship with one another
- Apply the information I have read in a real life context
- Synthesize knowledge and information I have learned
- Apply the information I have read in a real life context
- Evaluate the arguments and make judgements based on the evidence in the text

The textbook(s) for your current course is interesting.

(Strongly agree/Agree/Not sure/Disagree/Strongly disagree)

Fig. 3.2 (continued)

The textbook(s) for your current course is informative

(Strongly agree/Agree/Not sure/Disagree/Strongly disagree)

Challenges

You have difficulties understanding your textbook.

(Strongly agree/Agree/Not sure/Disagree/Strongly disagree)

You have difficulties retaining information from your textbook.

(Strongly agree/Agree/Not sure/Disagree/Strongly disagree)

From your experience, what makes reading the texts challenging?

- Difficult vocabulary
- Do not have enough background knowledge on the topic
- Unable to relate content to real life experience
- Unable to understand relationships among concepts
- Unable to understand the structure/organization of the text
- Instructors do not provide sufficient guidelines for reading the text
- No problem at all with readings
- Instructor does not require reading the text

What are the reasons for not completing your assigned readings?

- Lack interest in reading
- Cannot afford the textbook
- Cannot put the readings in meaningful/relevant contexts
- Lack reading strategies
- Not good at reading comprehension
- Text is too difficult
- Text is not interesting
- Cannot retain information
- Reading is not required to pass the course
- Course is not required

Strategy Use

I use strategies to read the assigned texts.

(Yes/No/Not sure)

Which reading strategies do you use?

- Mark/underline text

Fig. 3.2 (continued)

- Highlight text
- Annotate text
- Note-taking
- Visual-drawing/Mapping
- Re-read difficult parts
- Generate and answer questions
- Make mental pictures
- Other (please specify)

Language and Reading Background

English is your first language.

(Yes/No)

You are currently taking a developmental reading course.

(Yes/No)

Reading Habits

I read books, magazines, articles, or newspaper for pleasure.

(Yes/No)

How often do you read for pleasure?

When was the last time you read a book for pleasure?

Print/Electronic Texts

Of the following, which do you prefer?

- Print textbooks
- Electronic textbooks

Explain your preference for print textbooks.

Explain your preference for electronic textbooks.

Please describe what college reading is to you. Do you have any comments about reading in college that you would like to contribute?

Fig. 3.2 (continued)

The survey involves a metacognitive process in which students reflect on what and how they read, which helps them develop self-awareness when they learn through texts. From the outset, it is important to foreground their self-awareness of the relationship between reading and their college success. Students who do not consider reading as important in college learning may not have developed the habit of learning through texts in high school. Even when they are required to complete assigned readings, they seldom engage in deep and meaningful reading before they change their perceptions.

Students who struggle with reading often cannot articulate or identify the precise difficulties they encounter while approaching disciplinary texts. From the students' responses, faculty can understand the areas of struggles while they are reading and tackle the specific obstacles. Some of the difficulties can be overcome, depending on the needs demonstrated, through scaffolding the reading assignments by familiarizing students with difficult and specialized vocabulary, developing students' prior knowledge of the topics, and providing guidelines and setting a purpose for reading. In addition, teaching text organization and structure and helping students relate content to real-life applications are also crucial to promoting meaningful learning from texts. Since there is a wide range of strategies and practices that can be used in the content area classroom, it is important to select the ones that are most essential and address the literacy needs of the students. As the survey is conducted across the disciplines, it identifies both general and discipline-specific areas of concern and the tools and resources to address them.

From the survey, faculty can also find out students' attitudes toward and levels of commitment to completing assigned readings. Despite that most content area faculty routinely assign readings for their courses, they do not frequently assess if their students have completed the readings and understood the contents. Student feedback in specific disciplines can drive faculty to approach assigned readings differently to foster engagement in learning, especially among students who lack interest in reading. These can include active reading and learning activities that involve visual and creative components to motivate student reading. For instance, based on the information revealed in student responses, READ biology faculty designed collaborative class activities such as word/concept mapping and poetry writing from selected lessons to engage students in analyzing and articulating complex concepts in groups. Student presentations of readings that require higher-order thinking, as a form of authentic assessment (Lund, 1997) rather than lecturing of content knowledge that is acquired from reading can have a lasting effect on building students' interests in reading disciplinary texts.

Content area instructors often complain that students do not read their textbooks. This can be attributed to many factors. As READ faculty evaluate the causes reported by their students, they can begin to look for solutions. A good example is that several READ courses offer students free access to electronic textbooks through Open Education Resources (OER). The decision was made because most students in these courses, mainly in STEM, identified high cost as the main reason for them to refrain from using the textbooks. As these free resources are available online, we also monitor how the use of electronic textbooks affect student reading as opposed to print texts.

Getting to know the students and their literacy needs is also pivotal to implementing student-centered instruction. It is common to see a large number of students in STEM and professional studies classrooms. As a result, it becomes challenging for faculty to get acquainted with individual students and their language and literacy backgrounds, as well as their needs for literacy and reading support. The survey can provide information on the percentage of English learners and struggling readers who find comprehending and navigating the texts challenging. With this information, content area faculty can pace their lessons and support student reading accordingly.

For instance, we have seen a consistent trend in the survey responses that students find difficult vocabulary as the top obstacle to accessing disciplinary reading. In some courses, such as biology and chemistry, around 50% of the first-year students reported that they had difficulty understanding the vocabulary in their textbooks. This prompted the READ faculty to pay special attention to developing students' vocabulary strategies and syntactical analysis to help students to extract meaning of the words from the contexts. Showing novice students how words can be broken into parts and getting them into the habit of looking for prefixes and suffixes of vocabulary words are especially useful to enhance comprehension in many STEM courses. In courses where a high percentage of students reported problems with retaining information they learned from lectures or readings, admit slips or low-stakes short quizzes can be implemented at the beginning of each class period, asking students to recall main points and key concepts they have learned in the previous lesson or assigned readings. This can help students retain information in the long run.

The READ survey was designed as both a research tool and an assessment instrument to improve disciplinary literacy practices. With both quantitative and qualitative data, the survey information can be used flexibly to guide pedagogical decisions to enhance learning in the disciplines. As we compare the responses in the student survey to that in the initial faculty survey, we can identify mismatched perceptions and erroneous assumptions about student reading. When used with the READ assessments, this information can provide a broader picture of the effectiveness of strategies used in the content area classrooms. We also analyze and correlate student reading and their course performance. This can effectively direct our professional development decisions. Our survey results revealed that there were strong correlations among students' strategy use, their completion of assigned readings, and their academic performance (Kwon, Xu, & But, 2016).

3.7   Formative Assessment and Strategy Development

Pedagogical content knowledge, as Shulman (1986) observed, is required specifically *for* teaching. It includes educators' "understanding of what makes the learning of specific topics easy or difficult" and "knowledge of the strategies most likely to be fruitful in reorganizing the understanding of learners" (p. 10). The READ assessments and student surveys are instrumental in informing the development of instructional practices that enable students to overcome obstacles in disciplinary learning. Based on the assessment and survey results, faculty are able to modify their teaching practices and apply appropriate pedagogies.

The strategies applied in the READ content area classrooms serve both as developmental tools and formative assessments of student learning in the disciplines. For instance, in an architecture course, visual notetaking is used as a tool to assess students' understanding of concepts and relationships between textual components, including visual, written, and graphic representations. It serves to cultivate students' engagement in text-based learning as well as evaluate their proficiency in learning and application of the architectural language. In accounting courses, students learn to connect and analyze the network of knowledge by using concept maps. Concept mapping is embedded in these courses as an ongoing instructional routine to organize ideas and information. At the same time, it is a useful tool for the instructor to monitor students' progress in learning, comprehension, and mastery of key concepts. The instructor can then revise and reinforce instructional routines and provide relevant feedback accordingly. In addition, learning logs and exit slips are widely used by READ faculty across the disciplines to foster metacognitive skills. They are also useful tools to assess student learning at various stages.

In courses where students have difficulties analyzing concepts and evaluating information in the problem-solving process, instructors develop students' inquiry skills to address these areas of learning. For example, in mathematics and engineering courses, our faculty use questioning activities to help students reflect on their problem-solving process and evaluate any misconceptions they may have. Modeling the questioning process in the disciplines can help students explore specific ways of approaching the subject matters. As students are put in the position not only to answer but to generate questions, they begin to examine the topics with various perspectives and orders of thinking. They are also "pushed to evaluate and articulate their own thinking beyond a level they could attain on their own, and actually influence and enhance the learning of others" (Caram & Davis, 2005, p. 23). Student-led questioning can be done in different classroom settings. Instructors can assess students' knowledge and their level of familiarity with the language and meaning-making processes in the disciplines.

Many students tend to rush to try to solve the problems before they take time to recognize the types of problems and the methods required to solve them. To encourage deep learning, some READ faculty ask students to document their problem-solving process by writing out and justifying each step of the solution. Focusing on the problem-solving process rather than emphasizing the actual solution is a more effective form of assessment.

In addition to classroom assessments, faculty give students self-assessments in some READ courses. For instance, a checklist based on the required ABET student outcomes in areas of knowledge, skills, and teamwork was used to help engineering students evaluate their learning based on a set of academic and professional standards. This also enables the instructors to gain insight into students' abilities and their confidence in succeeding in the discipline.

3.8   Assessments for Learning
in Multiple Dimensions

Assessment always occupies a central place in learning and education. With the increasing institutional and accreditation demands for assessment of student outcomes, one impediment to widely implementing disciplinary literacy assessments is that it will divert existing mainstream assessment efforts to what is considered to be an area of specialty. It is not because disciplinary literacy is not a critical concern in content area learning, but it has not been adequately recognized among college educators as essential for disciplinary learning in college-level courses (Armstrong & Stahl, 2017). To leverage the time and efforts dedicated to assessments, READ assessments serve the dual purpose of informing and supporting disciplinary literacy teaching and learning and measuring the effectiveness of strategies and practices. They are discipline-specific and often embedded in the curriculum, rather than separate measures that potentially impose additional assessment burdens or fatigue on the faculty and the students, which could negatively affect evaluation efforts (Davies & Ferdous, 2005).

As assessment of learning is not our ultimate goal, we do not rely on a single summative assessment. In a disciplinary literacy program, formative evaluations engage students in self-reflective learning and establish student agency, as well as provide faculty directions for planning and instructional development. The strategies and practices, including formal and informal assignments, are developed and used as learning tools for students and means of evaluating teaching and learning. READ also incorporates traditional and non-traditional measures, including students' self-evaluation of their learning and formal assessment of their disciplinary literacy practices in-class and out-of-class. Continuous and systematic reviews of the assessments also help monitor the strengths and areas that need improvement in the program.

Since the inception of the program, READ assessment outcomes have been included in City Tech's regional and programmatic accreditation review processes. This inclusion emphasizes the relevance of reading and disciplinary literacy in higher education and refocuses the assessment efforts on an aspect that is significant but has been overlooked. With systematic and ongoing engagement in disciplinary literacy assessment, the institution is taking an important step toward improving disciplinary literacy practices.

References

Accreditation Board for Engineering and Technology (ABET), 2019–2020 Criterion 3 student outcomes. Retrieved from: https://www.abet.org/accreditation/accreditation-criteria/criteria-for-accrediting-engineering-technology-programs-2019-2020/#GC3

Afflerbach, P., & Cho, B. Y. (2011). The classroom assessment of reading. Handbook of reading research, 4, 487–514. New York: Routlege.

Armstrong, S. L., & Stahl, N. A. (2017). Communication across the silos and borders: The culture of reading in a community college. *Journal of College Reading and Learning, 47*(2), 99–122.

Boylestad, R. L. (2010). *Introductory circuit analysis.* Upper Saddle River, NJ: Prentice Hall Press.

Caram, C. A., & Davis, P. B. (2005). Inviting student engagement with questioning. *Kappa Delta Pi Record, 42*(1), 19–23.

Chappuis, S., & Stiggins, R. J. (2002). Classroom assessment for learning. *Educational Leadership, 60*(1), 40–44.

Conley, D. T. (2007). Redefining college readiness. Eugene, OR: Educational Policy Improvement Center.

Davies, A. (2000). *Making classroom assessment work.* Merville, BC: Connections Publishing.

Davies, J., & Ferdous, A. (2005). *Using item difficulty and item position to measure test fatigue.* Washington, DC: American Institute for Research.

Foust, D. (2006). Krispy Kreme: Still no sugar coating. *Bloomberg Business News.* Retrieved from https://www.bloomberg.com/news/articles/2006-09-12/krispy-kreme-still-no-sugar-coatingbusinessweek-business-news-stock-market-and-financial-advice

Gallagher, J. (2015). Antibiotic resistance: World on cusp of 'post-antibiotic era', *BBC News.* Available at https://www.bbc.com/news/health-34857015

Gillis, V., & Van Wig, A. (2015). Disciplinary literacy assessment. *Journal of Adolescent & Adult Literacy, 58.* https://doi.org/10.1002/jaal.386

Kwon, O., Xu, C., & But, J. C. (2016, August 2). *Reading matters in an electrical circuits course.* Paper presented at First-Year Engineering Experience (FYEE) conference. Ohio State University, Colombus, OH. July 31–August 2, 2016. Retrieved from http://fyee.asee.org/FYEE2016/index.htm

Livingston, S. A. (2009). *Constructed-response test questions: Why we use them; how we score them.* R&D connections. Number 11. Princeton, NJ: Educational Testing Service.

Lund, J. (1997). Authentic assessment: Its development & applications. *Journal of Physical Education, Recreation & Dance, 68*(7), 25–28.

Martinez, M. E. (1999). Cognition and the question of test item format. *Educational Psychologist, 34*(4), 207–218.

Roth, L. M., & Roth Clark, A. C. (2013). *Understanding architecture: Its elements, history, and meaning.* Boulder, CO: Westview Press.

Sadler, R. (1989). Formative assessment and the design of instructional systems. *Instructional Science, 18,* 119–144.

Shepard, L. A. (2000). The role of assessment in a learning culture. *Educational Researcher, 29*(7), 4–14.

Shulman, L. S. (1986). Those who understand: Knowledge growth in teaching. *Educational Researcher, 15*(2), 4–14.

PART II

Strategies and Practices in STEM and Professional Studies

CHAPTER 4

Literacy Strategies and Instructional Modalities in Introductory Accounting

Rachel Raskin

4.1   INTRODUCTION: ACCOUNTING AS A DISCIPLINE

Although introductory accounting courses do not involve complex mathematics or technological skills, many students have difficulties in learning the material. The courses are required for most business majors, and in some institutions, it is considered a general education course. Nevertheless, the pass rate is relatively low, and many students must repeat the course multiple times to pass, which can result in high attrition in business programs (Lay, 2008). The Principles of Accounting course is a gatekeeper course for most business majors. It is often taught as rote memorization of rules; consequently, failure rates are high (Sargent, Borthick, & Lederberg, 2011). When students try to "wing it" by memorizing instead of engaging the material and truly learning the concepts, they lose motivation and fail. The culprit may be students' common misconception that studying accounting requires minimal reading and writing. To the contrary, accounting is considered "the language of business", a language that

R. Raskin (✉)
New York City College of Technology, City University of New York, Brooklyn, NY, USA
e-mail: rraskin@citytech.cuny.edu

© The Author(s) 2020
J. C. But (ed.), *Teaching College-Level Disciplinary Literacy*,
https://doi.org/10.1007/978-3-030-39804-0_4

records and communicates financial information to various stakeholders. Therefore, principles of accounting classes introduce to students a foreign language. Learning a foreign language requires more than memorizing words, but building a vocabulary for effective communication. Similarly, accounting proficiency requires disciplinary literacy, or the ability to engage in the discourse and practices of the discipline (Shanahan & Shanahan, 2012). Disciplinary literacy builds an understanding of how knowledge is produced in the disciplines, rather than just building knowledge (Moje, 2008, p. 97). Accounting students must engage in disciplinary learning that very often can only be achieved by the deep reading of a variety of accounting-related texts, as well as the use of a range of cognitive and metacognitive learning skills (Byrne, Flood, & Willis, 2009). However, instructors often find it challenging to balance the time and efforts devoted to covering core topics and developing students' active reading and thinking skills. This becomes increasingly challenging as more accounting courses are being offered online and in hybrid classroom settings, where the modes of instruction and delivery of materials are different from those in traditional face-to-face instruction (Bryant, Kahle, & Schafer, 2005). This chapter will discuss ways to optimize student learning in introductory accounting courses using research-based active learning strategies, describing the implementation of varying approaches and strategies to develop students' disciplinary literacy. The effectiveness of the pedagogical designs and strategies used will be elaborated. As data science and technology are gradually shaping the accounting industry, the future trends of accounting education and the evolving literacy needs in the discipline will also be discussed.

4.2   Skills Gap in Accounting Education

The push for reform in accounting education dates back to 1986, when the American Accounting Association's (AAA's) Bedford Committee published a report, "Future Accounting Education: Preparing for the Expanding Profession", calling for major innovation in accounting education that would adapt to the current and future needs of the evolving profession. The report states that the focal point of accounting education should be students' learning how to learn'—the knowledge and skills required to meet the broad set of accounting functions demanded by the industry are more than just having technical expertise. To be able to understand and analyze vast amounts of varying information, on the economic and social climate in which an organization operates is crucial. The report states that the role of an accountant has become broader yet more specialized—the scope of services performed by accountants is expanding and so is the specialization required to provide expertise in various functions. The committee called for a focus on the development of students' skills of *analysis, problem solving,* and *communication* to succeed in a complex economic society where merely technical expertise is insufficient, corroborating the dire need to, above all, be able to pursue lifelong learning (American Accounting Association, 1986).

The nature of accounting education is reactive, not proactive—there will always be a lag between what the industry needs and how education will adjust to satisfy that need (Courtis & Zaid, 2002). In support of this assertion, a plethora of research concludes that over thirty years after the initial push for reform, accounting programs are still not doing enough to teach the importance of the professional skills that are crucial to accountants. Accounting classes emphasize the mastery of accounting principles and, with the abundance of content to cover during the semester, the critical value of nontechnical skills is bypassed.

As technology has enabled companies to become global in the era of information, an outpouring of data has surfaced. Accountants are in the position to analyze these data and use them to provide business intelligence. With technology replacing routine accounting functions that are being packed into accounting curricula, it is vital that academia recognize the current industry needs. Accounting programs need to train graduates who can be both accountants and business consultants equipped with *critical thinking, problem solving, technology* and *communication* skills. Currently, accounting education is broken due to the gap between what is taught and the additional competencies that are required to succeed in the industry today (Tatikonda, 2004). There is an evident concern of a skills gap in the workforce and a need to develop competencies to prepare students to succeed in the industry that calls for strong skills to perform data analysis. As Albrecht and Sack (2000) stated, the current textbook-based rule intensive lecture method should not remain the main mode of teaching. Their study claims that a majority of accounting practitioners and educators would not choose to major in accounting again due to the fact that the business world has undergone significant changes while accounting education has not.

The international accounting firm PriceWaterhouse Coopers stated that "technical knowledge will become commoditized and professionals will need to provide insight to stay relevant" (Agnew, 2016). Therefore, an understanding of how to record and report information is important, but the ability to analyze the information and communicate it for decision making is vital. A report by the Institute of Management Accountants (IMA) and Robert Half (2016) pointed to a talent gap due to a shortage of accountants with technical and nontechnical skills needed for data analytics. Although the technology is available, it cannot be leveraged without employees who possess the proper competencies and business knowledge. The report claims that non-technical or soft skills used to be nice to have but now they are mandatory. Thus, educators must strive to develop independent, lifelong learners who will be able to adapt to the rapid changes in the business environment. Shah (2013) asserts that the ability to integrate foundational accounting knowledge to solve business problems requires a skills set that is broad and flexible enough to evolve with the industry and includes communication, analytical and team-work abilities. Employers want new hires to write coherently, think creatively, and analyze quantitative data. However, on a national test of writing and reasoning skills, business majors had the lowest scores and score lower than other majors on the GMAT exam. Business majors also spend the least time studying and often do not read the textbooks (Glenn, 2011). Myers (2016) states that recruiters are looking to hire candidates who are non-business majors as these graduates possess cross-disciplinary knowledge and complex skills that business majors lack. He adds that to produce innovators, college courses must be innovated to encompass cross-functional skills.

Students' lack of deep learning of accounting continues throughout their undergraduate and even graduate years. The low Certified Public Accountant (CPA) exam pass rates shed light on the reality that even among the students who survived the accounting program and are determined to achieve CPA licensure, only 45–60% manage to pass the exam (AICPA, 2019).

As accounting is inherently linked to an organization's operational, administrative, and strategic endeavors, accountants must be able to leverage data to provide action-oriented information (Harper & Dunn, 2018). Thus, accounting educators should aim to shift classroom dynamics to student-centered learning that goes beyond the transmission of accounting knowledge to cultivate students' intellectual, critical thinking, professional, and interpersonal skills.

The Joint Curriculum Task Force of the Institute of Management Accountants (IMA) and the Management Accounting Section (MAS) of the American Accounting Association (AAA) stipulates that accounting education should equip students with a set of adaptable skills to meet the demands of long-term careers rather than preparing them for entry-level positions or passing entry-level exams. Secondly, students should be prepared to succeed in a myriad of careers outside of public accounting and be trained in applying accounting knowledge to the broader business to add organizational value in a wide range of functions (Lawson et al., 2014). Therefore, accounting education should not focus on the silos of GAAP rules and principles, but should instead be integrated to see the big picture—what is the purpose of the rule and how does the accounting information impact the business? Students need to gain skills not just for the first job out of college, but for careers five years down the road, possessing vital skills needed to be able to evolve with the global economy (Myers, 2016). The modern definition of success has shifted from granular expertise in a specific field to the ability of adapting transferable skills (Smith, 2010). Accounting education should thus be a catalyst for self-directed learning to develop students with a malleable and broad-based skill set. This notion is reflected in the Accounting Education Change Commission's (AECC) statement, *The First Course in Accounting: Position Statement No. Two*. The AECC states that the first course in accounting should be an introduction to accounting, not introductory accounting, primarily teaching the subject as an information development and communication function that supports economic decision making. The course should focus on interpersonal skills such as group work, case studies and should ultimately teach the student how to learn independently (Accounting Education Change Commission, 1992).

Contrary to the AECC's recommendations, the first course in accounting in most institutions continues to be rules heavy and dense with the volume of material that must be covered in a short semester. Thus, the transformation can be a daunting task. Principles of Accounting is a foundational course and many programs require a uniform final exam across all sections, which could make instructors even more hesitant to sacrifice class time to any activities that steer away from the required material. However, as the traditional mode of teaching accounting is proving to be inadequate, the role of the instructor must shift from presenter of facts to facilitator of active learning (Jackson & Durkee, 2008).

4.3   LITERACY AS A CATALYST
FOR HIGHER-ORDER THINKING

The data analytics hype is ubiquitous, and it will only continue to grow and shape the accounting profession. The literature shows that accounting graduates are not prepared to perform the high-level functions required in the current market and as a result a skills gap exists. At the heart of being able to analyze data is metacognition, and the ability to learn how to learn. To be data literate, or be able to read, understand, and communicate data as insight, one must be content literate. Data literacy is not just the ability to read the numbers, but the ability to find meaning in the numbers (Bryla, 2018).

Accounting is the process of identifying, recording, and communicating business information. Thus, communication has historically been considered accountants' most important skill. Pritchard, Romeo, and Muller (1999) assert that even back in 1968 the American Accounting Association (AAA) stated that no other quality is more important to an accountant than having the ability to communicate well both in writing and orally. Though reading ability is the foundation of technical communications and business literacy, assessing reading skills has been overlooked. There is a direct correlation among the competencies in reading, thinking, and communication. Pritchard et al. (1999) state that students who read well are generally organized thinkers who comprehend what needs to be said, connect thoughts logically, examine the importance or meaning behind things, and are more likely to demonstrate the empathy or see the other person's point-of-view. Their study reveals statistically significant relationships between students' reading comprehension, reading vocabulary, and calculated reading grade equivalent and their cumulative GPAs.

Reading and writing together facilitate higher-order thinking such as synthesis and evaluation of information to clarify, refine, and extend one's internalization of content. Effective comprehension and academic success depend on metacognitive processing, which during reading is pronounced by use of procedural and focused strategies invoked by the reader (Taraban, Rynearson, & Kerr, 2004). Direct instruction of course material paired with active reading and writing assignments provides a platform for effective learning, while the lack of active engagement with content often results in poor comprehension. Educators must implement tools and techniques to help students become engaged with the text to reach a level of deep learning, which is characterized by a personal commitment to learning and an interest in the subject. Students adopting this approach set out with the intention of understanding the material; they interact critically with the arguments put forward and relate them to their prior knowledge and experience (Byrne et al., 2009).

This promotes disciplinary literacy, or the ability to synthesize information to create and communicate knowledge (Shanahan & Shanahan, 2012). For instance, I assigned an article and a series of questions about the accounting problems of Groupon, a growing publicly traded company, to a class of first-year accounting students. One of the questions asked students to analyze the article to identify the factors that contributed to Groupon's internal control weaknesses based on the elements and evidence they found in the text. A prime factor was the company's rapid expansion that made it difficult to maintain and monitor internal controls. Later in the semester the class discussed Etsy, an online retailer of handmade crafts that dealt with material weaknesses in its internal control over financial reporting during its Initial Public Offering (IPO). I asked the class why Etsy might have had troubles with poor internal control. A student responded that perhaps like Groupon, Etsy expanded rapidly and it was difficult to keep track of consistent internal controls. This is an example of disciplinary literacy—the student grasped the underlying principal in the Groupon assignment and was able to apply the concept to a new context and make meaningful connections. Strategies that guide students to think more effectively in a discipline-specific manner could empower them to go beyond a superficial understanding and to grasp deeper and more sophisticated ideas (Shanahan & Shanahan, 2008). The ability to make connections and apply disciplinary knowledge in other contexts advances learning by participating in the practices and engaging in the disciplinary thinking and discourse.

4.4   Disciplinary Literacy Strategies in the Reading Process

Many undergraduate students come into college with weak reading skills and have difficulty reading disciplinary texts due to lack of sophisticated reading processes and strategies. Students read with limited breadth and depth, thus failing to comprehend whole-text arguments. Students' understanding of the material is habitually assessed by exams; however, when foundational reading issues are not addressed such assessment is inherently flawed (Davies, 2017). Instead, students must be taught to decode, analyze, and discuss disciplinary texts to apply specific concepts in analyzing business practices. These skills are critical in a scenario where students will have to use quantitative and qualitative data to influence business decisions. Accounting professors are typically not reading as literacy specialists, and they are usually in a race to cover all the course content in a short semester. However, when accounting instructors are introduced to disciplinary literacy strategies and practices, they can start integrating them into their teaching. Relevant strategies used prior to assigning a reading, during reading, and after reading can make students active readers who approach the text with meaning and purpose. Integrating assignments that target the development of students' reading processes help them move beyond superficial understanding of lecture content (Davies, 2017). Digging deeper into the text is a win for content knowledge.

4.5   PRE-READING TO SCAFFOLD PRIOR KNOWLEDGE

Pre-reading strategies set out a focus and direction for the reading. When introducing pre-reading strategies, I ask the students if they had ever visited a restaurant before looking up its menu online. As everyone shakes their head answering "no", I ask them to explain why not. The most common answer is they would not know what to expect once they got there, and that would impede on the dining experience. From there, I explain that not doing a precursory review of the text before reading will impede on the reading experience in the same manner. Whenever the brain tries to absorb new information, it tries to relate it to something it already knows (McGuire, 2015, p. 25). Thus, learning is a process where new knowledge builds upon existing knowledge. As accounting curriculum scaffolds on prior knowledge, previewing the text and setting a purpose for the reading is vital to enhance learning. Doing a precursory scan of the headings, sections and vocabulary can help students use what they already know to understand the new material. For instance, a pre-reading of the chapter about accounting for long-term operational assets should activate a student's prior knowledge of accrual accounting, the adjusting entry for depreciation, and how it relates to the book value of long-term assets presented on the balance sheet. Students need to be guided on how to pre-read effectively. I find visual organizers that prompt pre-reading such as anticipation guides to be helpful in framing the application of prior knowledge to new content or clearing up misconceptions in prior knowledge that would inhibit learning the new material.

I leave time toward the end of class for students to begin looking at the next chapter to be covered. I instruct the students to read the introduction and the subchapter headings, writing down in a completely unorganized manner the items that stood out to them and the terms they do not understand. Then I distribute an anticipation guide handout, or a tool that prompts students to become active seekers of important information and ideas by encouraging them to make predictions before reading and check their understanding after reading (Fisher, Brozo, Frey, & Ivey, 2015, p. 12).

As seen in Fig. 4.1, the guide consists of a list of about ten statements based on the text. The students must agree or disagree with the statement and explain their choice. After reading the text, students return to the guide and re-evaluate their responses, citing the page number or statement in the reading that either affirms or disaffirms their initial response. If this pertains to a chapter of the textbook, students finish the second part of the anticipation guide as part of homework and submit it at the next class meeting. If the guide relates to a non-textbook classroom reading, the students gather in groups of three to discuss their initial and post-reading responses. Students enjoy discussing their initial responses because at that point, they are just sharing opinions. This sparks interest in the topic and students begin the reading with prior knowledge and differing viewpoints, approaching the text with a variety of interpretive strategies. During the reading they are enthusiastic about seeking evidence to support their initial responses. Of course, often the evidence disproves their initial thoughts, but the hands-on experience contributes to effective learning. The anticipation guides activate students' prior knowledge, set a purpose for the reading, and enable reflection and discussion after the reading in groups and as a class.

4.6 Strategies Motivating Students to Read

Introductory accounting courses rely heavily on the textbook to provide organization and course content (Phillips & Phillips, 2007). It is not enough to assign readings and let them linger in the background—active reading should be a pronounced part of the course. Students need to be taught through modeling, direct instruction, and discussion how they should read the texts they are assigned (Davies, 2017).

Accounting for Partnerships

1. A partner who actively participates in a limited partnership has limited liability.
Before: After:
Explanation:
2. When a partner invests noncash assets into a partnership the assets are recorded at their book value, net of accumulated depreciation.
Before: After:
Explanation:
3. After noncash assets are sold in liquidation, the remaining cash is allocated to partners based on their income ratios.
Before: After:
Explanation:
4. If a partner with a capital deficiency cannot pay the amount owed to the partnership the deficiency is allocated to the other partners based on their income ratios.
Before: After:
Explanation:
5. If a new partner's investment is less than his/her capital credit, the bonus to the new partner reduces the old partners' capital balances.
Before: After:
Explanation:
6. Mutual Agency makes the act of one partner binding on all other partners.
Before: After:
Explanation
7. A limited partnership requires filing with the state but offers limited liability to all members.
Before: After:
Explanation:
8. A general partnership burdens all partners with unlimited liability.
Before: After:
Explanation:
9. An LLC is a hybrid between a partnership and a corporation.
Before: After:
Explanation:
10. When a partnership liquidates, all noncash assets must be sold.
Before: After:

Fig. 4.1   Anticipation guide: Accounting for Partnerships

Annotation for Close Reading

During the reading stage I stress the importance of annotation, which is an inseparable part of the reading process for reading college-level textbooks, not something done in addition to reading (Davies, 2017). I explain to students that annotating shows what you are thinking as you read and analyze the text and if you cannot concisely express your thoughts then you are not really understanding the content. As part of homework, students read the textbook chapter being discussed. Students must underline or circle important terms and write a short summary of each subsection in the margins, placing check marks next to sections they understand. The brief summaries facilitate reflection of each piece of the text and how it fits into the chapter. They should also jot down any questions that arise even by simply placing a question mark next to the sections they do not understand.

To connect knowledge and experiences, I ask students to create their own scenarios with solutions/journal entries in the margins like the examples given in the textbook to illustrate their understanding of the technical material and note any connections between the information and knowledge from other readings or class discussions.

Annotation ensures that students do a close reading of the chapter rather than a quick scan, coming to class with background knowledge of the topic and with questions for clarification and further discussion. Thus, instead of just reading the chapter, students actively engage with the text. Accounting textbooks are condensed, and each chapter builds on the previous one. Skimming through the text is not an option. It is important to understand each section of the chapter, as the knowledge is key to grasping the material in the subsequent chapters.

Prior to making chapter annotation a part of the homework grade, many of the students did not read the assigned text and during lectures. I stood at the chalkboard for the entire class period frantically trying to cover the vast amount of technical material to a room of students who looked at me as if I were speaking a foreign language. In addition to annotated chapter submissions, students are required to complete an online chapter quiz that closes twenty minutes prior to the start of the in-person class. The quiz is simple for those who read and annotated the chapter, and because these quizzes comprise a portion of the final grade, they provide an additional incentive to read the text before class.

Connecting the Dots

Accounting knowledge is presented systematically according to the way it is structured in the textbook. The labyrinth of accounting concepts challenges students who often struggle to make meaningful connections between the topics. This struggle ultimately hinders cognition. For instance, students often fail to see how the key accounting assumptions are reflected in the journal entries. They may memorize the definition of accrual accounting but they cannot connect it to the time period assumption, revenue recognition principle, or the matching principle. As such, students do not truly understand the purpose or context of adjusting entries or how to recreate the entries based on principles over memorization. They cannot articulate the difference between a deferral and an accrual and the types of transactions that result in each type of entry. There is a great volume of technical information in this unit and it is foundational to accounting knowledge. The material seems tangled, yet the relevant connections cannot be made or evaluated. Meaningful learning requires that new information be integrated with and connected to existing knowledge with broader concepts presented first followed by details that provide support.

Concept maps are graphic tools used to organize and represent knowledge in a hierarchical structure that include cross-links to show relationships between concepts in different segments of the concept map (Novak & Cañas, 2006). Structure is inherent in all knowledge, so understanding the structural foundation of any content domain improves comprehension as structural knowledge is essential to problem solving (Jonassen, 2006). Concept maps are a way to develop logical thinking and study skills by revealing connections and helping students see how individual ideas form a larger whole (Greenberg & Wilner, 2015). This is essential as accounting is innate to the various operational and strategic activities of a company and accountants must synthesize it all to produce business intelligence. Leauby, Szabat, and Maas (2010) claim that the accounting domain is well-suited to the underlying learning theory of concept mapping as knowledge is organized into a hierarchical framework where learners build upon elementary knowledge and add more ideas and concepts to what they know. Through integrative reconciliation, learners ultimately identify how concepts are linked together and relate to other knowledge. Concept mapping tools are valuable in the rationalization process as accounting moves from a rule-based to a principles-based environment.

Utilizing conceptual maps in introductory courses allows students to develop a skill that can be used throughout the entire educational process and even after school (Balaciu, 2015). I introduce concept maps in the Principles of Accounting course by distributing an incomplete map and having students fill in the missing parts as a chapter quiz at the beginning of the lecture. This serves a dual purpose—it ensures students read the chapter prior to class and it familiarizes students with the notion that they need to engage in deeper learning to connect the knowledge within the reading.

Once students are comfortable with the idea of mapping, I ask them to create their own concept maps to be submitted as a quiz, first in groups and then individually, as seen in Fig. 4.2a, b.

Students can use their lecture notes, the annotated textbook chapter, and PowerPoint slides to help them complete the maps. I give the students general guidelines and tips as to how to construct the map:

1. Make a list of all the concepts you think are relevant and identify the core concept to use as the base of the map.
2. The core concept can be broken down into more specific concepts in a hierarchical order. Go back to the list of all concepts and create groups and sub-groups by placing the most important concepts on top and closely related concepts next to each other. Use lines and arrows to show the relationships between the various concepts. Illustrate using examples.
3. Use words to link and cross-link concepts within the map to establish their relationship.

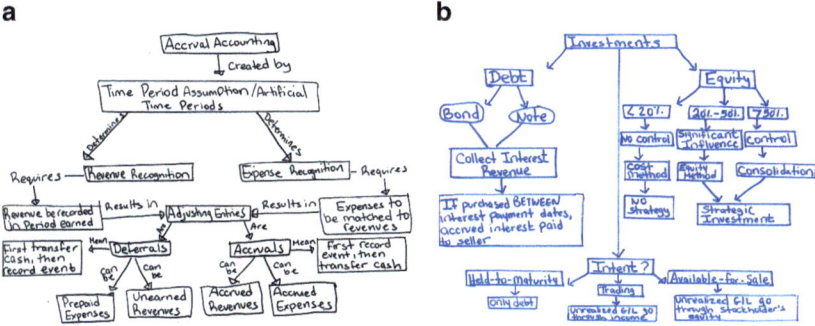

a **b**

Fig. 4.2 (a, b) Concept map illustrating Accrual Accounting and Accounting for Investments

Creating concept maps is a challenging task, which is why I have the class work in groups for the first half of the semester. The students are overwhelmed having to break down the vast material to a handful of concepts and link them using just a few words. It is very different from what they are accustomed to, be it solving a defined problem or furiously taking disorganized notes of everything discussed in class. Many of the students' concept maps, especially in the beginning, lack any direction, hierarchy, and meaning. The relationships between the concepts are incorrect and the hierarchy of items is not clear. Students tend to put the same concepts in different areas of the map instead of linking them to other related concepts. The linkages are often flawed and examples are missing. The flaws in the concept maps reflect the gaps in their understanding of the information presented in the chapter and present an opportunity for me to provide feedback and correct the misconceptions.

After a few weeks of practicing this exercise with continuous feedback, students' concept map submissions usually improve as they become more comfortable with the mapping framework and the thought process required to create an accurate and comprehensive map. As a result, it is evident that they are better able to formulate responses to questions that involve the use of integrated knowledge. For instance, after reading an article on the collapse of Lehman Brothers, I asked the class which ratio might indicate the bank's risk when borrowing money to invest in mortgage securities. As many of the students were thinking, one student scoured through his notes and pulled out the concept map he had made a few weeks back, mapping the financial ratios. Overwhelmed with excitement, he yelled out that a leverage ratio such as the debt to assets ratio would be a good indicator as corporations can finance investments using debt or equity. He continued to reason that if the debt to assets ratio is high, it means that debt was used to finance the mortgage investments and that creates a risk especially if the value of the assets decreases. The student used the concept map to connect a real business phenomenon with its financial statements. And the explanation was perfect.

Creating concept maps urges students to scaffold the linear information presented in the textbook. Concept maps constitute a metacognitive learning strategy that empowers students to construct their own knowledge rather than memorize a mass of definitions or solve problems by the routine plugging-in of numbers or symbols into abstract formulas (Novak, 1991, p. 48). Thus, concept mapping encourages students to think critically and independently to form connections between the different parts of their knowledge.

Accounting students tend to compartmentalize their learning and view the individual subjects in the program as discrete units, showing more reliance on surface approaches to learning than students from other discipline and as a result lose the knowledge in a short period of time (Irvine, Cooper, & Jones, 2006). In contrast with rote learning, concept mapping enables students to engage in meaningful learning as they continually refine their knowledge structures, ultimately constructing complex frameworks of interrelated concepts with many levels of hierarchy, branching, and cross-linking. Thus, students can form connections between different areas of their knowledge as they highlight the relationship between what they have learned and what they already know.

Concept mapping is time consuming and allocating class time to the exercise when there is a mass of information and other skills to cover can be challenging. The quality of learning over quantity must be considered, in line with a strategy-based over knowledge-based curriculum. However, most accounting educators are reluctant to use it because it is so counter-intuitive to the way accounting is usually taught, by crunching numbers (Leauby et al., 2010). Also, reviewing each student's map and providing feedback is a time commitment. Timely feedback is essential for students to solidify the relevant connections before the class moves on to the next topic. As students receive their maps back at the next class, they are given some time to look over the feedback and discuss and compare their work. Concept mapping is an example of the type of activities accounting educators must introduce into the learning process to achieve a skills-based curriculum as advocated by the discipline (Leauby et al., 2010).

Using Game-Based Activities to Engage Students in Learning Content and Vocabulary

Teaching students how to actively read the textbook by annotating the chapters and using their own annotated work to complete a concept map quiz at the beginning of class motivates students to do the groundwork and come to the lecture prepared. Another way to stimulate the class is with fun concept review games that are designed to complement the lecture while alleviating the pressure of the intensive content. The literature shows positive results of game-based activities in accounting classrooms— the games help students apply concepts, reinforce and enhance students' learning, foster peer interactions, increase understanding of the content, and are entertaining and enjoyable (Moncada & Moncada, 2014).

I created a Jeopardy game as a review for each chapter using a templates found on http://www.superteachertools.us/jeopardyx/jeopardy-review-game.php?gamefile=1774860#.Xaf00JJKi71. The students play the game in groups, and the winning team gets a few points toward the next exam. I structure the activity to include the concepts that are most commonly misunderstood, capitalizing on the students' engagement and eagerness during the game to clarify and elaborate on the topic. The activity is a big hit as it acts like an ice-breaker, team-building exercise, warm-up and review and throughout the game the class is noticeably engaged and excited to learn.

4.7 Instructional Modes and Fostering Reading with the Flipped Classroom

Gravitating to technology, the current student body is stimulated in a visual, interactive environment. A variety of teaching techniques should be utilized to appeal to students' varying learning modes—lecture alone is no longer enough. A hybrid or blended form of instruction is optimal as it combines class lectures with online discussion forms, bolstering dynamic interaction with the content, peers, and instructor. It is considered to be the "dynamic education vehicle of our time" (Duncan, Kenworthy, & McNamara, 2012). Online and hybrid courses are important for accounting programs as many working students go back to school to obtain an accounting degree or take accounting classes to sit for the CPA exam (to meet the 150-credit requirement) and they rely on the flexibility of online instruction.

Virtual Classroom Activities

In a traditional classroom setting, it is difficult to get everyone equally involved in the lecture, and students receive credit for simply attending class. Normally, students sitting in front of the class have no interaction with students who choose to sit in the back, and vice versa. But in an online class, no one can slip through the cracks; everyone must contribute to the conversation, and as a result, students learn from one another, enhancing their understanding based on the responses of their peers. This also gives the instructor the chance to provide instant feedback, enhancing the scope of teaching. Instructors can drill into the responses of the students to see areas where they are lagging and prompt them to improve or to note meaningful responses and challenge them further. Such one-on-one interaction seldom occurs in a busy classroom full of students and thus there is a shift to student-centered learning. Blended instruction cultivates lifelong learners who take responsibility for their own learning and thus enhances students' motivation to learn. Research shows that because blended learning retains classroom contact, it provides the best of both worlds (Hiralal, 2012).

The hybrid or blended form of instruction allows the allocation of a significant part of the course to reading. In the course, relevant articles assigned in parallel with textbook material cultivate students' analytical reasoning and professional judgment as they are able to bridge the gap between theory and technical accounting and how the principles apply to real business issues. Students see the complexity of the business world and develop crucial skills such as team building, communication, analysis, and information literacy. Weil, McGuigan, and Kern (2011) found that accounting students felt that online discussion forums improved their ability to identify relevant data, think critically about issues, summarize available information, learn from other students, and think independently.

Many of the introductory accounting courses at the New York City College of Technology are taught as hybrid courses. The class meets in-person once a week and the rest of the meetings are virtual. The online component of the course is conducted on the Discussion Board in Blackboard, a learning management system. I upload articles and case studies to Blackboard that illuminate the material discussed in the textbook. Students must print out the reading, annotate it for submission, and then engage in a discourse on the Discussion Board by responding to a set of questions and commenting on the responses of other classmates. This exercise drives students to connect the theory in the textbook to accounting in practice, capitalizing on student reflection, evaluation, and critical thinking. The guided reading questions on the Discussion Board are designed with the Question-Answer-Relationship (QAR) strategy, a cognitive strategy in which students learn to categorize comprehension questions according to where they are likely to find the answers to the questions (Fisher et al., 2015, p. 66). The questions are divided into three categories. First, text explicit questions use wording from the text and the answer can be found right in the reading. Second, the answers to text implicit questions can be inferenced from multiple sections of the reading but students may need to look beyond what is stated in the text to construct a response. Finally, script implicit questions require prior knowledge and experiences to answer and the reading may or may not be needed. It is important to teach students how to strategically approach the reading and look for the answers in the text before requiring them to complete the QAR questions on their own. Prior to beginning the reading, I advise students to gloss over the questions so that they have a sense of the information they are seeking and where to focus their attention. Then, they should assess the questions and designate them as text explicit, text implicit, or script implicit. Students should consider the kind of information they will need to gather while reading, discerning whether they will be searching for facts, or using the reading or other sources to come up with their own answer. By recognizing a variety of question types, students are better prepared to answer them. They come to understand that a response may require them to dig deeper than what the text presents and retrieved some information they may have stored in their mind or become seekers of information they have not yet acquired. This type of training is conducive to approaching accounting problems, where students must combine foundational knowledge and more sophisticated techniques to formulate solutions.

For example, students are assigned a CNN article about Netflix's stock split (Egan, 2015) in parallel with the unit on corporate stock transactions being discussed in class. Students must first print the article, read, and annotate the text. Then they are asked to categorize the following questions into the QAR framework and formulate their initial responses to the questions.

1. Why did Netflix announce a 7-for-1 stock split? (Text Explicit)
2. What impact did the stock split have on existing shareholders? (Text Implicit)
3. Which sentence in the article describes why companies engage in stock splits? (Text Explicit)
4. If the goal of every public company is to increase share price, why then would a company announce a stock split and decrease share price? (Text Implicit)
5. What is the price-to-earnings (PE) ratio? What does it mean to have a high PE ratio? What is the risk of having a high PE ratio? (Script Implicit)
6. What can Netflix do to increase revenues? (Script Implicit)

Students post their responses directly onto the discussion forum and I post follow-up questions/comments to urge them to dive further into the text. While students always try to complete all questions, their responses often fail to reflect deep reading and understanding. The benefit of the discussion forum is that I can catch such responses right away and point the students in the right direction to make the relevant corrections and analyses. After a few weeks they take the readings more seriously, knowing that if their responses are not comprehensive I will post a comment urging them to re-evaluate their answer. To receive full credit for the week's post, students must thoroughly respond to my notes and comment on the posts of at least three other classmates.

Blended Instruction and the Flipped Classroom

The online component of the course frames a flipped classroom, a student-centered teaching model that capitalizes on technology to take instructional content outside of the classroom and active learning, problem solving, and collaboration into the classroom, incorporating formative and summative assessment and meaningful face-to-face learning activities (Milman, 2012). Millennials are accustomed to acquiring information via the internet but they lack the ability to focus and read in-depth to achieve understanding. Students avoid reading the textbook and feel that they can learn the material by looking it up on the internet, relying on the traditional class lecture to repeat all the textbook content. Hence, the lectures become a substitute to reading the text rather than a complement (Braun & Sellers, 2012). McGuire (2015, p. 42) challenges this method, asserting that "no one can solve problems using information he or she has only just read by looking it up online". Problem solving requires critical thinking that depends on having prior knowledge.

It is unlikely that students will read the required text without appropriate guidance and motivation. Students should not passively receive material in class; they must read to gather the information largely outside of class. Class time should be allocated to activities that are typically thought to be homework—solving problems with professors or peers, and applying knowledge to new contexts (Berrett, 2012). Rather than sending students home to struggle with a new concept, the instructors can hear and correct misconceptions as they arise. In class, students learn how to think, and instructors learn what they are struggling with. As such, the instructor's role shifts from a presenter of knowledge to a facilitator of unpacking the content, or from the sage on the stage to the guide on the side (King, 1993). A flipped classroom method can easily be implemented in other subjects, such as English where students must read the book outside of class. Although more challenging to implement in technical courses like accounting, a flipped classroom technique is beneficial for teaching procedural knowledge, such as solving an accounting problem (Phillips & Trainor, 2014). The flipped classroom allows the instructor to gauge if students engaged in deep reading and if they could master the material effectively. The challenge is getting students to deeply read the required text.

Accounting students tend to favor a "skimming" strategy over a "sinking" strategy of deep and active reading. Students' textbook reading should be viewed as motivated behavior, given that high performing students are more likely to read the textbook chapter prior to the lecture than lower performing students (Phillips & Phillips, 2007). Brown, Danvers, & Doran (2016) implemented guided reading questions in fully in-person intermediate accounting courses an attempt to flip the classroom and motivate students to read the textbook. They found that the reading questions *motivated* students to complete the reading assignments on time, kept them focused while reading the chapter material and answering the questions helped them to *better understand* the material. Students believed that completing the reading questions on a timely basis kept them *more engaged* in the class discussion, and they spent *more time reading* the chapters than they would have otherwise, if there were no assigned reading questions. The QAR strategy I implement in hybrid courses using the discussion forum meets many of the same objectives.

Accounting students value active learning and prefer to do different things in class other than listen to lectures such as engaging in problem solving and group activities (Phillips & Trainor, 2014). I can attest to this by observing my students lively and engaged when working on activities yet distracted and tired during prolonged periods of lecture. There absolutely is a plethora of material to cover in introductory accounting and all the content is important for the students to grasp. As we frantically try to cover all the content in a short lecture period, we see the students furiously taking notes (or pictures of the board, nowadays). But are they learning? Can they absorb all that information in a single class, seeing or hearing it for the first time without any prior knowledge? McGuire (2015) states that the human attention span is about ten minutes, so if an instructor lectures longer than that without stopping for an activity many of the students will be physiologically unable to absorb the information.

Accounting instructors need to stop the content race. We need to put the students in the driver seat and move to the passenger side. Students must be held responsible to do the background work at home and come to class prepared to dive into the material and engage in meaningful activities—that is when learning truly occurs.

Applied Group Work

By the time students have done the concept map quiz, the Jeopardy game, and a brief overview lecture the chapter content is solidified, they are ready for hands-on practice. For example, students split into groups to complete an assignment during the unit on investments. The students are asked to read parts of Coca-Cola's 10-K and answer the following questions:

1. What brands does Coca-Cola own? On what page of the 10-K is this shown?
2. Why does Coca-Cola have a strategic investment in bottling operations? How does it benefit the company?
3. How does Coca-Cola account for its investments in bottling operations (cost method, equity method, or consolidation)? How does the method of accounting impact its financial statements?
4. According to the 10-K, what are some of the business risks the company faces?
5. How much income (loss) did Coca-Cola recognize from its equity method investments?
6. What happened to Coca-Cola's net income between 2016 and 2017? Why?
7. Would you buy Coca-Cola stock? Why or why not?

To foster cooperative learning, the questions are divided among the group members so that each member is responsible for his or her portion of the task. I walk around the room as the groups work on the assignment, helping students as needed. This is a great opportunity to sit with students that are struggling and work through the problems. Analyzing Coca-Cola's SEC filing to examine its investments proactively is more conducive to learning than watching a PowerPoint presentation and hearing me lecture about accounting for various types of investments for the duration of the class. This type of low-stakes assignment aims to bridge abstract textbook knowledge with actual accounting issues by fostering disciplinary literacy. Students examine and become familiar with the financial statements while connecting the numbers with information from the annual report. The flipped classroom empowers the students and motivates them to learn as it gravitates toward experiential learning.

The Power of Reflection

At the end of class I leave time for reflection, which is fundamental to turn experience into knowledge both in the academic setting and in the practice of accounting, emphasizing the interdependence of knowledge, learning, thinking, reflection, and action (Brown & McCartney, 1998). Thus, reflection is a key component of knowledge and thought formation which ultimately leads to actions and decisions in the accounting practice. Accounting students do not seem to retain knowledge from one course to the next although each course is important. Reflection provides a way to help students retain knowledge and improves their critical thinking, analytical reasoning and writing skills as students look at things from a different perspective. It can help to structure an individual's theory about how principles and rules relate to actions and decisions, bridging the prevalent gap between theory and practice in many professions, including accounting (Guess, 2014).

Exit slips are an easy yet powerful way to incorporate the reflection component in the classroom while also providing the instructor guidance on how to structure the subsequent lesson based on the level and areas of student understanding. They are slips of paper on which students reflect upon what they know and what they are coming to know to invite students to become active, critical listeners to a discussion and, as a result, more reflective thinkers (Leigh, 2012). Instructors can choose various prompts for student responses, depending on the intended outcome. Prompts may be used to gather formative assessment data, stimulate student self-analysis, gather feedback on instructional strategies, or pave the way for students to state their concerns or criticisms (Marzano, 2012). An example of a student exit slip can be seen in Fig. 4.3.

Reading students' exit slips in my introductory accounting courses has become integral to lesson planning. Because I minimize lecture time in favor of active learning activities, it is important to understand any gaps of knowledge prevalent in the class to address and clarify in the next lecture. The exit slips are anonymous, but each student must hand in their slip upon exiting the classroom. Students are not required to adhere to any

Name :

Exit Slip

The most important thing I learned today was.....

-Financial Ratios
- How ratios tie into the
financial Statements.

I need help with.....

Asset turnover
vs.
Return on Assets

I would like to learn more about...

How to use financial ratios
to analyze stocks and make
decisions on creating a personal
Portfolio.

Fig. 4.3   Exit slip

grammar, spelling, or writing structure—they are simply asked to respond to the prompts thoughtfully and truthfully. As such, the students really do use this activity to voice their concerns or express their satisfaction when they finally grasp a concept. The exit slips help to identify trends in student learning, as often students will voice the same concerns. I experienced an instance where I was confident that I did a great job explaining the accounting for receivables and that the students mastered all the concepts and were ready to move on to the next chapter. Only after the class when I started reading the exit slips did I see that the majority of students did not grasp the purpose of allowance accounts and could not comprehend why uncollectible accounts are simply not written off. They went through motions to complete the pertinent classroom activity without truly understanding the purpose or meaning. This insight shaped my next lesson plan as I devised a different way to teach the topic, incorporating key foundational knowledge such as the matching principle that students may have overlooked when approaching the topic at hand.

After an information and action-packed class session, exit slips enable students to wind down, reflect and unpack their thoughts by evaluating and internalizing the lesson.

4.8   Providing Support for Student Motivation

The success of the instructor and the learning strategies is reliant upon student motivation. It is of utmost importance that an instructor provides a motivational environment where students feel they are supported and encouraged. From the early childhood years, students are segregated into groups in the classroom, each group corresponding to one's level of understanding. This fosters what is known as a "fixed mindset", according to Dweck (2007). A fixed mindset demotivates students and therefore inhibits learning and success. Instead, as educators we should aim to instill a growth mindset in our students, where they understand that intelligence grows, it is not innate or fixed. McGuire (2015, p. 10) highlights that high-school students are not prepared for the demands of college because they do not know how to study. Students never had to truly learn to get good grades and they come to college with unrealistic expectations. They lack the tools for effective learning and can be overwhelmed by the sheer volume of college-level material. At a critical and vulnerable point, the instructor's support, patience, and understanding are key to their success as learners.

My introductory accounting courses are comprised of mainly freshmen who are faced with the dual task of mastering the curriculum while learning how to learn. Along with all of their other responsibilities (work, family, other courses), the load can be hefty. Besides, introductory courses are usually taken by both accounting and non-accounting majors, who may not be passionate about the course, as they may feel it is unrelated to their future career. Establishing a welcoming environment where students are receptive to motivation will help change this perception and make the course more effective.

Ice-Breaker

I begin each semester with an ice-breaker activity allowing students take some time to think about the following questions and then discuss in small groups:

- Introduce yourself by sharing a talent or just something you are great at and what you have done to become great at it?
- Think about the career you always dreamed of having as a child. How does this dream connect with your current education path? How do you think you can connect your lifelong dream with an accounting degree?
- What accounting career path appeals most to you? Why?

The groups are rearranged a few times to give students a chance to connect with more classmates. From the very beginning, I ask students to envision their ultimate goals and understand where this course fits in their visions. I explain that each course is a stepping-stone to accomplish their dreams. Therefore, success is in their hands and it is my job to help them along the way.

Transparency and Formative Assessment Structure

I set clear expectations to guide and motivate students. On the first day of class, I carefully review the semester calendar containing all assignments and their respective due dates so that there are no surprises. I convey that an exam grade does not have to determine the course grade. Instead of just a midterm and a final, I administer biweekly exams after every two chapters covered in the text. Frequent exams along with weekly online and concept map quizzes, homework and online discussion forum keep students focused and continuously reviewing and practicing the material. The constant and varying formative assessments make students realize that there is so much at stake if they skip studying a chapter and therefore motivate learning. This technique is indispensable to technical subjects like accounting where each chapter builds on previous chapters. I use the following criteria to determine the final course grade:

Biweekly exams	20%
Final exam	20%
Online discussion forum	20%
Homework	15%
Concept map quizzes	10%
Class group activities	10%
Online quizzes	5%

Practice is key to learning introductory accounting. Homework is comprised of algorithmic multi-step problems completed on an internet-based learning management system which I program to give the students unlimited attempts until they reach the correct answer. An example homework problem may show a comparative balance sheet and ask the students to perform a horizontal and vertical analysis and then to elaborate on what kind of conclusions can be drawn from the data. Students must understand how to perform the analysis and think critically to extract meaning from the numbers in the context of the relationships among the balance sheet accounts. I note to the students that for this type of exercise, the concept map and annotated chapter they produced may be useful and if they spend more than thirty minutes on a homework problem and still do not understand how to approach it, they should reach out to me for guidance.

I convey to them that homework is their place to learn from their mistakes and prepare for the exams—getting the correct answer is not as crucial as mastering the concept. The homework problems I assign are more difficult than those on the exams—so if students master the homework, exams should not be challenging.

We openly discuss the importance of reading and how deep reading is the foundation for metacognitive processes. I model to them each of the reading strategies used in the course and provide timely feedback on their assignments. They often struggle with the strategies initially, but improve throughout the semester. The students learn to understand that if they do not put enough effort into leveraging the strategies to comprehensively complete the tasks, I will guide them in re-evaluating and resubmitting their work in lieu of giving them a poor grade. Consequently, they become more assiduous in how they approach assignments.

4.9   REFORMING TEACHING CONCEPTION

Disciplinary literacy strategies have become integral to my teaching philosophy. There is nothing more frustrating for a teacher than seeing a class of confused, helpless students who did not read the textbook and cannot comprehend the material despite the stellar lesson that you meticulously planned and delivered. I experienced this frustration semester after semester. I came to realize that among the core issues contributing to the disparity is a lack of structured reading which consequently inhibits deep learning. So I began experimenting with research-based literacy strategies. While some of the strategies did not have a significant impact on student learning, others helped tremendously and transformed students' approach to acquiring knowledge. Students foster disciplinary literacy by practicing the metacognitive strategies engrained in the course structure. As deep reading is a catalyst for higher-order thinking, it must be leveraged to develop cross-functional skills such as critical thinking, analysis, problem solving, and communication to cultivate the qualities demanded by the modern accounting profession.

REFERENCES

Accounting Education Change Commission. (1992). The first course in accounting: Position statement no. two. *Issues in Accounting Education, 7*(2), 249–251.

Agnew, H. (2016, May 9). Auditing: Pitch battle. *The Financial Times.* Retrieved from https://www.ft.com

Albrecht, W., & Sack, R. (2000). *Accounting education: Charting the course through a perilous future (Series 16).* Sarasota, FL: American Accounting Association.

American Accounting Association (AAA), Bedford Committee, Committee on the Future Structure, Content, and Scope of Accounting Education (The Bedford Committee). (1986). Future accounting education: Preparing for the expanding profession. *Issues in Accounting Education,* (Spring), 168–195.

American Institute of Certified Public Accountants. (2019). *CPA exam pass rates.* Retrieved from https://www.aicpa.org/becomeacpa/cpaexam/psychometric-sandscoring/passingrates.html

Balaciu, D. E. (2015). The importance of conceptual maps in accounting curriculum. *The Annals of the University of Oradea, Economic Sciences, TOM XXIV,* 1348–1356. Romania Ministry of Education and Scientific Research.

Berrett, D. (2012). How 'flipping' the classroom can improve the traditional lecture. *The Chronicle of Higher Education.* Retrieved from https://www.chronicle.com/article/How-Flipping-the-Classroom/130857

Braun, K. W., & Sellers, R. D. (2012). Using a "daily motivational quiz" to increase student preparation, attendance and participation. *Issues in Accounting Education, 27*(1), 267–279.

Brown, C. A., Danvers, K., & Doran, D. T. (2016). Student perceptions on using guided reading questions to motivate student reading in the flipped classroom. *Journal of Accounting Education, 25*(3), 256–271.

Brown, R. B., & McCartney, S. (1998). Using reflections in postgraduate accounting education. *Journal of Accounting Education, 7*(2), 123–137.

Bryant, S. M., Kahle, J. B., & Schafer, B. A. (2005). Distance Education: A Review of the Contemporary Literature. *Issues in Accounting Education, 20*(3), 255–272.

Bryla, M. (2018). Data literacy: A critical skill for the 21st century. *Tableau.* Retrieved from https://www.tableau.com/about/blog/2018/9/data-literacy-critical-skill-21st-century-94221

Byrne, M., Flood, B., & Willis, P. (2009). An inter-institutional exploration of the learning approaches of students studying accounting. *International Journal of Teaching and Learning in Higher Education, 20*(2), 155–167.

Courtis, J. K., & Zaid, O. A. (2002). Early employment problems of Australian accounting graduates: An exploratory study. *Accounting Forum, 26,* 320–339.

Davies, J. (2017). Getting to the root cause of the problem: Teaching reading as a process in the sciences. In A. Horning, D. L. Gollnitz, & C. R. Haller (Ed.), *What is college reading* (pp. 161–182). Retrieved from https://wac.colostate.edu/docs/books/collegereading/davies.pdf

Duncan, K., Kenworthy, A., & McNamara, R. (2012). The effect of synchronous and asynchronous participation on students' performance in online accounting courses. *Accounting Education: An International Journal, 21*(4), 431–449.

Dweck, C. S. (2007). *Mindset: The new psychology of success.* New York: Ballantine Books.

Egan, M. (2015). Netflix stock just got 'cheaper'. Will you buy? *CNN Business.* Retrieved from https://money.cnn.com/2015/07/15/investing/netflix-stock-split-earnings/index.html

Fisher, D., Brozo, W. G., Frey, N., & Ivey, G. (2015). *Fifty instructional routines to develop content literacy* (3rd ed.). Boston: Pearson.

Glenn, D. (2011). For business majors, easy does it. *The Chronicle of Higher Education, 57*(33), A1–A5.

Greenberg, R. K., & Wilner, N. A. (2015). Using concept maps to provide an integrative framework for teaching the cost or managerial accounting course. *Journal of Accounting Education, 33*(1), 16–35.

Guess, A. K. (2014). Reflection papers in accounting classes: Really? *Journal of Accounting and Finance, 14*(2). Retrieved from http://www.nabusinesspress. com/JAF/GuessAK_Web14_2_.pdf

Harper, C., & Dunn, C. (2018). Building better accounting curricula. *Strategic Finance.* Retrieved from https://sfmagazine.com/post-entry/august-2018-building-better-accounting-curricula/

Hiralal, A. (2012). Students' experiences of blended learning in accounting education at the Durban University of Technology. *South African Journal of Higher Education, 26*(2), 316–328.

Institute of Management Accountants. (2016, January). Building a team to capitalize on the promise of big data. *Institute of Management Accountants.* Montvale, New Jersey.

Irvine, H. J., Cooper, K., & Jones, G. (2006). Concept mapping to enhance student learning in a financial accounting subject. *Proceedings of the Accounting Educators Forum,* Sydney, November 2005, 1–19. Retrieved from https:// ro.uow.edu.au/commpapers/122/

Jackson, S., & Durkee, D. (2008). Incorporating information literacy into the accounting curriculum. *Journal of Accounting Education, 17*(1), 83–97.

Jonassen, D. H. (2006). On the role of concepts in learning and instructional design. *Educational Technology Research and Development, 54*(2), 177–196.

King, A. (1993). From sage on the stage to guide on the side. *College Teaching, 41*(1). Retrieved from https://faculty.washington.edu/kate1/ewExternal-Files/SageOnTheStage.pdf

Lawson, R. A., Blocher, E. J., Brewer, P. C., Cokins, G., Sorensen, J. E., Stout, D. E., et al. (2014). Focusing accounting curricula on students' long-run careers: Recommendations for an integrated competency-based framework for accounting education. *Issues in Accounting Education, 29*(2), 295–317.

Lay, S. (2008). Improving success of undergraduate principles of accounting students by exploring new methods. *The International Journal of Learning, 15*(4), 75–80.

Leauby, B. A., Szabat, K. A., & Maas, J. D. (2010). Concept mapping – An empirical study in introductory financial accounting. *Journal of Accounting Education, 19*(3), 279–300.

Leigh, R. S. (2012). The classroom is alive with the sound of thinking: The power of the exit slip. *International Journal of Teaching and Learning in Higher Education, 24*(2), 189–196.

Marzano, R. (2012). Art and science of teaching/the many uses of exit slips. *Educational Leadership, 70*(2), 80–81.

McGuire, S. (2015). *Teach students how to learn.* Sterling, VA: Stylus.

Milman, N. B. (2012). The flipped classroom strategy: What is it and how can it best be used? *Distance Learning, 9*(3), 85–87.

Moje, E. B. (2008). Foregrounding the disciplines in secondary literacy teaching and learning: A call for change. *Journal of Adolescent and Adult Literacy, 52*(2), 96–107.

Moncada, S. M., & Moncada T. P. (2014). Gamification of learning in accounting education. *Journal of Higher Education Theory and Practice, 14*(3). Retrieved from http://digitalcommons.www.na-businesspress.com/JHETP/MoncadaSM_Web14_3_.pdf

Myers, M. (2016). Building better skill sets. *BizEd, 15*(1), 60–62.

Novak, J. D. (1991). Clarify with concept maps. *The Science Teacher, 58*(7), 45–49.

Novak, J. D., & Cañas, A. J. (2006). *The theory underlying concept maps and how to construct them* (Technical report IHMC CmapTools 2006-01 Rev 01-2008). Florida Institute for Human and Machine Cognition. Retrieved from http://cmap.ihmc.us/Publications/ResearchPapers/TheoryUnderlyingConcept Maps.pdf.

Phillips, B. J., & Phillips, F. (2007). Sink or skim: Textbook reading behaviors of introductory accounting students. *Issues in Accounting Education, 22*(1), 21–44.

Phillips, C. R., & Trainor, J. E. (2014). Millennial students and the flipped classroom. *ASBBS Annual Conference: Las Vegas*. Retrieved from http://abbs.org/files/ASBBS2014/PDF/P/Phillips_Trainor(P519-530).pdf

Pritchard, R., Romeo, G., & Muller, S. (1999). Integrating reading strategies into the accounting curriculum. *College Student Journal, 33*(1), 77–81.

Sargent, C. S., Borthick, F., & Lederberg, A. (2011). Improving retention for principles of accounting students: Ultra-short online tutorials for motivating effort and improving performance. *Issues in Accounting Education, 26*(4), 657–679.

Shah, S. Z. A. (2013). The use of group activities in developing personal transferable skills. *Innovations in Education & Teaching International, 50*(3), 297–307.

Shanahan, T., & Shanahan, C. (2008). Teaching disciplinary literacy to adolescents: Rethinking content area literacy. *Harvard Education Review, 78*, 40–59.

Shanahan, T., & Shanahan, C. (2012). What is disciplinary literacy and why does it matter? *Top Lang Disorders, 32*(1), 7–18.

Smith, A. K. (2010). New jobs, new skills. *Kiplinger's Personal Finance, 64*(11), 31–31.

Taraban, R., Rynearson, K., & Kerr, M. S. (2004). Analytic and pragmatic factors in college students' metacognitive reading strategies. *Reading Psychology, 25*(2), 67–81.

Tatikonda, L. U. (2004). Naked truths about accounting curricula: Here is a rallying cry for revamping undergraduate accounting curricula to prepare students to be certified management accountants and not only certified public accountants. *Management Accounting Quarterly, 5*(4), 62.

Weil, S., McGuigan, N., & Kern, T. (2011). The usage of an online discussion forum for the facilitation of case-based learning in an intermediate accounting course: A New Zealand case. *Open Learning, 26*(3), 237–251.

CHAPTER 5

Teaching a Broad Discipline: The Critical Role of Text-Based Learning to Building Disciplinary Literacy in Architectural Education

Jason A. Montgomery

Architecture is an ageless part of the human condition, with great depth and breadth of history and theory, with rich debates on aesthetics, technique, meaning, and purpose. While architecture is experiential and material, it is also conceptual, driven by critical analyses and theoretical constructs. To fully immerse oneself in this field, in this domain, one must seek out the direct experiences with the seminal works and rich vernacular environments, but one must also seek out the seminal works of authors exploring this great discipline in text. Through reading, we learn that the art of architecture experienced in great buildings contributes to our mental well-being, our sense of pleasure (Ruskin, 1989), reinforces our sense of order in the world, and stirs our sense of beauty (Le Corbusier, 1986). In the midst of debates on aesthetics, style, and historical relevance in the late

J. A. Montgomery (✉)
New York City College of Technology, City University of New York,
Brooklyn, NY, USA
e-mail: jmontgomery@citytech.cuny.edu

© The Author(s) 2020
J. C. But (ed.), *Teaching College-Level Disciplinary Literacy*,
https://doi.org/10.1007/978-3-030-39804-0_5

twentieth century, we find arguments that support a tectonic basis of architectural form and articulation, where the craft of making is the foundation for imitation that transcends mere building through artistic distance and perspective (Porphyrios, 1991). These explorations of the unique nature of architecture to human culture are fundamental to the study, research, and practice of architecture. The writing of architects, historians, theorists, critics, building scientists, engineers, and scholars is an inextricable piece of the great ageless discipline of architecture, linking the reader to an ancient past or thrusting her into the promise of a better future.

Access through this threshold stands open to all who seek the richness and cultivation encapsulated in the literature. Indeed, across the globe, architecture students for generations have delved into this literature, seeking a sense of belonging within the intellectual culture of this venerable discipline. This literature provides a central component of the critical path to disciplinary literacy in architecture, with the commensurate ability to fully participate as a practitioner, theorist, or scholar. But not all students cross this threshold easily, as it is text-based, with active, careful reading required for successful entry. Contemporary students of architecture, like many students in other disciplines, face myriad reading and text-based learning challenges or competing interests blocking passage: frustration from poor comprehension, unsuccessful application of learning strategies, conflicting priorities between academic work and personal time, work-avoidance goals, sense of the lack of intrinsic value of reading (Hoeft, 2012).

Like other disciplines, many architecture courses rely on student reading as an important component of learning. Less common are the courses where faculty explicitly help students with the reading challenges they face. Architecture faculty may believe reading skills are the students' responsibility and should have been already acquired and developed (Hoeft, 2012; Lei, Rhinehart, Howard, & Cho, 2010b; Wambach, 1998). Where reading is resisted and/or rare in a student's education, deep learning and awareness of the meaning and significance of architecture is hampered, thereby impeding the growth of students' disciplinary literacy (Fang, 2012). While other forms of communication and media may provide alternative sources for learning and developing disciplinary literacy, texts remain the primary repository par excellence of the rich and diverse body of knowledge and ideas available to the twenty-first-century architecture student (Plattus, 2012).

This chapter seeks to provide a guide to engaging students with architectural texts to facilitate building their disciplinary literacy. It focuses on helping architecture faculty work explicitly and implicitly to increase their students' dedication to reading and reading effectiveness to support this goal. The importance of expanding reading integration and support is discussed and exemplified in case studies as central to the facilitation of developing disciplinary literacy, both through course work and self-directed learning. Much of this chapter applies to undergraduate students, but it may be useful for consideration of graduate teaching as well. Ultimately, this purposeful emphasis on reading in architectural education can help faculty build a teaching culture that enables students to grow confidently in their engagement with the rich literature that widens and deepens their appreciation, understanding, intellectual growth, but, most importantly, full immersion in the noble discipline of architecture.

5.1   BREADTH OF ARCHITECTURAL EDUCATION AND THE ROLE OF TEXT-BASED LEARNING

Architectural education has inherent challenges stemming from the breadth of this discipline that seeks balance between science and art. The wide range of required skills for successful practice outlined by Vitruvius is carried into the twenty-first century by reflection on contemporary architectural education and practice and codified in registration (NCARB, 2018) and accreditation boards (NAAB, 2014). Vitruvius emphasized that the architect should be a person "of letters, a skillful draughtsman, a mathematician, familiar with scientific inquiries, a diligent student of philosophy, acquainted with music; not ignorant of medicine, learned in the responses of jurisconsults, familiar with astronomy and astronomical calculations" (Vitruvius, 1995, p. 9). Joan Ockman outlines the complexity of architectural education as combining "technics and aesthetics, sciences and humanities." She goes on to describe the "highly disparate types of knowledge" schools must impart, "negotiating the architect's multiple identities as craftsman, technician, and creative artist; professional and intellectual; public servant and businessman" (Ockman, 2012). The National Architectural Accreditation Board requires accredited degree programs to provide evidence of student learning in the categories of Critical Thinking and Representation, Building Practices, Technical Skills and Knowledge, Integrated Architectural Solutions, and Professional Practice (NAAB, 2014). From the list of skills and knowledge from the ancient world to Joan Ockman's recent summary, the individual seeking the professional title of architect needs to be well-rounded and capable of analysis of complex and multifaceted issues and synthesizing broad knowledge through a focused creative process.

In this breadth of concerns and complex identities, the discipline demands more of the student than mere content knowledge. The student must come to an awareness of the role of architecture in society, in the history of diverse civilizations, its meaning and significance to each culture, the way it communicates ideas and mirrors or enhances culture, the iconographic potential of architecture, the tectonic language that ties architecture to history, material, methods of making and crafting. Without this literacy, architecture loses value and meaning in culture. Indeed, critiques of the consumerist/formalist crisis in architectural practice in the twenty-first century may be linked to a lack of deep disciplinary literacy that starts with the education of architecture students (Salingaros & Masden II, 2008).

Professional architecture degree programs are required to expose their students to the broad scope of the discipline. Non-professional degree programs are typically more focused on particular aspects of practice, but still contend with a broad scope of skills and knowledge. In either case, reading, especially reading outside the classroom, persists as a critical activity expected by the faculty for the acquisition of knowledge and understanding of discipline content. Reading also is likely implicitly relied on to provide the foundation for disciplinary literacy in most degree programs, where the deep learning of the meaning and language of architecture, the development of cognitive processing at increasingly higher levels of sophistication is expected to originate and be nurtured. Students who are challenged by learning through text, however, are placed at a significant disadvantage in their development of disciplinary literacy in these conditions.

5.2   Challenges to Reading in Architectural Education

In the highly competitive employment marketplace, disciplinary literacy offers students an opportunity to distinguish themselves, with the ability to participate in broad or deep discussions of architecture, analyzing and synthesizing ideas simultaneously with their demonstration of technical proficiency. This literacy can be acquired to a large degree through active, guided engagement with the rich literature on architecture. Although reading skills are foundational to the development of disciplinary literacy, they are likely to have effectively diminished in the last few decades, following trends across disciplines in higher education (Hoeft, 2012; Ryan, 2006). Indeed, a broad examination of architectural education reveals students struggling to communicate in professional settings, a symptom of challenges with skills and knowledge linked to disciplinary literacy and reading (Boyer & Mitgang, 1996). This trend will undoubtedly continue without a change of approach to curriculum development and teaching. Curiously, however, reading in architectural education is a rare topic in disciplinary literature. The lack of attention to student reading in the literature or the classroom is not necessarily resulting from any conscious change of pedagogy, but from a number of factors prevalent in the contemporary architecture classroom.

Factors That Undermine Reading in Architectural Education

Many factors undermine reading in architectural education, thereby impacting the depth of students' disciplinary literacy. These include the overarching emphasis on the design studio, the prioritizing of hard skills, the tactic acceptance of students' lack of engagement with texts, the nature of architectural texts, and deficient cultural literacy demanded by texts.

Impact of the Domination of the Design Studio
The design studio remains the heart of architectural education (Anthony, 1991; Boyer & Mitgang, 1996; Ockman, 2012; Salama & Wilkinson, 2007). The creative process of design captivates students and demands significant time and effort on their part. Faculty apply their experience of the design studio to their courses, with expectations centered on long hours of creative exploration, development of ideas, and sophisticated presentations. Reading in this mode of architectural education is not commonly integrated, leaving text-based learning relegated to other parts of the curriculum. Students recognize the importance of design studio to their education and give it priority, leaving little time and energy for reading in their other courses.

Impact of Emphasis on Hard Skills
There is a persistent historic culture of architectural education that centers on hard skills as the key to employment and a career (Boyer & Mitgang, 1996; Johnston, 2005). In the past these skills centered on mechanical drafting; today they focus on digital tools for drafting and modeling,

building information modeling (BIM), rendering, and fabrication. The dichotomy between practical and theoretical knowledge that emerges where hard skills dominate in architectural education can diminish the emphasis on historical, theoretical, and general education learning and contribute to the reduction of the exploration of ideas and concepts through architectural texts.

Implicit Acceptance of Avoidance of Reading

Diminished dedication to reading in architectural education can result from the combination of student and faculty inattention and/or implicit acceptance of performance goals that allow reading to become effectively optional (Lei, Bartlett, Gorney, & Herschbach, 2010a; Wambach, 1998). The development of the course syllabus and the tools for grading and assessment may have the intention of requiring student reading, but may actually allow students to bypass this requirement (Hoeft, 2012). Students seeking the most efficient path to a passing grade will focus their reading efforts in such a way as to be able to perform on a quiz or exam or in a class discussion, thus determining their reading persistence and depth of engagement (Ambrose, Bridges, DiPietro, Lovett, & Norman, 2010; Roberts & Roberts, 2008). Tensions impacting student motivation may also affect their dedication to reading (Ambrose et al., 2010).

Diverse Types of Texts in Architectural Education

Active reading is foundational to entry-level access and higher levels of learning in a wide range of subtopics that pertain to the discipline. These subtopics include the history of the art of building; the evolution of aesthetic, compositional, and conceptual ideas that drive architectural design, refinement, and innovation; the broad questions relating to human habitat and urban/rural settlement; the science of materials and assemblies; the ethical urgency and strategies to reduce global warming and responsibly practice in response to climate change; the social implications of planning and development; and the legal regulations that ensure health and safety. The use of language and vocabulary as well as the functions and purposes of these texts vary considerably, thereby requiring students to use different cognitive strategies in the reading process. For example, reading and interpreting the legal language of the building code is a very different activity from reading historical analysis of architectural design. Where faculty do not explicitly assist students in navigating this diverse and challenging disciplinary literature, students may struggle to meaningfully engage with these texts.

Continued Prominence of Architectural Texts in Print
Reading in architectural education is also impacted by the nature of and access to architectural texts. While access to free online journals is increasing, a significant portion of important architectural literature online is still found behind paywalls while print books still occupy a central place in disciplinary publication (Alger, 2010). The expense of accessing books or online journals is a first-level impediment to student reading, but it is not the only one. Library collections supporting architecture programs are most likely well stocked with the seminal works, but even free access does not ensure use (Alger, 2010). Efficient internet searches for information erode the students' interaction with print texts while a lack of information literacy can result in the loss of quality control on the reading that students *actually* do. Students need motivation and explicit encouragement to engage with the curated texts found in college libraries. The library should serve as a critical space for architecture students' learning, but it likely does not happen organically in the twenty-first century.

Cultural Literacy Demanded by Architectural Texts
Architectural texts also commonly assume a "cultural literacy" that the reader brings to the text. When familiarity with the common knowledge, background knowledge, cultural codes in architecture is lacking, it creates a disconnect between the text and the reader that is difficult to counteract (Bean, 2011). Similarly, vocabulary and syntax present significant barriers to reading effectiveness (Bean, 2011); when vocabulary needs to be understood in terms of both definition and disciplinary context that is not yet presented as part of the curriculum, students struggle, impacting their motivation and persistence to learn through texts (Bean, 2011). If reading is to be a vibrant, persistent, meaningful activity that is central to student development of disciplinary literacy, faculty must consciously reflect on these issues and apply strategies to address them.

5.3   Key Learning Principles Impacting Text-Based Learning in Architectural Education

The revitalization of text-based learning to support disciplinary literacy in architectural education should start with special attention to entry-level students. These students have the highest potential for significant variation in college preparedness and established skills. Entry-level students also have the highest potential for benefiting from the positive impacts of specific strategies to engage them and help them become better learners (Kuh, 2007; Kuh et al., 2008). This obliges faculty to pay attention to the factors that impact the effectiveness of student learning in general and learning through text specifically. Outlined below are four principles that are particularly important to developing strategies that support text-based learning in architectural education: prior knowledge, knowledge organization, student motivation, and meaningful learning.

Prior Knowledge of Architecture and Its Role in Society

Faculty need to be cognizant of the students' prior knowledge of the discipline at the beginning of each semester (Ambrose et al., 2010). Entry-level architecture students' prior knowledge of the discipline may be insufficient, inaccurate, or inactive (Ambrose et al., 2010). These students may not see architecture as a rich discipline where science and art are synthesized but more like a trade involved in building construction. Their first-hand experience of great buildings may be limited and/or cursory. To improve the reception of new knowledge and the students' ability to learn, faculty must be aware of the sufficiency and accuracy of student prior knowledge and to ensure that it is activated and developed when the new material is presented in the course (Ambrose et al., 2010).

Knowledge Organization of the Myriad Concepts in the Discipline

Students need to learn how to structure the new knowledge they are obtaining in their courses. They need to visualize the relationships, associations, and connections between this new material and what they already know and develop an "organized representation" of the larger body of material (Ambrose et al., 2010, p. 42). This learning principle is particularly important to architectural education where the diversity of the sub-topics results in an exceptionally large body of material to synthesize and fit together into an organized understanding of the discipline. As the practice of architecture demands synthesis of complex requirements and concerns, seeing the connectiveness of the many issues at play, and organizing them into a cohesive whole, the development of knowledge organization is critical to architecture students' growth in the discipline.

Student Motivation in the Discipline

With the emphasis on the design studio, it is important to consider the motivations that impact the study habits of architecture students. Student motivation impacts the "direction, intensity, persistence, and quality of the learning behaviors in which students engage" (Ambrose et al., 2010, pp. 68–69). When students are not in the classroom, many competing interests will impact how they study and how they see the connections between out-of-class work and their overall learning. Where students are motivated to perform well in the design studio, much of their time out of the classroom will be dedicated to this work and may lead to the sacrifice of other modes of studying and learning required for their other classes. If most of their text-based learning takes place in classes other than studio and this reading work requires significant time that competes with the design studio work, this component of learning hinges significantly on each students' motivation and the specific goals that direct her behavior.

Meaningful Learning as a Path to Disciplinary Literacy

Dedicated and motivated engagement with the text is an important step, but it does not ensure meaningful learning on its own. Architecture faculty need to reflect on the nature of learning through the diverse texts of the discipline and how to cultivate deep learning through them. Richard Mayer (2002) offers three possible outcomes as a result of student reading: no learning, rote learning, or meaningful learning. The outcome of student reading is dependent on the cognitive processes students are applying when they read. Students are conditioned to see memorizing as the core goal of reading, but recalling information alone does not lead to meaningful learning, especially in a discipline with a broad range of knowledge that needs to be synthesized. Meaningful learning requires students to move beyond the basic activity of memorizing to the higher-order cognitive processes of understanding, applying, analyzing, evaluating, and creating (Mayer, 2002). This in turn requires faculty to reflect on the way they organize their course and the activities they plan for students, with special attention dedicated to fostering active reading and developing students' disciplinary literacy.

5.4   STRATEGIES TO ENHANCE DISCIPLINARY LITERACY IN ARCHITECTURAL EDUCATION

As text-based learning is a central activity for developing disciplinary literacy in architectural education, below there are a number of strategies for the integration and enhancement of text-based learning in courses with the potential to facilitate students' increasing engagement with architectural texts and compliment and deepen their learning. Two case studies are provided as examples of the application of these strategies in two of the critical courses in architecture curricula: the design studio and building science courses.

Strategies Especially Applicable to Early Years in the Curriculum

New students in undergraduate architecture programs may have varying skills and knowledge of the discipline as they start their studies. The strategies below seek to provide early students with foundational development of disciplinary literacy to help them succeed as they progress into higher levels of the curriculum.

Formative Assessment and Course Adjustment

In first-year courses in architectural education, it is important to consider some sort of assessment that can help the faculty member gain perspective on the students' preparedness for deep learning in the discipline. The findings of assessments can guide faculty adjustments to the curriculum, course content, and teaching methods to the needs of the cohort, which may vary year to year, in particular bridging any gaps in prior knowledge and base skills. For example, a common challenge for new students is their proficiency in understanding architectural concepts and ideas presented in texts and architectural drawings. Texts may be challenging if they require prior knowledge and vocabulary new to the students. Architectural drawings may be more challenging for the students to "read" and understand than faculty appreciate, especially two-dimensional drawings, due to their abstract nature. These challenges often coincide with a lack of vocabulary and terminology related to architectural drawing concepts, conventions, and techniques. These challenges can have a profound impact on students' understanding of readings, drawing assignments, and discussions if they are not explicitly addressed.

To understand the preparedness of the students in the course, an initial short reading assessment can be designed to measure the incoming students' reading skills and general knowledge of the discipline as well as specific vocabulary and terminology, usually consisting of two–three pages of text and six–ten short answer questions designed to address reading comprehension, analysis, context, and evaluation. This can be combined with an assessment designed to measure students' experience with reading architectural drawings. The drawing assessment can ask groups of students to sort scrambled drawings of a group of buildings, identifying each unique building and grouping the drawing sets accordingly (Fig. 5.1). Together these assessments offer insight into students' disciplinary knowledge and their preparedness for building a foundation of disciplinary literacy.

(Source: Photo by Jason Montgomery)

Fig. 5.1   Students sort drawings into organized sets to assess their experience of reading architectural drawings

The results of these assessments can guide the faculty in the development of discussions focused at the right level for the cohort on how architects communicate ideas through text and drawings. Where the assessments reveal students struggling with both text and drawings, the professor can scaffold cognitive skills while addressing prior knowledge gaps. One strategy is to integrate a seminar in class where a foundational reading that provides critical base knowledge is read out loud and discussed, with the faculty member guiding students through the reading while actively modeling engaged interaction with the text through diagramming and annotating. This can be followed by group activities that build familiarity with two-dimensional and three-dimensional architectural drawings with an annotation component that can help students build their vocabulary of architectural elements and understanding of terms related to drawings and drawing conventions. The faculty member can prime the students with a Socratic discussion that probes why text-based learning and reading architectural drawings are so challenging for first-year students, helping them reflect metacognitively on their learning needs.

Scaffolding Knowledge Organization
Student disciplinary literacy is critically linked to their skill of organizing the broad knowledge of architecture, linking new knowledge to existing knowledge in a structured way. There are explicit strategies that support the development of architecture students' skills to organize knowledge. One strategy is to map the course content directly in the syllabus, illustrating the concepts presented and how they relate to each other. This map can help students build a mental picture of the concepts they are going to learn and allow them to anticipate each transition from one concept to another (Fig. 5.2). This map serves as an armature for the course readings, giving the students a critical overview before they move into the readings (McGuire & McGuire, 2015). It also models strategies the students can apply to their study techniques.

Concept mapping, diagraming, and graphic organizers are particularly useful as study tools in architectural education where visual learners can use them in a structured way to build a more sophisticated knowledge organization. These tools can help facilitate students' navigation of the broad complexity of architecture as a discipline and place their learning in one course in the broader context of the discipline, or to organize the detailed concepts presented in an assigned reading. Concept maps, diagrams, and graphic organizers can help students focus on the bigger

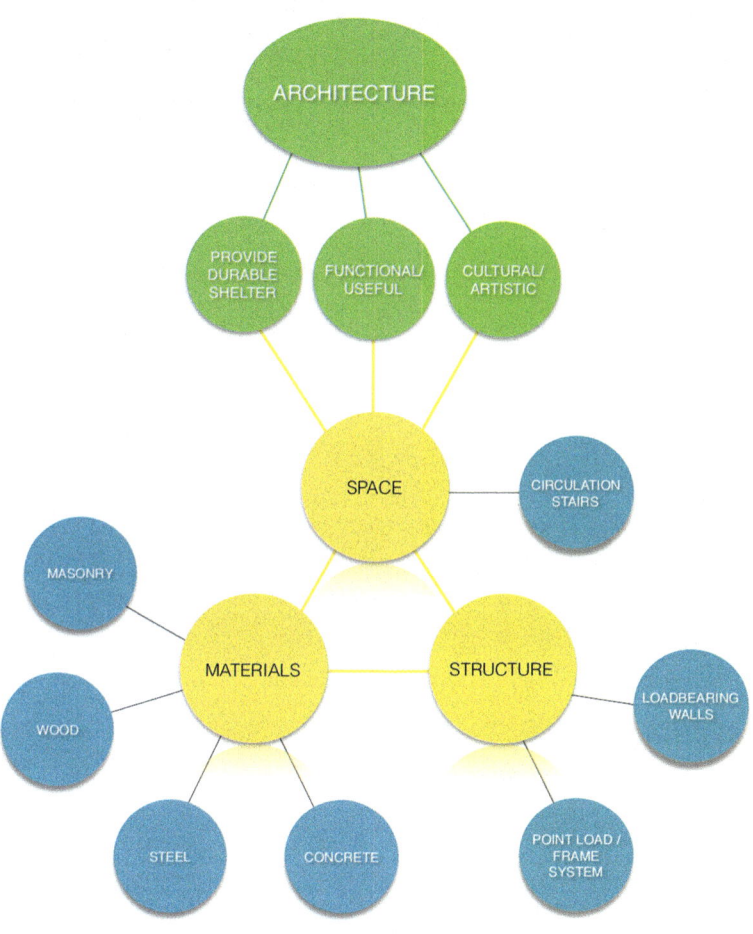

(Source: Jason Montgomery)

Fig. 5.2 Concept map for an introductory building science class course content

picture understanding of the *relationships* between the concepts discussed in class and in the readings, counteracting the students' tendency to focus merely on rote memorization of information. Faculty can require this approach to note-taking (Fig. 5.3), emphasizing that concept maps can be applied at any scale of information, zooming out to see the whole and zooming in to see the detail, much as they do in the development of

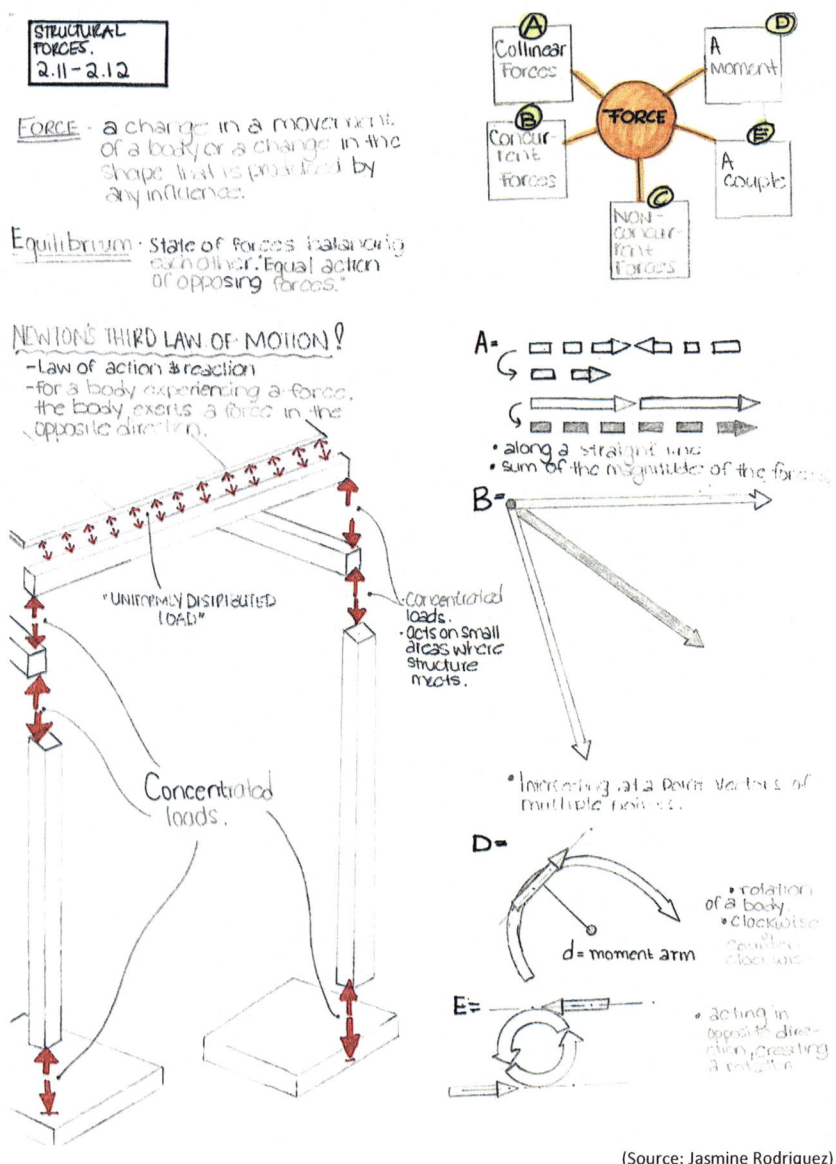

Fig. 5.3 Example of student application of graphic diagramming and concept mapping to their note-taking

architectural drawings. Faculty can model mapping for the students as an integral part of class lectures and discussions and explicitly stress knowledge organization as a critical activity for growth in disciplinary literacy.

Motivating Student Reading
With reading and learning through text serving as a central activity for building disciplinary literacy in architecture, every course in architectural education offers the opportunity to find ways to build the students' motivation to persist and commit themselves to reading and learning through text. As student motivation is often linked to grades, one strategy can leverage this motivation by tracking student reading through note-taking, graphic organizers, and concept maps that are submitted on a regular schedule (see note-taking tracking discussion below). This strategy demonstrates the importance the faculty member places on reading in the course, holds the students accountable, and helps establish a base value of text-based learning for the students (Ambrose et al., 2010).

Another strategy for motivating students to commit themselves to text-based learning is to require regular reflections on the readings. Asking students to reflect on each reading helps them contemplate and recognize the value of reading to their learning. Reflection can also serve to increase confidence in reading and learning through the text, working toward a positive feedback loop motivating increased commitment to reading (Ambrose et al., 2010). Reflection can also promote analysis and synthesize skills that build disciplinary literacy.

Architecture faculty can also seek to motivate students to read by linking the course content to real-world issues to help students see the higher value of their academic learning to their future professional career path (Ambrose et al., 2010). Faculty integration of recently published articles or studies on important issues concerning the built environment demonstrates the relevance of the course content to the students. The use of articles or studies published through mainstream media sources, trade publications, and academic journals expands the available reading materials to this wider range of literature beyond the classic textbook.

For example, in a course presenting materials and structural concepts, the reinvigoration of the use of timber for its environmental benefits and innovative use in urban high-rise construction can be presented through mainstream media articles in outlets like the BBC. While the textbook outlines the well-established properties of wood and its typical applications, the news articles can report on cutting-edge applications written for a general audience. This strategy provides text that is less intimidating than the technical density and style of the textbook prose, serving as a scaffolding strategy to build reading motivation and confidence.

Deeper Learning Through Linking Text, First-Hand Experience, and Visual Thinking

Deeper learning in the discipline is enhanced when students can associate text-based knowledge with other contexts. One strategy is to include direct experiences of the built environment as a purposeful component of the course. At a building or construction site, students can apply their skills of careful observation and visual thinking to construct knowledge from first-hand experience and see connections between this knowledge and the concepts and ideas discussed in the readings. Visual thinking provides an excellent alternative approach that balances with text-based learning, and acts as a scaffold to help visual learners improve their reading effectiveness (Arnheim, 1969).

Local sites can be selected for their relationship to the course readings. For example, a course on structures can incorporate site visits to bring students up close to salient examples of the concepts and systems reviewed in the text, such as the compressive and tensile stress in the structural components of a bridge. A visit to a renovated historic warehouse offers the study of walls, arches, lintels, beams, joists, and posts working together as an integrated system. Standing below the arches while observing carefully the post and beam system that structures the space for modern offices allows the students to connect directly to the volumetric nature of the elements, sense their distribution of the heavy loads of the building, see them in a contemporary context, and analyze the role of each component as they are prompted by probing questions of the faculty member. This approach is intended to embolden the active participation of students, where discussion and careful observation in the field draw them into a high level of engagement with the concepts and vocabulary discussed in the course (see the discussion of the walking seminar below).

Applying Metacognition to Reading Strategies

In order for text-based learning to be meaningful to the development of disciplinary literacy, reading skills must be nurtured and developed incrementally (Bean, 2011) in combination with metacognitive skills that help students look at their reading and study habits with a critical eye (McGuire, 2007). Explicit discussions with students can help them understand that reading may be challenging and that there are strategies and various approaches to the reading process that may help them (Bean, 2011). This discussion should include the presentation of the taxonomy of different types of learning to help students recalibrate their views of the learning process and their role in it (Ambrose et al., 2010; Bloom, 1956; Mayer, 2002; McGuire, 2007, McGuire & McGuire, 2015). Strategies can be applied to the course that embed the metacognitive aspect, such as learning logs and exit slips.

The metacognitive skills that improve reading effectiveness enhance disciplinary literacy in architecture more broadly. The discipline of self-critique and metacognition helps architecture students develop their strategies for problem-solving and design process through a critical lens, evaluating the effectiveness of their strategies progressively so they can improve their learning (see problem-based learning discussion below). It creates a synergy between improving text-based learning and their overall development and application of metacognitive processes in the discipline.

Developing Active Reading Strategies
Among the most important strategies for enhancing disciplinary literacy through improving student reading effectiveness is the integration of active reading strategies. While common strategies such as annotation of the text are useful for developing discernment of the hierarchy of information and keywords and definitions, strategies that focus on the big picture and the connections between topics are particularly useful for this broad discipline.

One active reading strategy that helps focus the students on the big picture of the text is SQ3R (Survey, Question, Read, Recite, Review). This strategy guides students of architecture to start their engagement with the text at a macro scale, supporting their formulation and focus on the overarching nature of the topic, establish its context, and see the critical relationships of the topic before delving into details. Surveying technical readings on building performance, for example, by previewing headings, drawings, diagrams, and photographs, helps the students understand the nature of this technical concept as well as the multiple layers of subtopics that fit within this category before tackling the highly technical concepts such as R-value, thermal bridging, or condensation. Similarly, architectural history texts can be surveyed and previewed to help students move beyond a chronological understanding of periods and memorization of names and dates to see more universal themes of stylistic characteristics, cultural contexts, and theoretical movements. When they are not clear on context and big relationships, this strategy encourages them to identify questions and actively search the text to answer them. This strategy can be facilitated with worksheets and guides provided to the students. The worksheets can be reviewed together and demonstrated in class with a sample text. Students can be encouraged to submit their completed worksheets for extra credit. The discipline of seeing the whole and understanding its nature before diving into the details promoted by SQ3R is a synergistic skill valuable to managing the complexity and diversity of architectural texts and making connections across the discipline.

Concept mapping, noted above for its benefits to knowledge organization, should also be noted as an active learning strategy that has similar benefits to SQ3R. The graphic mapping of concepts and their relationships expressing a hierarchal order is a powerful tool for students to mine the meaning of the reading and to activate an analytical cognitive process while reading (Bean 2011; Lei et al., 2010b). Concept mapping, like SQ3R, naturally links to core aspects of architectural thinking, like the analysis of design problems and client space and flow requirements, where organization and study of relationships in a hierarchal structure are critical skills.

Active reading documents (ARD) are another variation of these strategies that offer a structure for student interaction with the text. ARD prompt student attention to genre, hierarchy, organization of the text, identification and definition of keywords, concepts, vocabulary, and activation of cognitive analytical processes seeking connections both within the text and beyond the text. This strategy encourages faculty to develop customized worksheets that guide the students reading, encouraging multiple levels of interaction with the text. For example, students can be asked to answer questions focused on foundational knowledge found in the text and identify the genre of the text. They can then be asked to construct a lecture to teach the content in the reading to others. Finally, they can be prompted to diagram how the reading content integrates with larger themes in the course or across courses (Barkley & Major, 2018). This strategy also encourages the use of diagramming and sketching that allow visual learners to explore the relationships graphically (Dubas & Toledo, 2015). Like the other active learning techniques discussed, ARD are well suited to the support of disciplinary literacy in architectural education, especially through the emphasis on identifying the genre and relationship of the text to the larger discipline so that students keep this context and awareness of intent and purpose in the foreground while they read (Cabral & Tavares, 2002).

5.5 Design Studio Pedagogy: Applying Problem-Based Learning to Integrate Text-Based Research and Apply Metacognitive Skills

The heart of contemporary architectural education, the design studio, is an environment for learning that stresses the creativity and aesthetic vision of the student but also their conceptual, analytical, and synthetic thinking and the logic of their argumentation. The history of architectural education reveals a wide range of possible modes of learning while recent examinations of architectural education encourage innovation and creativity in the reform or remaking of design studio pedagogy (Anthony, 1991; Boyer & Mitgang, 1996; Ockman, 2012; Salingaros & Masden 2008). There is room for exploration, integration, and application of approaches to learning that either draw from enhanced historical modes or from other disciplines, including learning through observation and research, problem-based learning, experiential learning, and inquiry-based learning (Salama, 2010; Ware, 1866). Within this range of approaches, there is likely significant untapped potential for both leveraging the unique nature of text-based learning in architectural education and explicitly supporting active reading and overall disciplinary literacy.

Problem-based learning (PBL) offers a structure that can guide the integration of text-based learning into the design studio as a regular and significant component. PBL is intended to be structured as an explicit cycle of learning that includes the following steps: establish problem scenarios, identify facts, generate hypotheses, identify knowledge deficiencies, apply new knowledge, abstraction, and evaluation (Boud & Feletti, 1999; Hmelo-Silver, 2004). The application of this structure offers a solution to a common critique of design studio pedagogy: the potential for students to come to see their efforts to solve the problem as the end in itself, without consciously building on their existing skills and knowledge and integrating new knowledge and skills as they progress in their education. In this way, studio exercises may become rote rather than meaningful, self-referential rather than transferable (Anthony, 1991; Salama & Wilkinson, 2007). Application of PBL to design studio pedagogy addresses this critique through the critical steps of the learning cycle of identifying the limits of existing knowledge, identifying what new knowledge is necessary to solve the problem, conducting the research that constructs this new knowledge, and reflecting on the learning process to prepare for higher-level execution in the next project. Research here is a key strategy that many reformers recommend for integration in the design studio (Anthony, 1991; Salingaros & Masden, 2008). The integration of text-based research in combination with an explicit metacognitive learning approach has great potential to be a central feature of the reform of the design studio, taking advantage of PBL pedagogy.

Another significant critique of the current culture of the design studio education is that studio pedagogy creates a barrier to synthesis of knowledge, as the focus on abstract and subjective creativity "seduces" students to the extent that they are unable to see links between the practical and evidence-based knowledge from other parts of the curriculum, reinforcing the silo effect (Salingaros & Masden, 2008). To counter this subjectivity and reinforce integration of knowledge, studios can apply the PBL learning cycle with an integrated seminar that combines with an initial assignment to serve as the research component of the learning cycle, providing a review of the key literature on the studio topic, exposing students to critical thinking on the topic through text-based learning, and offering a foundation of knowledge that they can apply more objectively to their design process.

Case Studies on Restructuring Design and Technical Courses with Text-Based Components

With the above explorations of enhancing disciplinary literacy in architectural education, two case studies are presented here as examples of the application of a number of these strategies in live courses in an undergraduate architecture degree program.

Urban Design Studio with an Integrated Research Seminar

In a studio that introduces students to urban design, the PBL cycle was applied to explore the question of how to develop new neighborhoods in urban centers. As a starting point, a literature review would provide students with grounding in urban theory to begin to formulate guiding principles for their design approach. To this end, a research seminar was integrated to provide a review of seminal writing on cities and urban design including Camillo Sitte, Le Corbusier, Jane Jacobs, Colin Rowe, Leon Krier, and Rem Koolhaus. In addition, an interdisciplinary module was introduced, focused on happiness research and its application to cities. This seminar and module ran parallel to a series of studio assignments that started with neighborhood analysis and led up to a large-scale masterplan.

Students who are working at the urban scale for the first time often lack the knowledge base and experience that allow them to shift from the architectural project to the neighborhood or city scale. To address this lack of knowledge and experience, faculty lead the students through a process of reflection and analysis that facilitate their development of a list of key principles to guide their neighborhood masterplan. Together these activities comprised the initial stages of the PBL cycle, with the establishment of the problem scenarios, identifying base facts (site analysis), and developing a hypotheses (design principles).

Reflection on prior knowledge and experience continued in the PBL cycle, identifying the limits of existing knowledge. Initial reflections revealed the students had little knowledge and experience of thinking about and designing at the neighborhood scale. The first assignment worked to address this. It asked students to research their neighborhoods, documenting the key features: urban structure, building and block typologies, use patterns, nodes and networks, boundaries, public space, centers of activity, and so on. Moving from the larger scale of the urban structure to the block itself, the students analyzed a typical block in their neighborhood, documenting building mass, the figure-ground relationship of built and unbuilt space, the various building types found within the block, and the section of the streets that define each edge of the block. This research assignment provided students with a deeper knowledge of urban neighborhoods and helped them understand what knowledge they needed to continue to acquire to design a new neighborhood in the city.

Parallel to this initial assignment, the seminar introduced them to a wide range of theoretical views of cities and neighborhoods, serving as the literature review of the research. This included the interdisciplinary module on happiness scholarship, which consisted of seminar discussions, a visit to a museum exhibition, and outside-the-class readings. The contrasting urban theories and happiness research presented the students with multiple theoretical viewpoints to draw upon while the neighborhood analysis gave them an objective understanding of an extant urban condition to help them interpret and evaluate the urban theories. The seminar, while serving this critical role in the PBL cycle, also facilitated enhancement of the reading effectiveness and text-based learning through discussion, argumentation, and evaluation, challenging the students to think and interact with the texts at higher levels of learning taxonomy (Mayer, 2002).

From this stage of the PBL learning cycle, the students began in earnest to develop their projects, applying the new knowledge gained from the research seminar and assignment. Working in teams the students reviewed their initial set of principles and re-evaluated them with the new knowledge they gained from the neighborhood analysis and the seminar. Their revised set of principles then guided their execution of the masterplan, representing the abstraction and summary of their new knowledge.

The student reflections on the seminar experience provide important insight into their view of this approach, and the key impacts on their learning. A range of responses reveals that some students benefited from the seminar as they would not likely have read the text independently while a few expressed discomfort with reading out loud in the classroom. The students also gravitate in their reflections to the module on happiness studies, noting that this contemporary research made the project feel more relevant and helped them understand how urban design impacts people's daily life. It was also more accessible to many students compared to the urban theory presented in the seminal works. Overall, the students reflect positively on the benefit of the research seminar to provide context and alternative viewpoints that can help them form a deeper view of the subject of urban design and help them develop a design strategy that builds on this new knowledge.

Integration of reading through the PBL learning cycle in the studio is a natural response to the critique of the shortcomings of contemporary design studio pedagogy and supports four important goals:

- Text-based research in the studio allows faculty to embed seminal scholarship in the studio pedagogy, elevating students' critical thinking past the practical or form centered concerns of the presented problem.
- Second, it emphasizes research as a standard component of the design process. This is particularly important as disciplinary knowledge is rapidly expanding with new techniques for a building based on the changing environmental conditions across the globe.
- Third, it encourages students to build their knowledge base in a directed manner following the PBL cycle, both in and outside the classroom.

- Fourth, with the dominant position of the design studio in architectural education, integration of reading as a critical component of learning in the studio is a significant opportunity to improve student reading effectiveness for architecture students.

Focused Text-Based Learning in Building Science Pedagogy

A first-year building science course in an open enrollment architectural technology degree program provides a case study of the factors that may impede text-based learning in these important courses. In open enrollment programs, many students are less prepared for college and have not developed strong study habits and skills in their high school years. Working while taking classes, an increasingly likely condition for many college students facing high education costs, may compound these students' challenges, resulting in reduced time for out-of-classroom work, especially weekly reading. Students facing these challenges are often eager for the least demanding and most efficient path to pass the course. Additionally, students who are inexperienced with self-directed learning may take a relatively passive approach to their coursework, waiting at each stage of the class for the professor to tell them what they need to do. The combination of the desire for efficiency and passive dependency on the professor does not serve the interest of the student developing meaningful learning goals and self-directed learning skills, and likely results in neglect of text-based learning outside the classroom.

This course previously followed a traditional building science course format, including weekly lectures, out-of-class readings, and quizzes in combination with drawing assignments where the concepts presented in the lectures are applied. The quizzes were administered with the intention to "force" the students to read each week. A final exam of 60 questions largely taken from the quizzes was given on the last day of the semester. A study of three sections totaling 56 students over two semesters revealed a 69% average across the 9 quizzes. The average on the final exam in the same three sections was 64%. The passing rate for this course, below 70%, was among the lowest in the department.

The poor performance in these sections raised the question of the effectiveness of the learning in general, and in particular, the dedication to the weekly reading assignments and the effectiveness of student reading. The results of the final exam were evidence of poor understanding of important concepts presented in the course and/or poor study habits and exam preparation. Depending on motivations and learning goals, students may have been choosing the path of least resistance and accepting a low score on a quiz in exchange for the release from spending out-of-class time reading and preparing for the quiz (Ambrose et al., 2010; Burchfield & Sappington, 2000; Roberts & Roberts, 2008). Alternatively, students may ascertain from experience that everything they need from the text is presented in the lecture, relying on the professor to sort and provide a structure of the information covered in the text, thereby making actual engagement with the text superficial or in their view unnecessary (Bean 2011; Wambach, 1998).

In addition, the lecture format suffers from the general critique of the tendency for a passive learning environment (Bligh & Cameron, 2000; Michel, Cater, & Varela, 2009; Roehl, Reddy, & Shannon, 2013; Werner, Scovotti, Cummings, & Bronson, 2018). The combination of lecture-focused class time and poor reading dedication out-of-class generates a feedback loop, where faculty tend to try to compensate for the lack of reading by covering the material in their lectures (Bean, 2011; Wambach, 1998). If students neglect the reading, the efficacy of learning through lecture-based courses is adversely impacted and opportunities for students to practice and improve reading effectiveness are diminished. Faculty and students alike can fall into a trap of conscious but tacit acceptance of insufficient or outright abandonment of reading (Carkenord, 1994; Hoeft, 2012; Ryan, 2006). Lecture-based building science courses, therefore, are likely fertile places for exploration of re-emphasis on engagement with the text and nurturing meaningful text-based learning.

In lecture courses like this where students struggle with out-of-class reading and perform poorly on summative assessments, a number of strategies could reinforce the central role of the text in the learning process and, through close monitoring of student engagement, help build increased reading dedication and effectiveness. Five strategies were adopted to refocus the dedication to text-based learning in the course: a major emphasis on note-taking, reflection utilizing open pedagogy (post a reflection and/or summary), application of reading material directly into the lab assignments, on-site investigations/seminars (the walking seminar), and guided discussion rather than lecture.

Note-Taking from the Text Out-of-Class
With students often neglecting out-of-class reading, finding a mechanism that motivates students to engage with the text is important. Note-taking

can be a scaffolded process that builds a structure and method for student interaction with the text with multiple benefits. As students may not have good techniques for effective note-taking entering college, scaffolded strategies can provide a step-by-step guide that builds this skill for application in any course (Katayama & Robinson, 2000). As care and completeness of notes co-relates to higher levels of achievement, emphasis on tracking note coverage supports students' learning beyond the particular course (Jairam, Kiewra, Rogers-Kasson, Patterson-Hazley, & Marxhausen, 2014). Note-taking while reading offers students an active reading study strategy with the opportunity to build a concept map that organizes the new information (Ambrose et al., 2010). It is a central activity to the encoding and recall of knowledge (Dyer, Riley, & Yekovich, 1979; Katayama & Robinson, 2000; Kiewra, Dubois, Christensen, Kim, & Lindberg, 1989), especially students lacking prior knowledge (Kiewra, 1989). Note-taking combines with reading strategies like SQ3R (described above) or SOAR to help students work through a text with deeper learning (Huber, 2004; Jairam et al., 2014; McGuire & McGuire, 2015). The SOAR study method is particularly useful for architecture students as its process utilizes cognitive practices that are highly applicable to disciplinary practices (Fang, 2012; Jairam et al., 2014).

In this course, readings are carefully selected from Francis Ching's *Building Construction Illustrated*. The reading assignments take advantage of the organizational structure of the textbook, where topics are covered in short focused and heavily illustrated sections, often one to two pages in length. This focused subdivision of the text in the assigned readings allows more meticulous tracking of student reading through their note submissions, with points allocated for each focused topic. Each submission of notes can earn points against a rubric score they are given at the beginning of the semester to make clear the expectations for their submissions. For example, students can earn points for their note organization, paraphrasing, and summary, as well as section coverage (Fig. 5.4). Models of note-taking best practices (Cornell notes, graphic organizers, concept mapping) are presented to the students to scaffold the development of a clear structure for their notes that reflects the hierarchy and structure of concepts discussed. The models also reinforce the benefits of paraphrasing and the value of summarizing. Coverage can be measured based on the inclusion of the major and minor headings in the text with key concepts noted or diagramed and key vocabulary defined. With the fine grain coverage tracking, students see grade value in covering all the

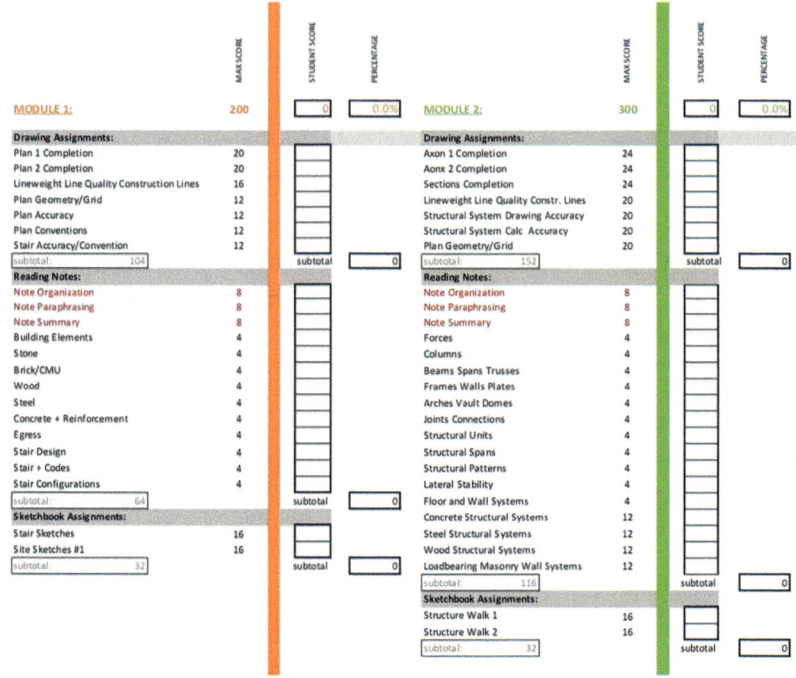

(Source: Prof. Montgomery)

Fig. 5.4 Fine-grained tracking of assigned readings in student grade spreadsheet

sections of the required readings, and the faculty can monitor directly how engaged the students are with the text. This approach, similar to the emphasis in the SOAR study method, places a priority on the completeness of the notes (Jairam et al., 2014).

Student notes for grade credit can be submitted directly through collection of the notebooks, but this requires a quick turnaround in the review and grading process as the notebooks are an everyday tool throughout the semester. An alternative strategy is to require scans or careful photographs of the notes organized in a pdf file for digital submission.

This strategy of note-taking from the text is enhanced when note-taking is handwritten for similar reasons that handwritten notes during lectures have been shown to have an advantage over typed notes (Mueller & Oppenheimer, 2014). In addition, architecture students are able to integrate sketches and diagrams from the text into their notes, combining text-based and visual learning. Handwritten notes encourage discernment in the information recorded, helping students recognize the hierarchy of information from the text. This is particularly important in technical texts on topics like building science, where major concepts need to be understood before nuanced details can be grasped.

The notebook in this strategy serves as a critical tool in class lectures or discussions. Note-taking out-of-class builds experience that can be leveraged when taking notes in class during a lecture or discussion, encouraging more active engagement. Faculty can continue the scaffolding of note-taking with in-class activities, including reflection on learning at the end of the class.

Note-taking from the text as part of the grade for the class generates a personal learning artifact in the hands of the students that they can use every day and carry forward, building on knowledge from one class to the next. This strategy can be coordinated across multiple courses either within a linked sequence of technical courses on building science or across all courses, including design studio.

The out-of-class site visits (like the walking seminar mentioned below) offer opportunities for developing the skill of taking visual notes, capturing data from observed conditions in the built environment. This reinforces a core activity for architecture students, serving as a critical tool and process for visual thinking and learning (Arnheim, 1969; Crowe & Laseau, 1986). Linking visual note-taking and text note-taking cultivates an integration of learning across domains and contexts in the architecture curriculum, breaking down silos and encouraging students to transfer and apply knowledge from one context to another.

Note-taking strategies are powerful tools that contribute to building disciplinary literacy. The SOAR study method, in particular, with its focus on selection, organization, association, and regulation, mimics steps commonly applied in a design process where selection and organization are key activities in the formation of the parti or design concept. The SOAR method also includes overlapping components with place-based learning where associations are made between text-based learning and real examples in the field, as well as problem-based learning where metacognitive reflection critically identifies what was learned through the design process (Jairam et al., 2014).

Open Pedagogy: Posting Reflections and Summaries
Faculty can further track student engagement with the assigned readings through reflections and/or summaries of the readings posted to an online course site. These posts can be made public so students can see each other's posts to motivate their participation and to provide some peer perspectives on learning in the course. Reflections serve as a learning log, aiding the development of a critical view of their learning process (Baker, 2003; Wagner, 2003).

Application in Drawing Assignments
Application is an excellent measure of student understanding of the critical concepts presented in the text. Assignments can be tailored to require specific knowledge from the text, with variables added to avoid rote reproduction from the text. One example is a structural exercise using a case study building as a base for the exploration of span, material, and structural system configurations. The assignment builds on a series of readings from Ching's *Building Construction Illustrated* that start with the materials of construction and their properties for use in structure, discussion of forces and fundamental structural elements, spans, and finally structural systems. Each student is assigned a specific structural system and set of variables. Each structural system description includes rules of thumb that students can use to size each element. The variables and different assigned systems provide a diverse set of solutions across the class, facilitating a rich discussion in the review of the assignment.

To complete the assignment, students must have acquired the requisite knowledge from the text for their assigned system. They also need to demonstrate both two- and three-dimensional understanding of the element in axonometric views of the system as well as dimensioned sections of each structural component (Fig. 5.5). Each student is further required to include their calculations for all elements of the system and to provide a reference for the page(s) in the text where they found the rules of thumb. The drawing assignment replaces the quizzes as the tool for motivating both engagement with the text and assessment of the quality of that engagement.

The Walking Seminar: Adapting a Form of Experiential Learning
The dual goal of addressing the shortcomings of the traditional lecture and the cultivation of students' text-based learning offers the opportunity to seek strategies that link these learning modes with each supporting the

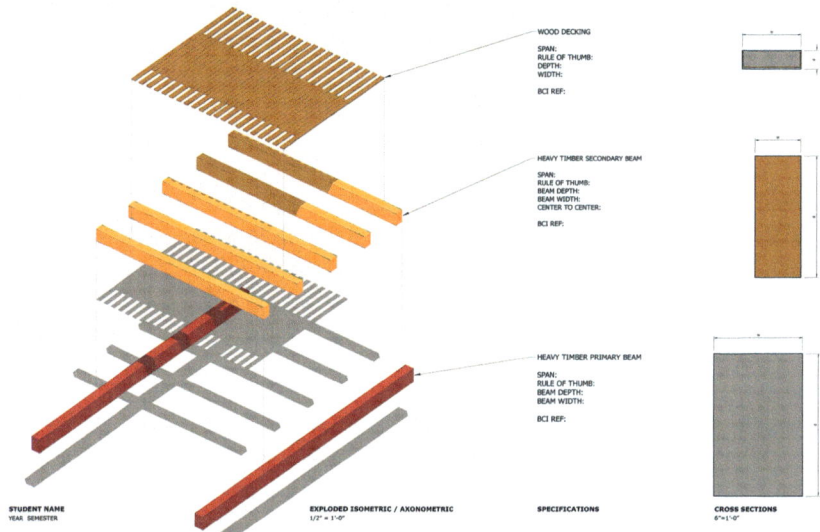

(Source: Prof. Montgomery, Spring 2017)

Fig. 5.5 Structural component assignment example

other. In architectural education, the built environment is a laboratory for learning that provides direct experience that can be a powerful aid in activating prior knowledge (Salama, 2010). Students of architecture may understand that the built environment is the focus of their education, but they may not be experienced in looking carefully and making observations when they are out in the streets of their neighborhood, town, or city. In addition, they may not intuitively draw from their prior experience of the built environment until prompted. Direct experience of the built environment is particularly efficacious for building science courses. Taking the students out of the classroom into the streets offers students sensory and dynamic interaction with the built environment, helping them see aspects of it that they have not really paid attention to in the past, and make real-world associations with the concepts in their readings. This approach has great potential to activate what they know about buildings and gives them a platform to construct new knowledge.

The lecture taken out into the streets becomes a "walking seminar" where the faculty member can coordinate an active experiential learning environment that either supplements the classroom lecture or replaces it altogether (Salama, 2010). Working with the students in the field, the faculty member can actively assess the prior knowledge of the students, determining its accuracy and if it is sufficient for the concepts and topics presented in the course. Where it is insufficient, the gaps can be filled through drawing special attention to particular aspects of the buildings in the field, using direct sensory experience, careful observation, sketchbook documentation (visual and text notes) as the tools for learning. This experience is supported by and in turn supports engagement with the text, linking the text to the real world and helping students visualize concepts that may have otherwise challenged them.

The walking seminar can be highly interactive, with the Socratic dialectic method of questioning and probing used in place of didactic methods. Students can see and feel the elements and spaces discussed in the text, directly experiencing their materiality and volume. The directness and specificity of this experience connects the walking seminar to the practice of place-based learning, where students can begin to construct knowledge for themselves rather than merely receive knowledge (Smith, 2002). It models self-directed and independent learning where the students can begin to pay attention to the built environment they experience every day in a new way on their own, making their day-to-day experience of the built environment a part of their life-long learning (Salama, 2010).

Faculty can curate the walking seminars to hone in on particular content of the course. In this building science course, many aspects of building systems and performance are observed and studied in the field, including a survey of the commonly used building materials (wood, brick, stone, concrete, and steel), or structural systems (lightwood frame, load-bearing masonry, steel, or concrete frame), or building envelope approaches (masonry cladding, curtain wall, window wall). For example, to explore exterior envelopes, students in the case study course were taken on a walking seminar of the neighborhood of downtown Brooklyn, where buildings of various age and construction type offered a close-up examination of the performance of their exterior walls. Students were able to examine buildings exhibiting signs of problems in the envelop, including a curtain wall with severe condensation buildup inside the insulated glass unit and an exterior cladding with impact damage revealing its delicate cross-section of Styrofoam insulation with a thin stucco outer layer which made plain its vulnerability in an urban environment. The student observations and discussion were highly animated, demonstrating a high level of engagement.

Student reflections confirm that these experiences motivate them to pay more attention to the built environment on a regular basis.

The walking seminar, while an obvious approach to teaching architecture, is not leveraged as much as it can be, with logistical steps required, time limitations, and inclement weather as potential barriers. Nonetheless, this approach is a powerful model for learning and offers a rich experience that reinforces, clarifies, and illustrates the topics learned through the text.

Discussion Rather Than Lecture
Although the distinction seems subtle, it is important to recognize the difference between a lecture and a class discussion. Faculty focused on discussion rather than lecture can reconfigure the classroom to de-emphasize the hierarchical arrangement and bring the students into a more intimate setting. Discussion opens the door to a less formal sequence of review of the topic and the use of questions to draw out students' knowledge from the readings. Faculty can work through the topic with a series of prompts and questions to the students, who can use their notebooks to bring their knowledge gained from the text into the discussion. This approach holds students more accountable for their engagement with the readings and their preparation before class. Discussion can eliminate the passive presentation of the same content as the reading material and focus more on helping students with the difficult concepts brought up through their feedback.

5.6   Student Testimonial on the Impact of These Strategies on Her Learning

Student feedback on the integration of many of these strategies demonstrates they appreciate the impact it has on their study habits and growing confidence with disciplinary literacy. This architecture student was eager to share her feedback:

> The understanding of summarizing, highlighting and sketching in any reading is important for a student's education. In my second year of college, I was taking many classes, most of them requiring reading. One of the courses caught my attention, Building Technology II with Professor Montgomery. This class combined drawing assignments and weekly reading. This course required us to take notes, highlight the text, and sketch important concepts from the paragraphs, sentences, and words in the book. At the beginning,

because of my lack of knowledge, I thought it was a waste of my time as a student; I thought 'it's a lot of work'. Little did I know that later on while I was constantly doing this, my brain was capturing and understanding how building codes, materials, wall details, and construction all come together when buildings are assembled. At the end of the semester I was able to engage in conversations that I was avoiding before taking Building Tech. The learning process was difficult but the reward I will carry with me for a lifetime. Although summarizing, highlighting and sketching is not a requirement in other classes or in my daily life I use it as a weapon against my mental laziness. Every time I apply summarizing, highlighting and sketching my mind holds the information unconsciously; now I just don't memorize, I learn. (Arianna Kevelier, personal communication, Sept 20, 2019)

5.7   GENERAL CRITIQUES OF ARCHITECTURAL EDUCATION AND THE ROLE OF READING IN CURRICULUM REFORM

A number of critical examinations of architectural education call for reform of curriculum and pedagogy (Anthony, 1991; Boyer & Mitgang, 1996; Ockman, 2012; Salingaros & Masden 2008). An extensive survey of architectural programs published in 1996 revealed a deficiency in the emphasis on a liberal education balance to the practical and technical teaching in architectural curricula, with general education skills lacking, especially among students graduating from undergraduate architecture programs (Boyer & Mitgang, 1996). A more recent study charts the role of text in architectural education but ponders the current and future role of text-based learning (Plattus, 2012). These studies document a well-understood reality in architectural education: design education dominates, with other courses seen as expendable by students. Students make the effort to pass these courses but meaningful learning is sacrificed for efficiency so that more time can be dedicated to the design studio work. General education skills, especially writing and communication skills, are particularly called out as deficient by both faculty and professionals working with new graduates (Boyer & Mitgang, 1996). Disciplinary literacy stands at the core of these critiques, where students are not just struggling to communicate but to think and communicate like experts. Reading is rarely explicitly mentioned in these critiques but is clearly linked to the students' deficiencies in disciplinary literacy. But text-based learning is also linked to the deficiencies scholars find in design studio pedagogy. Reform of architectural education that responds to these critiques would see text-based learning permeating the full curriculum with explicit support and close attention to its meaningful integration. Placing reading and text-based learning at the core of architectural education opens up its full potential to help students both balance their skills and also go deeper into the discipline.

To reflect on architectural curriculum at the macro level, it is useful to finish this chapter using an armature of key conditions for effective higher education learning to guide thinking on architectural curriculum reform. This armature includes cumulative learning, integrated learning, progression in learning, and consistency in learning (Engel, 1999).

Cumulative learning emphasizes the repetition of concepts and skills, following a model of introduction and reinforcement with increasing sophistication. Information that is only presented once in a degree program and never applied is hardly useful to students. Student reading will trend toward the superficial if students perceive its relevance is short-lived in the curriculum. This is where coordination of text-based learning around critical texts across multiple courses can provide a structure for building knowledge and a more sophisticated knowledge organization that is appropriate for the complexity and breath of architecture as a discipline.

Integrative Learning requires effort to bring important concepts to bear on the problem at hand anywhere in the curriculum, breaking the barriers that separate content knowledge in architectural education. This issue has been adopted by NAAB as a central component of student performance criteria used to evaluate architecture programs for accreditation. Text-based learning offers a means of bridging gaps and transferring concepts through their application in different contexts. Using multiple texts or text-based research can engage students in developing interdisciplinary connections and a deeper understanding of the interdisciplinarity of architectural practice (Klaassen, 2018).

Progression in Learning requires the expectation of deeper and broader knowledge and skills exhibited in the student work as they move higher in the curriculum. Higher-order thinking should become apparent. This is especially important in the design studio, where the range and depth of issues explored should be increasing with each project. Text-based research is uniquely positioned to support this growth through the learning cycle structure offered by problem-based learning.

Consistency in Learning can be applied to faculty working together across the curriculum in a coordinated effort to support and motivate student learning through texts. Faculty need to be trained and supported to facilitate effective, active reading in their classrooms, collectively empha-size its importance to their students, and, through application of agreed-upon strategies, enable students to engage in the reading process with consistent discipline-specific literacy strategies (Engel, 1999).

It is also important to reflect on the impact of divergence in architec-tural education where disciplinary literacy or lack there-of can perpetuate a lack of diverse representation and participation in the discipline. Guided text-based learning, since the establishment of the earliest architecture col-legiate programs in the United States, offered a step ladder to higher sta-tus in the profession for students that previously may have been relegated to the role of a draftsman. A profession seeking increasing diversity needs to pay critical attention to the educational structures that impact the development of disciplinary literacy for students from all backgrounds and at different levels of academic preparedness.

This review of reading effectively in architectural education to promote disciplinary literacy demands both a micro and macro examination of ped-agogy and curriculum. Reading effectiveness supporting text-based learn-ing and disciplinary literacy cannot be handled or solved in a small corner of the curriculum; it must become a pervasive, ever-present component that offers access to knowledge and fosters growth. Only then will reading be able to fulfill its structural role in each students' educational foundation for disciplinary literacy and a life-long career in the discipline.

REFERENCES

Alger, J. (2010). The value of architecture and design branch libraries: A case study. *Art Documentation: Journal of the Art Libraries Society of North America, 29*(2), 48–52.

Ambrose, S. A., Bridges, M. W., DiPietro, M., Lovett, M. C., & Norman, M. K. (2010). *How learning works: Seven research-based principles for smart teaching.* San Francisco: Josey-Bass.

Anthony, K. H. (1991). *Design juries on trial: The renaissance of the design studio.* New York: Van Nostrand Reinhold.

Arnheim, R. (1969). *Visual thinking.* London: University of California Press.

Baker, J. H. (2003). Teaching tip: The learning log. *Journal of Information Systems Education, 14*(1), 11.

Barkley, E. F., & Major, C. H. (2018). *Interactive lecturing: A handbook for college faculty*. San Francisco: Jossey-Bass.

Bean, J. C. (2011). *Engaging ideas: The professor's guide to integrating writing, critical thinking, and active learning in the classroom*. San Francisco: Jossey-Bass.

Bligh, D., & Cameron, B. J. (2000). What's the use of lectures? *The Canadian Journal of Higher Education, 30*(1), 192.

Bloom, B. S. (1956). *Taxonomy of educational objectives: The classification of educational goals*. New York: D. McKay.

Boud, D., & Feletti, G. (1999). *The challenge of problem-based learning*. London: Routledge.

Boyer, E. L., & Mitgang, L. D. (1996). *Building community: A new future for architecture education and practice. A special report*. California Princeton Fulfillment Services; 1445 Lower Ferry Road, Ewing, NJ 08618.

Burchfield, C. M., & Sappington, J. (2000). Compliance with required reading assignments. *Teaching of Psychology, 27*(1), 58–60.

Cabral, A. P., & Tavares, J. (2002). Practising college reading strategies: First-year students' choices. *The Reading Matrix: An International Online Journal, 2*(3), 1–16.

Carkenord, D. M. (1994). Motivating students to read journal articles. *Teaching of Psychology, 21*(3), 162–164.

Cindy E. Hmelo-Silver, Problem-Based Learning: What and How Do Students Learn? Educational Psychology Review, 16(3), 235–266.

Crowe, N., & Laseau, P. (1986). *Visual notes for architects and designers*. New York: John Wiley & Sons.

Dubas, J. M., & Toledo, S. A. (2015). Active reading documents (ARDs): A tool to facilitate meaningful learning through reading. *College Teaching, 63*(1), 27–33.

Dyer, J. W., Riley, J., & Yekovich, F. R. (1979). An analysis of three study skills: Notetaking, summarizing, and rereading 1. *The Journal of Educational Research, 73*(1), 3–7.

Engel, C. (1999). Not just a method but a way of learning. In D. Boud & G. Feletti (Eds.), *The challenge of problem-based learning* (pp. 17–27). London: Routledge.

Fang, Z. (2012). Language correlates of disciplinary literacy. *Topics in Language Disorders, 32*(1), 19–34.

Hmelo-Silver, C. E. (2004). Problem-based learning: What and how do students learn? *Educational Psychology Review, 16*(3), 235–266.

Hoeft, M. E. (2012). Why university students don't read: What professors can do to increase compliance. *International Journal for the Scholarship of Teaching and Learning, 6*(2), 12.

Huber, J. A. (2004). A closer look at SQ3R. *Reading Improvement, 41*(2), 108–113.

Jairam, D., Kiewra, K. A., Rogers-Kasson, S., Patterson-Hazley, M., & Marxhausen, K. (2014). SOAR versus SQ3R: A test of two study systems. *Instructional Science, 42*(3), 409–420.

Johnston, G. B. (2005). Drafting manuals and manual training: Rouillion and Ramsey's architectural details. *Journal of Architectural Education, 58*(4), 41–52.

Katayama, A. D., & Robinson, D. H. (2000). Getting students "partially" involved in note-taking using graphic organizers. *The Journal of Experimental Education, 68*(2), 119–133.

Kiewra, K. A. (1989). A review of note-taking: The encoding-storage paradigm and beyond. *Educational Psychology Review, 1*(2), 147–172.

Kiewra, K. A., Dubois, N. F., Christensen, M., Kim, S. I., & Lindberg, N. (1989). A more equitable account of the note-taking functions in learning from lecture and from text. *Instructional Science, 18*(3), 217–232.

Klaassen, R. G. (2018). Interdisciplinary education: A case study. *European Journal of Engineering Education, 43*(6), 842–859.

Kuh, G. D. (2007). What student engagement data tell us about college readiness. *Peer Review, 9*(1), 4–8.

Kuh, G. D., Schneider, C. G., & Association of American Colleges and Universities. (2008). Introduction, Part 1 and Part 2. In *High-impact educational practices: What they are, who has access to them, and why they matter*. Washington, DC: Association of American Colleges and Universities.

Le Corbusier. (1986). *Towards a new architecture*. New York: Dover.

Lei, S. A., Bartlett, K. A., Gorney, S. E., & Herschbach, T. R. (2010a). Resistance to reading compliance among college structures: Instructors' perspectives. *College Student Journal, 44*(2), 219–229.

Lei, S. A., Rhinehart, P. J., Howard, H. A., & Cho, J. K. (2010b). Strategies for improving reading comprehension among college students. *Reading Improvement, 47*(1), 30–42.

Mayer, R. E. (2002). Rote versus meaningful learning. *Theory Into Practice, 41*(4), 226–232.

McGuire, S. Y. (2007). Using the scientific method to improve mentoring. *Learning Assistance Review, 12*(2), 33–45.

McGuire, S., & McGuire, S. (2015). *Teach students how to learn: Strategies you can incorporate into any course to improve student metacognition, study skills, and motivation*. Herndon, VA: Stylus Publishing, LLC.

Michel, N., Cater, J., & Varela, O. (2009). Active versus passive teaching styles: An empirical study of student learning outcomes. *Human Resource Development Quarterly, 20*(4), 397–418.

Mueller, P. A., & Oppenheimer, D. M. (2014). The pen is mightier than the keyboard: Advantages of longhand over laptop note-taking. *Psychological Science, 25*(6), 1159–1168.

NAAB. (2014). *2014 conditions for accreditation*. Retrieved from https://www. naab.org/wp-content/uploads/01_Final-Approved-2014-NAAB-Conditions-for-Accreditation-2.pdf

NCARB. (2018). *Education Guidelines*. Retrieved from https://www.ncarb.org/sites/default/files/Main%20Website/Data%20&%20Resources/Guidelines/EducationGuidelines.pdf

Ockman, J. (2012). *Architecture school: Three centuries of educating architects in North America*. Cambridge, MA: MIT Press.

Plattus, A. (2012). Books. In J. Ockman (Ed.), *Architecture school: Three centuries of educating architects in North America*. Cambridge, MA: MIT Press.

Porphyrios, D. (1991). *Classical architecture*. London: Andreas Papadakis Publisher.

Roberts, J. C., & Roberts, K. A. (2008). Deep reading, cost/benefit, and the construction of meaning: Enhancing reading comprehension and deep learning in sociology courses. *Teaching Sociology, 36*(2), 125–140.

Roehl, A., Reddy, S. L., & Shannon, G. J. (2013). The flipped classroom: An opportunity to engage millennial students through active learning strategies. *Journal of Family & Consumer Sciences, 105*(2), 44–49.

Ruskin, J. (1989). *The seven lamps of architecture*. New York: Dover Publications.

Ryan, T. E. (2006). Motivating novice students to read their textbooks. *Journal of Instructional Psychology, 33*(2), 135A.

Salama, A. M. (2010). Delivering theory courses in architecture: Inquiry based, active, and experiential learning integrated. *Archnet-IJAR: International Journal of Architectural Research, 4*(2–3), 278–295.

Salama, A. M., & Wilkinson, N. (Eds.). (2007). *Design studio pedagogy: Horizons for the future*. Gateshead: The Urban International Press.

Salingaros, N. A., & Masden II, K. G. (2008). Intelligence-based design: A sustainable foundation for worldwide architectural education. *International Journal of Architectural Research: ArchNet-IJAR, 2*(1), 129–188.

Smith, G. A. (2002). Place-based education: Learning to be where we are. *Phi delta kappan, 83*(8), 584–594.

Vitruvius. (1995). *On archictecture* (F. Granger, Trans.). London: Harvard University Press.

Wagner, C. (2003). Put another (b) log on the wire: Publishing learning logs as weblogs. *Journal of Information Systems Education, 14*(2), 131.

Wambach, C. A. (1998). Reading and writing expectations at a research university. *Journal of Developmental Education, 22*(2), 22.

Ware, W. R. (1866). *An outline of a course of architectural instruction*. Boston: Press of John Wilson and Sons.

Werner, J. M., Scovotti, C., Cummings, R. G., & Bronson, J. W. (2018). Building a case for active learning: The use of lecture vs. other classroom activities at LMBC. *Journal of Learning in Higher Education, 14*(1), 7–15.

CHAPTER 6

Poetry in Biology: Enhancing Science Education with Creative Writing

Robert Ostrom, Michael Gotesman, and Juanita C. But

6.1 INTRODUCTION

College biology is the gateway to further studies in life and health sciences, so it is crucial for students to understand the disciplinary thinking, relationships among concepts, and specialized vocabulary in this foundational course. At New York City College of Technology, Introductory College Biology II (BIO1201) is a reading-intensive science course that prepares students planning to pursue a career in health sciences and the medical field. In Biology 1201, students have to learn a vast network of complex biological concepts and medical terminologies. In general, the course is taught with a didactic approach in which the instructors teach with lecture slides. This allows for limited student engagement; therefore, students in this class often struggle to process a large amount of specialized vocabulary that deals with conceptually dense information. Many of the concepts and organisms discussed in the course are abstract and

R. Ostrom (✉) • M. Gotesman • J. C. But
New York City College of Technology, City University of New York,
Brooklyn, NY, USA
e-mail: rostrom@citytech.cuny.edu; mgotesman@citytech.cuny.edu;
jbut@citytech.cuny.edu

© The Author(s) 2020   147
J. C. But (ed.), *Teaching College-Level Disciplinary Literacy*,
https://doi.org/10.1007/978-3-030-39804-0_6

challenging to learn for incoming students who may be underprepared in college reading and writing and lack strategies to navigate the biology texts, which have very high readability levels.

In Biology 1201, to explore methods that may improve student learning and engagement, we applied "alternative" teaching approaches to enhance student performance. We developed a sequence of lessons that focused on fostering students' ability to understand and articulate complex biological concepts and processes using figurative language and creative expressions. The lessons aimed to create a student-centered environment that enhances participation and disciplinary literacy for Biology 1201 students. This chapter discusses the design, implementation, and effectiveness of the lessons, and the ways in which they effect student learning in both the cognitive and affective domains. The results of the study indicate that the use of "alternative" teaching methods is an engaging tool that can be used to enhance students' performance.

6.2   CHALLENGES IN THE COLLEGE BIOLOGY CLASSROOM

Lack of Prior Knowledge

Many students enter Biology 1201 with limited prior knowledge in the subject and, therefore, lack the ability to properly achieve expected learning outcomes. Even though students have taken biology courses in high school, the topics and contents covered at college level are much more complex. In this introductory biology course, students learn various topics such as phylogeny, homology, and bacteriology as well as the description of main organ systems in animals and their function in humans which can be used to prepare students for advanced biology topics taught in subsequent courses. Traditionally, the subject draws on prior knowledge that students should have been exposed to in high school biology. Unfortunately, many of our students have never learned or do not recollect studying these important topics.

Lack of Motivation in Reading

Due to different constraints such as time restrictions, low reading ability, and the lack of prior knowledge in the subject matter, many of our students find it difficult to find the motivation to read their textbooks. It is especially challenging for students to study introductory biology when using an e-book for the first time. They often lack the skills to navigate the digital texts, especially when they are not used to taking notes when they read.

Conceptual Density and Text Complexity

To fully understand biological concepts involves more than reading; students must learn how to read actively. To read actively means students have to engage with the text by using a range of strategies to help them understand complex concepts, make connections, and apply content knowledge. The density of specialized vocabulary is also a challenge for students. At times even reading the definitions is difficult for students who do not have sufficient knowledge of scientific vocabulary (Snow, 2010).

It is imperative for students to understand the concepts and vocabulary to acquire disciplinary literacy in biology. To make biology more accessible to students, scientific terms need to be explained in simpler terms. Only after biological terminology is learned can a deeper understanding of biology be appreciated as it relates to concepts in other sciences. Students must have a good understanding of the dense syntax in biological writing, where sentences often consist of multiple clauses, long noun phrases, and technical terms (Fang, 2012; Thonney, 2016). In addition, they need to understand how information is organized in the text.

6.3 Reframing Biology Instruction at Reading Effectively Across the Disciplines (READ)

To reframe instruction in introductory college biology, we used a pre-assessment to evaluate comprehension and then we implemented reading strategies to enhance student learning. Various strategies were used including a fill-in-the-blank activity in which the students were required to complete missing portions of texts to enhance concentration and active listening. We also used the recap game Kahoot at the end of the corresponding class to support vocabulary building. In addition, group activities such as concept mapping followed by discussion were implemented. In the following sections, we focus our discussion on an organized sequence of lessons in poetry writing in the Biology 1121 classroom, which involved a design to promote creative thinking and student engagement. It provides a new approach to teaching the language of biology.

Why Is Poetry Used to Supplement Learning in the Biology Classroom?

Creative thinking has always played an important role in how we understand complicated scientific concepts. Analogy and metaphor are often employed in science in order to convey these ideas. For instance, neuroscientists refer to neurons as trees, biologists study the chambers of the heart, and environmental scientists study the greenhouse effect. The link between creative and scientific thought accounts for the long list of scientist-authors such as John Steinbeck, Johann Wolfgang von Goethe, Gertrude Stein, William Carlos Williams, and Michael Crichton.

Creative expressions such as poetry are powerful tools for processing scientific observation and assumption (Brown, 2015). By giving students in science classes the opportunity to explore these methods, they are able to demonstrate an understanding of complex ideas from their textbooks while gaining ownership of how they came to these understandings (Pollack & Korol, 2013). As opposed to rote learning, these methods encourage students to make connections to previous knowledge and thus deepen their understanding (Jensen, 2006). These critical thinking and analytical strategies can be particularly useful for non-science majors. Furthermore, such strategies can make tedious material more enjoyable. In teaching, it is our hope that students will figure out how they learn—although these methods might not work for all students, they add tools to their disciplinary learning toolbox. For some, this could be the key to success in their science classes.

A recent study to determine how biology experts explain concepts of molecular and cellular mechanisms showed that biologists contextualized explanations according to their biological and social significance, integrated explanations with methods and instruments, and used analogies in addition to narrated stories (Trujillo, Anderson, & Pelaez, 2015). Biological phenomena and processes are difficult to explain and understand; therefore, the use of analogies can enhance both communication and comprehension of complex concepts. Incorporating the use of figurative language and poetry, we aimed at building students' abilities to understand and write metaphorically, so they can find new avenues to understanding difficult biological concepts.

Assignment sequence

For each lesson, we first decided which chapter from which unit we would focus on. Then, we chose the concepts within that chapter. These were based on concepts students typically struggled with. After this, we designed the lessons which followed the typical scaffolding of explaining, modeling, working as a class, and finally writing the poem in small groups or individually. Last but not least, students were asked to reflect on their product and the experience. Each lesson was built on prior knowledge of poetry and literary devices from previous lessons; thus, the activities were subsequently more complex.

Note Key biological terms are italicized.

6.4 LESSON ONE: RESPIRATION METAPHORS

Objectives

For the first poetry in biology lesson, our goal was for students to gain a deeper understanding of content vocabulary through the use of simile and metaphor; therefore, we needed them to grasp the meanings of these essential poetic devices. Building this common understanding would also be useful for future lessons. Through collaborative learning, we wanted to motivate students to think deeply about biological concepts while working together in small groups.

Lesson

We began by discussing the meaning of simile and metaphor and then asked students to give examples. It is easier for students to understand a simile (using *like* or *as* to compare two things that share a common feature), so we started there; to simplify things, we explained that a metaphor can be the same comparison but without *like* or *as*. We then discussed student examples—what works better as a simile, what works as a metaphor, and why.

In pairs, students were assigned two vocabulary words from their unit on respiration. They were instructed to figure out what each word meant and then to create a simile or metaphor for that word. After this, they had to arrange their metaphors into a poem to share with the class. Before they began working on their own poems, we created a class poem for *gas exchange*. First, we defined *gas exchange* (as it occurs in the lungs) as "the process of air, which contains oxygen, crossing the lung tissues then entering the bloodstream and traveling to organs and tissues." Students were then encouraged to ask themselves, "What else behaves this way?" By thinking about transport and the idea of transfer we came to the idea that this is somewhat like a subway system. So, for our metaphor/simile, we wrote: "The oxygen is like people. The lungs are Grand Central Station and Penn Station. The bloodstream is the subway. And the organs and tissues are people's destinations." With this, we were ready to write our poem:

Gas Exchange

Oxygen like New Yorkers
travel into the lungs
of Grand Central and Penn Stations,
pass through the sliding doors
and into the *bloodstream*,
the New York City Subway Station,
to all the *organs* and *tissues*,
their destinations.

Results and Reflection

In order to create a simile or metaphor for each word, students had to find something that acted like each of their vocabulary words. For this reason, students had to first have a firm grasp on what that vocabulary word meant. After this came the hard work of finding something to compare it to. As we observed the students thinking and discussing, we could see that learning was happening. In their groups, students had in-depth discussions about whether or not this or that metaphor or simile worked. It also inspired discussions between the instructor and students. In addition to talking about the content vocabulary words, it gave us the opportunity to talk about metacognition as we encouraged students to see that understanding requires varying degrees of intellectual work. In the beginning, many of the students asked for help and expressed how "hard" this task was. "It's supposed to be hard," we explained to students, "because that means your mind is working to understand." Given the difficulty, the sense of reward the students had when they discovered an appropriate metaphor was also palpable.

For the most part, the poems the students wrote reflected a deeper understanding of the concepts. We were often astonished by the imaginative and beautiful metaphors students created.

Tree of Life

Like a mirrored tree,
Blooming in fall upon a crystal lake,
Leafless *bronchi's* grasping at the air;
Even when inverted and lacking crimsoned petals,
Still provides life living breath

The fact that the students came up with "a mirrored tree,/ Blooming in fall upon a crystal lake" in such a short period of time is impressive and might even change the way a reader sees bronchi. Unlike a tree, the bronchi have no leaves, though this doesn't stop them from doing their job of providing "life living breath," another lovely turn of phrase. The poem reflects an understanding of the vocabulary word, and the images deepen the reader's understanding of bronchi.

According to Taylor and Dewsbury (2018), "The language of science is largely metaphorical." It was interesting when students discovered this on their own. For instance, one group was assigned the word *larynx* which, in their notes, they defined as "voice box, a short passageway connecting the pharynx and the trachea." In this case, the students noticed two metaphors: box and passageway. Still, the group had to find a new metaphor that hopefully contained the different parts of their definition: a voice box, a short passageway, and a connector. They first chose to write a simile: "The larynx is like a hallway full of the first sounds of our voices." However, when it came time to write the poem, they revised this, making a more lyrical poem using a metaphor instead which detailed the branching aspect of trachea/bronchi system.

> Between the *pharynx* and the *trachea*
> the *larynx* is a hallway
> echoing the first sound
> of the songs we sing.

As striking as the metaphor is, this poem also functions as a way to understand the location and function of the larynx.

In contrast, while the students who wrote the following poem clearly understand that the pressure within the thorax is less than atmospheric pressure during inhalation and that breathing is based on pressure differences caused by muscle contraction and relaxation, this poem is a little more difficult to parse and for that reason, it probably wouldn't help readers understand the concept.

Thoracic Pressure Refresher

> The pressure within the *thorax*, a spacecraft's interior
> Astronauts and air both enter, leaving these pressures inferior
> But when inside the pressure rises, *exchange* of knowledge and *gas*
> Now to return to origin, increase of pressure will come to pass

This happened with a few of the poems—perhaps the students got carried away with the music of language—but even if the poems do not fully clarify for the reader what the vocabulary term means, the work the students did to write the poem was worthwhile to their own understanding. Perhaps students could be encouraged to clarify in a subsequent revision. Additionally, through presenting and discussing the poems, students could explain and thus deepen their understanding by sharing their ideas with others.

It is important to acknowledge that while metaphors can be powerful learning tools, there is the risk that they can lead to further confusion. Metaphoric comparisons might mislead students to make other incorrect connections between the vocabulary word and the metaphor, or the comparison could be altogether erroneous. Therefore, it is necessary to model this activity for students and to discuss ways that the metaphor works and where it falls short. Knowing the limitations of the metaphor will further help students understand the concept at hand. Moreover, because scientific language is full of metaphors, it would be interesting to provide common scientific metaphors and discuss the ways in which they are restrictive, insufficient, or problematic. Not only can established scientific metaphors lead to misunderstandings but also as Taylor and Dewsbury (2018) point out, they can also hold "remnants of colonialism" or they can be exclusionary. Again, bringing these types of metaphors to the students' attention can lead to exciting revelations about the power, pervasiveness, and complications that stem from using metaphors in science.

6.5   LESSON TWO: DIGESTION DRAMATIC MONOLOGUE

Objectives

While utilizing the same tools from the previous lesson, the goal of the second lesson was to motivate students to gain a better understanding of a biological process—namely, human digestion—through large-group collaboration.

Lesson

Before students were split into groups, we explained the activity. First, we had to discuss what a dramatic monologue is: a dramatic monologue involves a single person delivering a speech to an audience present or not present in the poem. The person speaking is clearly not the poet, and oftentimes, this is made evident from the onset by the title. Many students will be familiar with famous dramatic monologues such as Robert Browning's "My Last Duchess," William Wordsworth's "Tintern Abbey," or even Mary Shelley's *Frankenstein*. It is different from soliloquy because "Monologue is a personal and participatory speech act, even though only one person may be speaking. Soliloquy, however, is impersonal, in that no one other than the actor is intended to hear these words" (Davis, 2007, p. 178). The dramatic monologue allows students to insert themselves into the process being studied, and this shift in perspective opens up new means of understanding. After discussing dramatic monologues, we walked them through the steps of the writing activity. To help guide them through this, we gave the following handout:

Turkey and Cheese Sandwich: A Dramatic Monologue
Through poetry, your group will document the turkey and cheese sandwich's journey from entry into the human body to exit.
- Divide your group into smaller groups of two to three people.
- Throughout, incorporate as much vocabulary as you can, but be sure to **demonstrate an understanding** of the following:
  - *mechanical stage* – chewing, stomach churning
  - *transport* – peristaltic action
  - *enzymatic* – trypsin, amylase, enzymes
  - *absorption* – intestines (small and large)
  - *elimination* – colon, sphincter
- Your poem will be a dramatic monologue; therefore, it will be in the first person.
- Begin your poem with "The first thing I remember is…"
- Each small group must include at least one simile and one metaphor.
- Think colors, sensations, smells, sounds, but whatever you do, be sure to describe, in detail, what it was like for the turkey and cheese sandwich to go through each phase of digestion.
- Your poem will be at least 25 lines long.
- Be creative and have fun!

The following key terms were explained:

Dramatic Monologue: a poem in the form of a speech or narrative by an
imagined person, in which the speaker inadvertently reveals aspects of
their character while describing a particular situation or series of events.
Metaphor: a figure of speech in which a word or phrase is applied to an
object or action to which it is not literally applicable. "The world
is a stage."
Simile: the comparison of one thing to another of a different kind, used to
make a description more emphatic or vivid. Example: "The world is
like a stage."

Results and Reflection

In poetry classes, the persona poems or dramatic monologues are especially helpful for students who feel they do not have anything to write
about—the mask of a persona allows students to be someone else and, as
such, to think beyond their own experience and feelings. In the end, what
we often find is that the students' personalities show through the persona.
Imagining what another persona is thinking, how it would behave, and
how it would feel also encourages empathy and higher-level thinking. In
the sciences, where students rarely are permitted to insert their unique
personalities, this activity might give them a way into understanding while
exercising their individuality. Furthermore, by writing this kind of poem,
students are able to demonstrate their comprehension through first-person
explanation.

Speaking behind the mask of their assigned persona—in our case, the
turkey and cheese sandwich—allowed the students to explore, firsthand,
what takes place during digestion. While students were still utilizing
metaphor, this activity helped to develop more complicated disciplinary
thinking than the previous. Students had to understand the process:
what came before and what came next, and they had to understand what
exactly was happening within the stage that they were writing about.
Students were motivated and more engaged. We noticed that the creative writers immerged during this activity—indeed, the small groups
leaned on those students who were more comfortable writing poetry.
This kind of validation could be invaluable to such students. At the end
of class, students enjoyed sharing their collaborative poems and hearing
each other's work.

Similar to the metaphor activity, students sometimes struggled with concepts, but this struggle manifested itself as curiosity. In their textbooks, in their groups, or by asking their instructor, students sought out answers to their questions, which almost always had to do with content literacy rather than creative writing. The poem, which they titled "My Last Ride," shows that they gained a greater understanding of the concept.

> I'm scared, yet strangely intrigued
> There's a squeezing sensation, and I can feel a *membrane*
> closing in around me
> I compress upon myself and the
> tube pulls me down
> with all the speed of a tired snail
> It is an alien scene and landscape
> I descend lower into the unknown, like
> an explorer into uncharted territory
> As I continue to crawl, I sense the
> tube slowly ending
> An acidic smell becomes apparent
> What could that substance be?

In the above stanza, rather than using many of the technical terms, the group conveys what peristaltic action might feel like—"a membrane/ closing in around me" and "the/ tube pulls me down." They also describe the sandwich compressing itself, pointing to the way peristalsis creates a bolus or ball of food. While their images show an understanding of the transport stage, their description of what the muscles are actually doing during this stage could have demonstrated a higher level of understanding of the vocabulary.

In contrast, the authors of the following stanza chose to use the vocabulary words in their poetry.

> It felt like days being incased in this thing called *amylase.*
> Converting my sandwich into starch and *glucose* into *sugar.*
> Digestion about to start, like a violin. *Trypsin* breaking me down.
> This will be the last you hear from me.
> How did it come to this, stuck in this *enzyme.*
> Rest in peace in this catalyst.

Here, the students show a basic understanding that these enzymes are playing a role in digestion, and in a few cases ("Converting my sandwich into starch and glucose into sugar"), they demonstrate some knowledge of what the enzymes are doing, but they don't delve into the important function each of these enzymes are performing and where in the digestive system this is happening. While there are more keywords being used than in the previous stanza, they are not illustrated in any way that allows us to see that the students comprehend their meanings. Furthermore, the poetic devices being employed do not help us understand the function of the enzymes. For instance, why is digestion "like a violin" and what do they mean by "Rest in peace"? In hindsight, perhaps it would have been better to assign each student in the group a specific enzyme. Also, employing some sort of marginal definition or footnote detailing what biological concept is being described would have been useful for all of the students.

As they worked on the poem, we could readily observe that the students were wrapped up in the processes happening during their section of the digestive tract. As the process quickened, so too did their writing. From metaphor to rhyming, students employed a variety of literary devices to convey this. Notice, for instance, in the fourth stanza, the pace is accelerated by the use of alliteration and the verb suffix -ing.

> Going through the *duodenum* as if I'm in a Big Thunder
> Dropped in a dark small space
> Going through the roller coaster, *enzyme* breaking me down.
> Seeing my shrunken family floating through me.
> Slowing down as I see a large opening
> Being one with my family with a different form.

By the end of the activity, students had a greater appreciation of how food is transformed from something edible into something nutritious. While sharing their work, the students explained that food is transformed into a *bolus* which is partly absorbed in the stomach and processed further into *chime* for either subsequent digestion and absorption or elimination.

After we shared and discussed the poems, students filled out a brief reflection. Nearly all of the students responded that they found the activity enjoyable. When asked what their favorite part of this activity was, students often stated that they appreciated the opportunity to be creative in biology. One student wrote, "Favorite part – The ability to get creative as we would want." Another responded, "My favorite part of this activity [was] being able to experience a different type of learning on a creative side. I don't have a least favorite part." Others enjoyed the opportunity to work together: "My favorite part of this activity is the ability to make us come together and interact with our classmates to form a poem." One student relished the opportunity to "spill bars." This same student wrote, "It was difficult at first, then I channeled my inner Rakim (the greatest MC of all times) and we were alright." This activity enhanced students' learning of biology through close reading. Students were more invested and involved in a learning process; they not only took ownership of the content knowledge but also the process of expressing it creatively.

Some students wrote that they didn't have enough time or that they felt rushed. Next time we do this activity, we will allow more time for students to write their stanzas. Also, when we do this again, after they read their poems, we will make time for each group to explicate their stanzas, explaining to us what is happening during that stage of digestion. In order for this activity to be successful, students must be allowed ample time.

When asked if the activity was helpful, one student wrote that it helped her remember the process better: "I had forgotten some steps of the digestion system. For example, the location of some of the enzymes." And on whether it was as helpful as a traditional lecture: "For me personally it's better because it's hands on. I'm more of a tactile and visual learner than just listening." Another student wrote, "Learning through the traditional lecture, the information is usually there, whereas this activity one has to obtain the information which helps us. I would prefer this activity." "I prefer this activity," wrote another student, "because I got to express my creativity rather than listening to a lecture that I'm not interested in." Not all the students found this as helpful as a traditional lecture. One wrote, "I prefer lecture because I'm not much of a writer." This same student wrote that his least favorite part was the "creative process." It's interesting that his favorite part was seeing how it all came together—which is, in fact, one of the most rewarding parts of the creative process.

Last, our favorite response to whether it was as helpful as a lecture: "I understand it in a different way." This shift in perspective signifies a possible breakthrough, one that can generate new meanings and deepen comprehension. Having the ability to find new paths to understanding can benefit students in countless ways.

6.6   Lesson Three: Reproduction Poems

Objectives

For the final lesson of the semester, our goal was for students to better understand biological concepts by connecting them to their personal narratives, poignant experiences, and/or current moods and feelings.

In the previous activities, the poems students wrote were secondary to the content they were learning. Even though the two activities triggered interesting and creative products, poetry was still the tool used to remember and understand. In our final assignment, we wanted to try to let both the content and the poem share the stage. Of course we tried to give students another opportunity to access ways to understand and retain information, but we also wanted to give them the opportunity for more personal and creative expression. The challenge was doing this in an hour and 15 minutes.

We decided to urge students to write poems that were more elliptical than the previous ones. Encouraging students to be abstract and to employ leaps in their poems would give them more creative freedom. Furthermore, we wanted to see if connecting a difficult biological concept to personal/emotional memory may help understanding and retention. When writing poems, restrictions often help to anchor students and give them things to write about; therefore, we also included specifics that must occur in their poems.

Lesson

First, students were given a list of vocabulary words to choose from such as *follicular phase, ovulation, metamorphosis, dioecious,* and *monoecious.* After they chose the word, they had to define it and list its characteristics. Then, they had to arrange this definition into seven to ten unrhymed lines of no more than ten syllables each. This stanza had to contain at least one simile or metaphor that begins on a line of its own, and this simile/metaphor could not occur at the beginning of the stanza.

Next, students were asked to brainstorm any feelings, experiences, and memories that were conjured while they thought about their vocabulary words. They each chose one, and with the same number of lines as before, they wrote about this. While there was much more freedom in terms of content for this part, students had to include at least one question and one undomesticated animal.

Finally, students were told to "zipper" these two stanzas together by alternating lines from each. After this, they could revise as they saw fit. The vocabulary word would act as the title of the poem.

Results and Reflection

Overall, the writing from the first part of the assignment demonstrated comprehension of the vocabulary words, while the final products showed competence in higher-order thinking. As we anticipated, this activity was challenging for many students. It is difficult for students to write about private/personal aspects of their lives, especially in a biology course; furthermore, students are not often encouraged to do non-linear writing. Both of these challenges yielded worthwhile results.

One of the surprises of this lesson was that we saw the students' very different perspectives when asked to write about their associations with the vocabulary words in the reproduction unit. Interestingly, these differences were somewhat gendered. Many of the female students wrote poems that were very personal and private, whereas several of the male students took a less serious, less personal approach. This observation may be explained by the unit—reproduction—and the simple fact that female students in this age range have more personal associations with the content.

Ovulation
by Ka Yi Lee

It is a crazy story.
This happens every month.
My mother speaks multiple languages.
Until all of the family members are released.
Last time we went to a plain.
One mature member is releasing each month.
A leopard tried to attack us.
From a big house to the tunnel
My mother blamed it immediately
Occurs when the *ovarian follicles* rupture
Just liked how she punishes me usually
Midway in the *menstrual cycle*.
Does my mom know how to speak an animal language

In a female's body.

From lines like "This happens every month," "Occurs when the *ovarian follicles* rupture," and the metaphor "From a big house to the tunnel," we can see the student understands the process of ovulation. It's interesting that the personal story conjured by the vocabulary word is one about her mother. Not only that, but it is one of mother as protector. The dynamic between these two—the vocabulary definition and the story—is intriguing, and the way they blend together is startling in those last two lines: "Does my mom know how to speak an animal language/ In a female's body."

In contrast, although his poem is quite interesting, this student may have lacked the personal experience and background knowledge to connect, both cognitively and emotionally, to his vocabulary word:

Metamorphosis
by Jonathan Youance

The process by which an animal
And sweaty people
Physically Develops
Overcrowded Train Carts
After Birth or Hatching
I should of just rode a lion
A new creation like caterpillar getting his wings
The Bus skipping my stop
It is the change
Change in Routes
Through the growth of cells
When will New York City fix their subway system?

Here, the student's comprehension of the vocabulary words is not apparent. While he demonstrates a rudimentary understanding of metamorphosis, it's not developed. In contrast to the previous, the experience it invoked is somewhat trivial, although the informal "I should of just rode a lion" is surprisingly rich.

We found this student's take on gender binaries interesting, and it was an astonishing turn when they directly address the snail at the end of the poem:

Hermaphroditic
by Briana Roldan

Slow, slimy, small
Reproductive organs
complete or partial
living in a shell, an apartment of their own
living like numbers in a code—
sandwiched
male & female
sometimes a delicacy in a fancy suit
possible in Humans
mostly invertebrates
But snail,
Tell me, How does it feel to evaporate,
within and without the binary,
in something of a salt lake?

This poem demonstrates uncertainty. The words "sometimes," "possible," and "mostly" are ways to defy the definitive binary of how nature and species are defined. "Within and without" the binary shows a wrestling between the scientific and personal constructs. While the student underlines that "binary" as the condition of the reproduction of species in science, she wondered how the existence of a species is possible without a binary. The result of the author's understanding did not end with a demonstration of full knowledge, but the beginning of a question. The question mark opens up an attempt to engage biology in a sociocultural dialogue, "sandwiched" between rigid concepts and processes and fluid identities.

Some of the poems revealed struggles the students were having in their lives. For instance, this student wrote about losing her passion in the sciences and wondering how she might get it back:

Follicular/Luteal Phase
by Assa Gory

What takes place in female
Memories of A&P 2 class arises
Shedding of the endometrium lining
Making my memory as sharp as a shark
Uterus now like a falling tree
Some information stayed

FSH to stimulate egg production
While others flew away
LH to stimulate the egg's release
Sparking my interest in medicine
Waiting to be fertilized
I miss the drive it gave me
The *Follicular/ Luteal Phase* continues…
How will I be able to bring it back?

As we can see from the last two poems, this activity gave students an opportunity to explore more delicate matters. Several of the students wrote about being tired and/or hungry while others told about more personal difficulties. Whether or not this helped students remember content material, much of this information could be useful to an instructor. Such activities may reveal the reasons why students are not doing well in their science class; consequently, the poems could give instructors a way to talk about possible solutions.

6.7   Poetry in Biology as Culturally Responsive Teaching

Moje and Hinchman (2004) emphasize that teaching needs to be responsive to the "many funds of knowledge and Discourse" (p. 322), which is unique to an individual's sociocultural and linguistic backgrounds (Gee, 2000). Discourses are defined as "ways of knowing" and "ways of words" (Heath, 1983). As a form of responsive teaching, poetry writing in biology allows students to incorporate their discourses into the learning of subject matters in unique and personal ways. For instance, situating "Gas Exchange" in a local context/metaphor, "The Grand Central Station" or associating "Ovulation" with a mother who "speaks multiple languages" inevitably merges the discourses of the students as persons and the discourses of the students as learners of new concepts, practices, and skills (Moje & Hinchman, 2004).

The advantage of this approach is that it readily engages students from diverse sociocultural and language backgrounds. It opens up the discursive space of academic learning and seeks to achieve the goals of a culturally responsive pedagogy: to forge a "bridge from everyday language practice to conventional content learning," to teach students "how to navigate cultural and discursive communities," and "to draw from students' experiences to challenge and reshape the academic content knowledge and literacy practices of the curriculum" (Moje & Hinchman, 2004, p. 322).

6.8   Conclusion

The application of the creative writing strategies and cooperative learning in the poetry lessons has shifted the teacher-centered approach in teaching biology lectures to a student-centered approach, extending the lab/doing part to the lecture, only offering more opportunities for students to tap into their creativity and personal experiences. After all, learning is most powerful when it is personalized and foregrounds everyday knowledge when developing discipline-specific knowledge. The poetry in biology lessons to a certain extent moved teaching and learning toward these goals. They provide access to discipline through creative activities and personal input, which can enhance student motivation. These strategies can also be used to assess where disciplinary learning takes place or not.

We also found poetry in biology can be a powerful tool to enhance student engagement. Students find the freedom to interact and engage the material at a level that they feel comfortable. This is especially helpful for underprepared students. As they find a way to relate their personal experience or make connections between things in the world, such as associating "a personal memory" or "an undomesticated animal" with a biology concept, they feel empowered to participate in making meaning of specialized knowledge.

The process of writing poetry on biological concepts is a composition that also involves the translation of scientific into personal or everyone's language. This creative process involves a multidimensional cognitive engagement that allows students to explore and negotiate access and ownership of content knowledge through personalizing disciplinary discourse. No matter how minute or extensive this engagement is, it charts a new way for students to participate and expand the possibility of a closer encounter with the scientific language, access content knowledge, and develop disciplinary literacy.

Acknowledgments Emerging Scholars Program Students: Nevila Kica and Anisa Shkembi. Biology 1201 for their help in organizing this chapter, and course coordinator Prof. Tatiana Voza and Biology Chairperson Prof. Andleeb Zameer for allowing freedom to pursue alternative teaching methods.

REFERENCES

Brown, S. A. (2015). Creative expression of science through poetry and other media can enrich medical and science education. *Frontiers in Neurology, 6,* 3.

Davis, J. (2007). Dialogue, monologue and soliloquy in the large lecture class. *International Journal of Teaching & Learning in Higher Education, 19*(2), 178–182.

Fang, Z. (2012). Language correlates of disciplinary literacy. *Topics in Language Disorders, 32*(1), 19–34.

Gee, J. P. (2000). Discourse and sociocultural studies in reading. In *Handbook of reading research* (Vol. 3, pp. 195–207). Mahwah, NJ: Erlbaum.

Heath, S. B. (1983). *Ways with words: Language, life and work in communities and classrooms.* Cambridge: Cambridge University Press.

Jensen, D. (2006). Metaphors as a bridge to understanding educational and social contexts. *International Journal of Qualitative Methods, 5*(1), 36–54.

Moje, E. B., & Hinchman, K. (2004). Culturally responsive practices for youth literacy learning. In *Adolescent literacy research and practice* (p. 321). New York: Guilford Press.

Pollack, A. E., & Korol, D. L. (2013). The use of haiku to convey complex concepts in neuroscience. *Journal of Undergraduate Neuroscience Education, 12*(1), A42.

Snow, C. E. (2010). Academic language and the challenge of reading for learning about science. *Science, 328,* 450–452.

Taylor, C., & Dewsbury, B. M. (2018). On the problem and promise of metaphor use in science and science communication. *Journal of Microbiology & Biology Education, 19*(1), 19.1.46. https://doi.org/10.1128/jmbe.v19i1.1538.

Thonney, T. (2016). Analyzing the vocabulary demands of introductory college textbooks. *The American Biology Teacher, 78*(5), 389–395.

Trujillo, C. M., Anderson, T. R., & Pelaez, N. J. (2015). A model of how different biology experts explain molecular and cellular mechanisms. *CBE Life Sciences Education, 14*(2). ar20.

CHAPTER 7

Engineering Technology: Engaging Disciplinary Thinking and Doing

*Ohbong Kwon, Chen Xu, Kenneth Markowitz,
and A. E. Dreyfuss*

7.1 INTRODUCTION

In today's world, the great majority of engineering systems and services consist of networks of integrated hardware and software applications. With the fields of technology continuously evolving and expanding, teams of trained engineers are needed to analyze and develop solutions and solve contemporary technical problems.

A portion of this chapter was excerpted with permission from "Reading Effectively in First Year Electromechanical Engineering Courses" (2015). *First Year Engineering Experience Conference Proceedings, 2015 (Roanoke, WV). American Society for Engineering Education.*

All the authors contributed equally to this chapter.

O. Kwon • C. Xu • K. Markowitz • A. E. Dreyfuss (✉)
New York City College of Technology, City University of New York,
Brooklyn, NY, USA
e-mail: okwon@citytech.cuny.edu; cxu@citytech.cuny.edu;
kmarkowitz@citytech.cuny.edu; ADreyfuss@citytech.cuny.edu

At New York City College of Technology (City Tech), the Computer Engineering Technology (CET) Department is committed to meet this challenge by providing students with an educational environment for learning the rudiments of the field, as well as instilling a platform to promote lifelong learning. Since 2013, CET faculty have been actively engaged in the college-wide Reading Effectively Across the Disciplines (READ) program in order to improve disciplinary literacy (Shanahan & Shanahan, 2012), critical thinking, and problem-solving skills in three first-year Electromechanical Technology (EMT) courses for the Associate in Applied Science (AAS) degree offered by the CET Department.

Even though reading proficiency is essential to learning in every discipline, in higher education institutions there has been insufficient effort in fostering disciplinary literacy through reading, especially in Science, Technology, Engineering and Mathematics (STEM) areas. Research in engineering pedagogy seldom addresses the importance of effective reading and its role in facilitating learning in the discipline (But, Kwon, & Laboy, 2015). The demand for higher-order cognitive skills through effective reading, such as application, analysis, interpretation, and evaluation, is ubiquitous throughout the learning process in engineering courses, as described in the Accreditation Board for Engineering and Technology criteria (ABET 2019). Reading is embedded in acquiring knowledge in every field, and the ability to read proficiently is indispensable in engineering, for "knowledge is the data base of a professional engineer" (Rugarcia, Felder, Woods, & Stice, 2000). The targeted engineering courses in the READ endeavor have included Electromechanical Lab (EMT 1130), Electrical Circuits (EMT 1150), and Electronics (EMT 1255). These three courses not only are required courses for the program but also provide the core principles and foundations needed by students to successfully complete the AAS degree. Students' motivation and self-confidence often result in a desire to continue their education and pursue a Bachelor's degree in Technology (BT) or Science (BS).

It is the intent of this chapter to describe each of the three courses, enumerate challenges faced by students and faculty, describe READ program strategies employed, and discuss group work and collaboration efforts, as well as highlight assessment efforts.

7.2   ELECTROMECHANICAL MANUFACTURING LAB

Students entering the AAS program in Electromechanical Engineering Technology are required to take EMT 1130, "Electromechanical Manufacturing Lab" in their first semester. This lab course contributes one credit and meets three hours per week during a 15-week semester. Enrollment capacity is limited to 22 students per section, who learn basic safety regulations, breadboarding skills, and the proper use of test equipment including the digital multimeter, oscilloscope, and function generator. These skills are required to build a digital trainer and also constitute the core foundations and principles for all the labs in the AAS program.

As listed in the syllabus of EMT 1130, the learning outcomes are the ability to

- understand, analyze, and safely use basic electrical and electronic circuits/systems and electromechanical devices;
- troubleshoot and fix problems in electrical circuits/systems and electromechanical devices;
- develop skills to use the tools and instruments to build electromechanical devices;
- function as effective contributing members of a team;
- recognize the physical laws that govern how all electrical circuits and devices work;
- apply fundamental mathematical principles to calculate current, voltage, resistance, power considerations as needed; and
- wire circuits using lab test equipment to test and troubleshoot circuits.

Breadboarding exercises expose students to different passive and active components used in electrical or digital systems, and require students to arrange these components in series, parallel, or series-parallel configurations. The test equipment is used to monitor circuit behavior as well as support troubleshooting (finding shorts and opens) when the need arises. Students are required to purchase the prescribed equipment and materials that they will use to build the digital trainer.

Challenges Students Face in Reading

Reading proficiency certification is not required for this course. However, many EMT 1130 students fresh from high school lack basic comprehension and analysis skills needed to succeed in this course and continue in the EMT AAS program. Even though students are required to read the lab manual before coming to class, those students who lack these basic skills come to lab unprepared and struggle to complete their assignments in a timely manner. Further compounding this problem is that most engineering texts are complex and often require multiple literacies in academic language, symbolic and visual expressions, and everyday language. This often results in declining motivation for students, and possible withdrawal or failure in this course.

Students who lack reading proficiency often rely on listening skills in class, rather than reading to learn (Schemo, 2006). Even among those who read their text material, many still cannot readily move beyond accumulating facts and memorizing the right answers to learn a level of abstract metacognitive thinking skills (Peters et al., 2006).

It is for these reasons that EMT 1130 was targeted for the READ discipline initiative in the fall of 2013. Various READ strategies were employed to motivate and help students, including incorporating the Peer-Led Team Learning (PLTL) model.

Peer-Led Team Learning in an Engineering Manufacturing Lab

Peer-Led Team Learning (PLTL) is a curricular model where groups of students, facilitated by a trained Peer Leader, work on course materials. The weekly "workshop" session is an integral part of a course that provides a scheduled structure to discuss and review materials which were introduced in the classroom, and practice problem-solving (Dreyfuss & Fraiman, 2015). PLTL has been implemented at City Tech since the mid-1990s, originally in the Chemistry Department, since 2001 in the Mathematics Department, and in 2011 in Civil Engineering (Dreyfuss et al., 2015). Incorporating PLTL in courses, especially the "gateway" courses that incoming students must take, has been demonstrated to improve retention rates, and promote persistence to higher-level courses, and an increase in majors (Wilson & Varma-Nelson, 2016).

The existing PLTL infrastructure at City Tech (Liou-Mark et al., 2013), with recruiting, selection, training, and supervising Peer Leaders, allowed for the addition of PLTL to departments that incorporated the READ initiative in 2013. The Peer Leader training course of one credit, listed in the Mathematics Department, was also listed as an Independent Study course for non-math majors. It prepared the first-time Peer Leaders, no matter what courses they were leading, in facilitating collaborative teamwork by building effective communication, questioning, and teamwork strategies, as well as introducing them to theories of learning. Working in groups facilitated by a "more knowledgeable peer" (Vygotsky, 1978) promotes learning among students who are encouraged to, and actively engaged in discussing the course material. The Peer Leader leads by questioning and fostering critical thinking, a vital difference from tutoring where students often do not have the benefit of listening to others' thinking. By working as part of a team, students become comfortable in asking questions, making mistakes that can then be examined, and finding their voice in expressing their growing understanding of the content.

In their first semester serving as Peer Leaders in EMT 1130, two undergraduate CET majors incorporated not only strategies for group work (process of facilitation), content (building the digital trainer), but used reading strategies to which they had been introduced in training and were designated as part of each week's curriculum in the steps of the lab work.

Pre-reading Strategies and Pre-lab Activities

As a weekly pre-reading strategy, anticipation guides were introduced. Students in EMT 1130 were asked to agree or disagree with statements to predict the information they were going to read in the lab manual before reading it; they then validated or revised their answers after reading the manual. The purpose of this set of pre-reading activities is to relate students' background knowledge to technical information they were about to learn. This not only served to motivate students to look for specific answers in the text, but also enabled them to reflect on the reasoning behind their predictions, especially when they were not accurate.

Numerous tools and processes are involved in assembling the digital trainer. Students are required to obtain precise information about the features, functions, and characteristics of different tools and components; they also need specific details for each step and how these fit into the entire assembling process. To help students retain information better and visualize the steps more clearly, feature analysis charts (see Fig. 7.1) were used as pre-lab assignments and assessment tools. These can be used repeatedly in varying formats to reinforce learning the lab manual.

Another assignment that helped students lay out a blueprint of the assembling process is the process map. It is designed as an intermediary step to translate instructions they read in the lab manual into a visual representation that could eventually guide them in accomplishing the process. Since there is more than one sequence of steps in which the digital trainer could be built, students had to critically evaluate the process and come up with a sequence that worked for them. To facilitate this, students were asked to generate a process map from the information they gained from the instructor and the lab manual. Figure 7.2 shows a version of the process map detailing the steps.

Class (Category) : Tools	For compressing or indenting metal	For flattening sheet metal from stretch or nicks	For marking measured lines (deep into sheet)	For pressing hole center into metal deep punch (turret press)	For widening increasing hole diameter of sheet metal	For removing small, sharp chips / burrs of metal
Ball Peen Hammer	+					
Mallet		+				
Metal Scriber			+			
Center Punch				+		
Hand expansion reamer					+	
Hand File						+

(Source: But et al., 2015, by Henry Laboy)

Fig. 7.1   Feature analysis chart

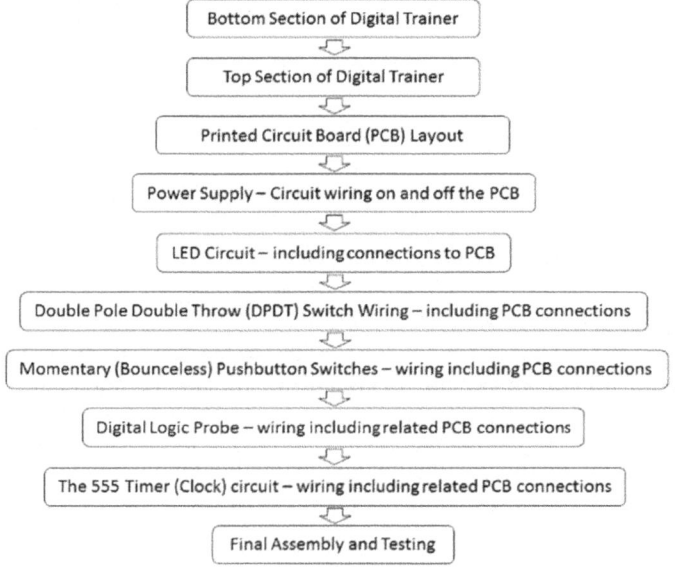

(Source: But et al., 2015, by Henry Laboy)

Fig. 7.2   Process map

General Literacy Strategies

Other general reading and vocabulary activities are also used to enhance students' reading proficiency and help them develop transferrable strategies for the AAS EMT program. These include note-taking skills and text annotation. The instructor with the help of the Peer Leaders took some lab time to introduce these skills in how to read the lab manual critically and formulate questions to bring to the next laboratory session. Further, exit slips at the end of the laboratory sessions proved to be an effective way to get feedback from students, as they check understanding, and even provide suggestions to the instructor. Exit slips can be designed as formative assessment tools, or they can provide information to determine what items need review.

Faculty find exit slips invaluable in planning future lessons, progressing through units and incorporating student ideas. Exit slips are not only beneficial for the professor, but students also enjoy having opportunities to reflect on their learning, ask questions, give input, and ultimately shape what happens in the classroom.

An early focus of the first-semester pilot was the need to rewrite the safety manual. This is the first lesson that students must absorb and the existing manual, used for several years, had proved hard to read as it was not in sequential order and had not been laid out in an inviting manner. A quiz format was updated to correlate with the safety manual instructions.

Among other concepts and practices, "troubleshooting" is at the center of engineering learning and practices. Students may not readily know the meaning of troubleshooting in the engineering context. This is particularly important in EMT 1130, where students need to troubleshoot each step of the way when building the digital trainer. To introduce this concept, a word map (see Fig. 7.3) is used to show how the word is used in the context of the course and the procedures that it involves.

Embedded Peer-Led Team Practice in Lab Learning

Implementing a peer-led workshop proved to be challenging. Because EMT 1130 is held in a laboratory, pairs of students share a workstation. There is no occasion for the Peer Leader to assemble a group as had been done in stand-alone PLTL workshops associated with lecture courses. Instead Peer Leaders circulated in the room, guiding the students in their assigned "group." One Peer Leader in the 2013 semester noted in his first

Troubleshooting is required most of the time when putting an electromechanical project together

Source:

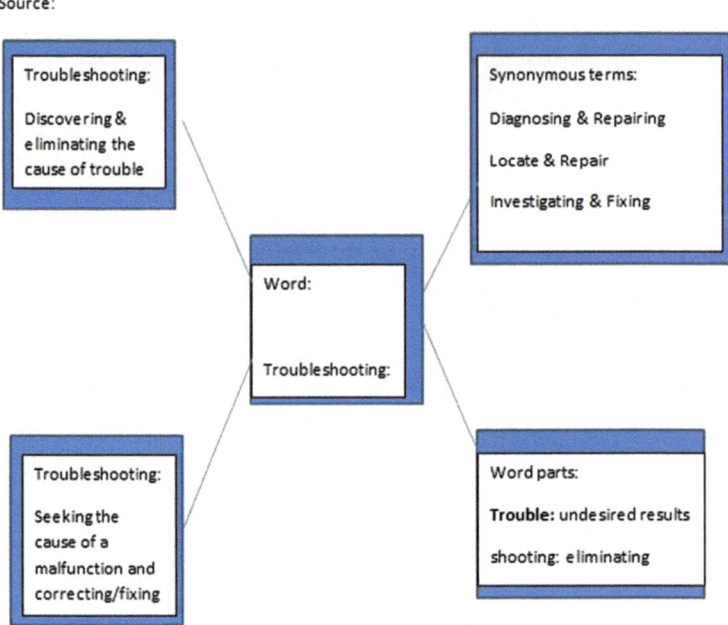

Two sentences using the word:
1. You may need to troubleshoot your most recent work from time to time.
2. When any testing shows an undesirable result, troubleshooting will be necessary

(Source: By Henry Laboy)

Fig. 7.3 Word map

journal that the EMT 1130 workshop was not what he had expected, since it was not separate from the laboratory session. Instead, he answered questions and explained what to do based on his experience in the same course. When he was able to talk with students in his group without the instructor's presence, the students appeared more enthusiastic and willing to engage with each other.

Since part of the task of the Peer Leader is to encourage asking questions and working with others as a team, the icebreaker set the tone and promoted the concept of interaction with classmates, which is not often found in college courses. Students needed to feel comfortable and be able to converse with their classmates—a first step to being able to ask for help, something many incoming students are loath to do. This helped to motivate students and keep them focused in an unfamiliar setting, as they were starting their first college EMT course. A Peer Leader's journal entry from a later week in the course notes the importance of communication and motivation:

Motivation is key in every aspect of life. If we did not have motivation, why would we do anything? One way which Chris Richard (2012) describes to encourage motivation is to have the students feel connected with what they are doing. If students understand the reasoning behind their action, they will be more motivated to follow through to their goal. Another way is to have the students set goals for themselves. Although the students are sometimes externally motivated, they feel motivation internally because they do not want to fail.

One way I try to keep the students motivated is by going to their workbench and asking questions. "How's everything going? What's the next step? So you have completed that, move unto the next step then!" I usually clap my hands to wake them up a bit if I see they are slacking. It is already loud in the lab so I am not singling out anyone. I am motivated because they continue to ask me for help. It is my motivation to help them.

To improve learning the workshop, I will encourage more communication. The more people communicate with one another, the less misunderstanding there will be. I do see some students rush through procedure[s] for some reason. Although a nice pace is encouraged, no one should have to rush. One student today had to re-bend his sheet metal simply because he was not paying attention.

The main challenge of the course is to translate what students read into what they do and to hone the ability to troubleshoot when processes do not function. The first instructor involved with READ gave the students worksheets and the Peer Leaders help guide students to complete these. These worksheets helped students familiarize themselves with the tools, understand important concepts, and troubleshoot problems in the course of building the digital trainer. The role of the Peer Leaders was in part to help students reflect on the procedures they take to build the box by questioning them on what they had done, as well as guiding activities by knowing what questions to ask. Students were guided to think critically through questions based on the stages of Bloom's Taxonomy (Fowler,

2004). The "exit slips" were developed as feedback questionnaires which mixed content knowledge and reflection on the process of learning. As one Peer Leader noted mid-semester:

> Our [written] feedback questionnaire consisted of questions relating to their acquired knowledge of skills, tools, and procedures in this workshop. We also asked a question concerning whether their comfort level is increasing or decreasing [each week]. Most students answered the questions positively and confidently. These answers correlate with their behavior in class. Most students seem very interested at their workbenches.

Even in the laboratory course where students must build the digital trainer correctly, and reading instructions is critical to their success, other factors came into play. After his second semester as a Peer Leader in EMT 1130, Pinkhasik (2015) wrote that active learning also needed reflection, to allow formulation of questions, connect current tasks with prior knowledge, and gain a wider understanding of the tasks with which students are confronted. He formulated, with the help of the instructor, the weekly survey with two general questions focused on the tasks of the week, and three questions regarding electronics and safety aspects. Students felt comfortable with answering task-based questions but hesitated to reflect as this was new to them. Pinkhasik recommended that reflection be formalized as a necessary component in engineering classes to promote problem-solving, reading, and writing to develop their professional skills.

Reading Assessments

Reading assessments were used both as formative and summative measures in the READ program. The assessments were administered twice in each semester of EMT 1130. Students took the "pre-READ assessment" at the beginning of each semester, and the "post-READ assessment" at the end of the course. Reading outcomes of four areas—comprehension, interpretation, analysis, and context—were assessed when students read and answered questions on passages from the lab manual for both the pre- and post-READ assessments. The results revealed significant improvement in all four areas in the READ assessments, particularly in comprehension, context, and analysis with a faculty target of 80%.

This improvement could be attributed to the effectiveness of the strategies used to foster reading proficiency and disciplinary literacy by engaging students in active learning. In addition, an OpenLab READ website was also created where faculty and READ administrators could share their ideas, best practices, and resources among each other to support teaching and learning in this collaboration. The READ EMT faculty had the opportunity to exchange best practices not only with colleagues but also with those in other disciplines.

7.3   ELECTRICAL CIRCUITS

Electrical Circuits (EMT 1150) is a foundational engineering course for freshman students that includes both lecture and laboratory components. The lecture portion of the course introduces the physical basis and mathematical models of electrical components and circuits. Topics include Ohm's Law, Watt's Law, resistance, series, parallel, and series-parallel circuits, network theorems, equivalent circuits, capacitive and inductive circuits, and sinusoidal ac inputs. The lab portion of the course is performed on a breadboard using the digital multimeter, oscilloscope, and function generator. To evaluate this course, City Tech uses the following student learning outcomes:

- demonstrate a basic understanding of engineering expressions and basic concepts, such as current, voltage, resistance, and power;
- understand Ohm's law and use it to analyze basic series, parallel, and series-parallel circuits;
- understand basic network theorems, especially using Thevenin's Theorem to find an equivalent circuit;
- recognize capacitors and inductors in series and in parallel circuits and understand simple AC circuits.

This course is identified as the critical course of Electromechanical Engineering Technology (EMT) AAS program and is required for all EMT students to continue their study in this program. The average enrollment for EMT 1150 is around 150 students per semester. Data showed that nearly a third of the students either failed or withdrew from the course by the end of semester. The high failure rate in EMT 1150 is one of the major reasons for the low retention rates for the CET Department, and it has consistently been identified as one of the most challenging courses in the department. The causes for the high failure rates were examined. It is the first course that introduces the formal engineering language to incoming students. The engineering language emphasizes the use of the scientific method and logic to express the problem. Similar to learning any language, students need to learn the new vocabulary words and concepts and will usually experience a steep learning curve at the beginning of the course. Moreover, EMT 1150 also requires good critical thinking and problem-solving skills. Students need to build these skills throughout the semester continuously.

Because this is the first lecture-based engineering course for students who just graduated from high school, many students do not easily adjust their studying habits from high school mode to college mode. Informal conversations with students revealed that habits in high school informed expectations in college: if students attended classes throughout the semester in high school, they would pass the course. Further, in high school, students generally had review sessions before exams, and the questions in the review sessions would appear on the exams. Consequently, some students simply waited for the review sessions at the end of semester. In the beginning of their college year, students followed the same pattern as in high school until they found out that they were falling behind. Some students can catch up after hard work, but many students dropped the course.

Finally, the withdrawal rate in EMT 1150 is almost double the failure rate. Many students dropped the course without taking the final exam. The main reason for the high withdrawal rate is that many students are either unable to follow the course or lose interest in the subject.

There are multiple sections of EMT 1150 in the CET Department. In general, EMT 1150 is taught with the conventional lecture-based approach. The instructors use either PowerPoint slides or whiteboard to introduce the concepts and provide examples. Students are expected to do homework and labs to practice what they learn in the classroom. To improve student performance and disciplinary literacy of EMT 1150, faculty members from the CET Department worked with the READ program to develop strategies to enhance active learning and reading. Many strategies were implemented, including PLTL, KWL charts, concept maps, as well as exit slips, note-taking skills, and annotations. These strategies can help students adjust to the steep learning curve and gradually build good learning habits to succeed in college courses.

Post-Lecture Peer-Led Team Learning Strategy

As noted previously, PLTL is a model of teaching undergraduate science, math, and engineering courses that introduces peer-led workshops as an integral part of a course, where the Peer Leaders meet with a group of the same students each week, for one to two hours, to discuss, debate, and engage in problem-solving related to the course material. PLTL promotes a friendly environment for students to discuss, review, and practice materials which they learned in the classroom. With support from STEM Faculty Development Funding from the City University of New York (CUNY), PLTL was adopted as a strategy in this course. Three aspects were emphasized. The first one was to truly integrate PLTL workshop as part of the course. Lectures were condensed to two hours weekly, and the other two lecture hours were used for the separate PLTL workshop, which is mandatory for all students in the course. This was a difference with the practice in EMT 1130, where the "workshop" was embedded in the laboratory classroom. The weekly peer-led workshop sessions provided additional time for students to discuss and practice the theory, and learn from their mistakes in a supportive environment.

Further, workshop materials were designed to correspond to each chapter in the textbook to provide scaffolding. Each module started by reviewing simple concepts, followed by applying those concepts to simple problems and progressing to more challenging questions. Some common mistakes which students tend to make were broken down into detailed steps to facilitate understanding.

The second change was the incorporation of seven Peer Leaders who themselves completed the EMT 1150 course with B+ or higher grades and were selected and trained with Peer Leaders from other departments in the Peer Leader Training course. They also worked with faculty to review the workshop modules and prepare questions regarding the course content for the weekly workshop session.

The third change was targeting the disconnections between lectures and lab sections. Previously, students registered for EMT 1150 lecture and lab separately through the online registration system (CUNYfirst) and often the lab and lecture sections in which they enrolled were taught by different instructors. The structure of lab materials might require students to do certain experiments even before they learned about those materials in the lecture. With the administrative support from the CET Department, a learning community format was piloted that linked the lecture and the lab together to be taught by the same instructor. As a result, some supplemental lab materials were developed to target specific problems observed in the lectures and homework.

In Fall 2017, one pilot section (N = 15) was implemented with restructured EMT 1150 materials while a second EMT 1150 section, taught by the same instructor, was used as a control section (N = 15). Throughout the semester, the pilot section implemented PLTL workshops and reading practices, and the labs and lectures were synchronized under the guidance of the same instructor. The control section covered exactly the same materials but did not include the PLTL workshop and synchronized labs. At the end of semester, a uniform exam, synchronized to ABET requirements, was given to all sections. The average grade of the PLTL section was 78.2, and the average grade of the non-PLTL control section was 67.8. The improvement in student performance in the PLTL section was over 10%, compared with the non-PLTL section (Xu et al., 2018). The results suggest that integrating PLTL workshop into EMT 1150 can help students bridge the learning gap and improve their performance. However, the withdrawal rates in the PLTL section and control section were comparable, but students expressed greater satisfaction rates in the PLTL section compared to the control section.

Enhancing Disciplinary Learning with General Reading Strategies

As noted previously, students experience a steep learning curve in EMT 1150. They need to form effective learning strategies to cope with not only this course but also other courses at the college level. Because no one can grasp all knowledge presented in a classroom completely, the practice outside the classroom is as critical as the work inside. Reading and literacy skills are important to help students learn the engineering language (Kwon, Xu, & But, 2016). However, many first-year EMT students do not demonstrate sufficient literacy skills and motivation to navigate the engineering texts and to learn effectively through reading. To tackle this problem, the READ program was initiated to introduce discipline-specific literacy strategies, and help students practice these strategies in and out of the classroom.

A KWL chart is a widely used strategy to track what a student knows (K), wants to know (W), and has learned (L) about a topic, and was used to foster students' independent reading. Through discussions with students, the faculty found that when students read their textbook and reviewed the material after the class, they were overwhelmed in the reading process by all the technical terms and forgot why they were reading. Their goal was simply to finish reading, but students did not retain anything. The KWL chart can help a student become an active reader. It facilitates their reading, promoting stopping and thinking. It can help connect their prior knowledge with current reading and monitor what they learn and the misconceptions they may have in the process of reading. They can also meaningfully connect the knowledge they learned and forge continuity between the topics and various laws they have learned and subsequently apply them more effectively. The strategy was suggested for students to use when they reviewed materials after each lecture. Since the lecture and lab were synchronized by the same instructor, students were asked to practice a KWL chart on one topic in the lab and to practice further at home. For technical subjects, often it requires students to think more thoroughly what they want to learn. At the beginning, students have a tendency to ask simple and superficial questions. As they progress in the course and accumulate more knowledge in the field, they begin to generate more in-depth questions that require more extensive answers. This routine, both done individually and in groups, can foster disciplinary thinking and inquiry. A model of the enhanced KWL chart with additional components that facilitate reading engineering texts is shown in Fig. 7.4. Some students thought it is useful and practiced this strategy in and out of the class.

Additional strategies were also introduced to enhance students' reading proficiency and learning efficiency, including note-taking, text annotation, concept mapping, and exit slips. Students learned various concepts and theorems in different chapters. Their biggest question is when to use which laws. Concept mapping is quite helpful to connect the laws and theorems from each chapter. At the beginning of the semester, students were provided with a blank map. Over time, they filled in the variables and formulas, and gradually they developed their own concept maps. One example of a concept map used in the class is shown in Fig. 7.5, which was posted on Blackboard (educational software). Each arrow indicates that there is a formula or relationship between linked variables. Students were asked to fill in all the relationships by themselves as part of their homework. [Then] The concept map was then reviewed in the next class session. Students especially liked the concept maps in their reviews prior to exams.

Exit slips, as described earlier, are an effective and efficient way to get feedback from students. They need only to include two questions: "The most important thing I learned today" and "One question I have about what I learned today." After reviewing the exit slips from students, the instructor had a better understanding of what students learned and what questions they have. It also can help the instructor plan the next lecture and review what is not understood.

Topic: Ohm's Law		
K What do I know about this topic?	**W** What do I want to know about this? What questions do I have?	**L** What have I learned from this?
Ohm's Law is a law that applies to electrical circuit. It is about electrical current. It is an important law.	Why is it called Ohm's Law? What does it look like? What are the main principles of this law? What is the use of this law?	Ohm's Law was named after a German scientist Georg Simon Ohm who discovered that the ratio of the potential difference (the change of voltage between two points) to the current is constant for any conductor **It looks like this**: $I = V/R,$ $V = I \times R$ $R = V/I$ I = current, V = voltage, and R = resistance **Principles**: The electrical current in a circuit can be calculated by dividing the voltage by the resistance The current is <u>directly proportional</u> to the voltage and <u>inversely proportional</u> to the resistance **Uses:** Ohm's law is used to calculate electric values (I, V, or R) when analyzing or designing circuit systems (e.g. in electronic devices)

What **additional** information I need to know?	
Units associated with Ohm's Law: 1 ampere $= \frac{1 \; volt}{1 \; ohm} = I$ 1 volt $= (1 \; ampere)(1 \; ohm) = V$ 1 ohm $= \frac{1 \; volt}{1 \; ampere} = R$	Definitions in my own words: Directly proportional = when I increases, V also increases, given that R is unchanged Inversely proportional = when I increase, R decreases and vice versa, given that V is unchanged

(Source: By Juanita C. But)

Fig. 7.4   Enhanced KWL chart

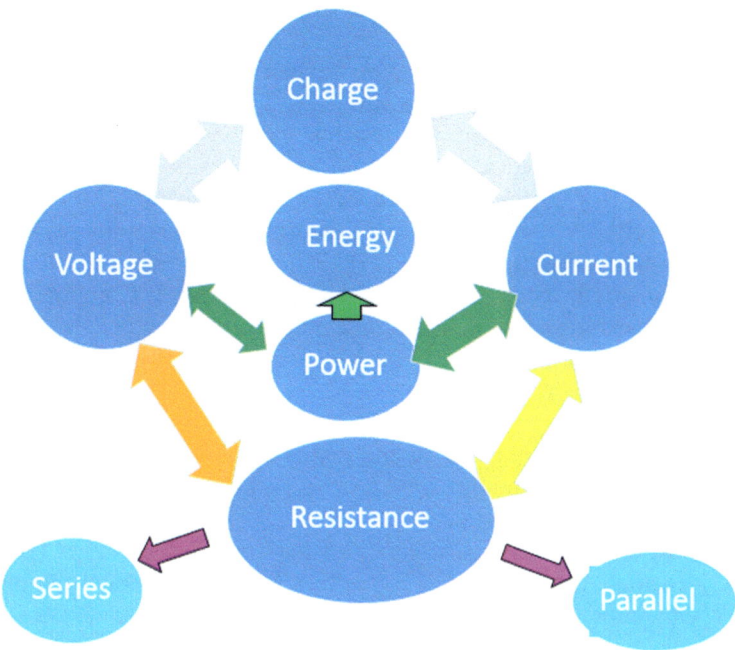

Fig. 7.5   Concept map

READ Assessment

To evaluate the results of incorporating reading strategies, two READ assessments were developed. One was administered at the beginning of the semester before any reading strategy was introduced, and the other was administered at the end of semester after students practiced these strategies throughout the semester. The READ assessments evaluate four different competencies in student reading – comprehension, analysis, context, and evaluation. The assessment results showed that by the end of the semester students improved 10–30% in all four categories. However, their improvement on evaluation was lower than their improvement in the other three categories. Evaluation is the highest level of critical thinking (Bloom, Krathwohl, & Masia, 1956) and the most difficult for students because it requires them to understand and analyze the problem, then select the theorem to solve the problem.

7.4   ELECTRONICS

Students entering the AAS program in Electromechanical Engineering Technology are required to take EMT 1255 "Electronics" in their first year. This course constitutes four credits and also has an embedded lab component. In this course students learn the behavior and characteristics of semiconductor devices such as diodes, voltage regulators, and half and full wave rectifier circuits as well as exploring in depth amplifiers (Bipolar, Field Effect Transistors [FETs], and operation amplifiers). Typical circuits are breadboarded, analyzed, and tested in the laboratory. Computer simulations are used for additional reinforcement of course materials.

As listed in the syllabus of EMT 1255, the following learning outcomes are summarized below:

- distinguish between analog and digital signals;
- draw, analyze, configure, and test basic diode circuits. Troubleshoot these circuits;
- draw, analyze, configure, and test basic amplifier circuits (Bipolar Junction Transistors [BJTs], FETs, and operational amplifiers [Op-Amps]);
- explain the frequency responses of low-pass, high-pass, and band-pass filters.

Although there are clear outcomes in the field of electronics, all technologists regardless of their disciplines share a considerable amount of common ground when it comes to comprehension, analysis, and problem-solving. EMT 1255 challenges students to integrate and apply principles learned in mathematics, physics, and circuit theory in order to comprehend, analyze, configure, and test practical electronic networks. EMT 1255 also provides the basic foundation knowledge to pursue other courses such as computer hardware systems, data communications, network design, and control systems.

It is for these reasons that EMT 1255 was targeted for the READ program. The first goal of the READ initiative was to select an appropriate text for the course. With feedback from the EMT faculty, a textbook was needed to actively engage students to explore, comprehend, analyze, and troubleshoot practical electronic concepts. *Analog Fundamentals: A Systems Approach* by Floyd and Buchla (2013) was selected to be the text for the course. It was chosen for the following reasons.

- Systems are emphasized in each chapter with appropriate and sufficient examples. This helps students see the "big picture" before going into specific details.
- Each chapter begins with a chapter outline, chapter objectives, and website references. This helps students to key into the course outcomes outlined in the syllabus and go deeper into subject matter.
- Each chapter ends with a summary and a problem set with different degrees of understanding. In addition, there is a detailed glossary for quick references at the end of the text. All these features help students become active readers and critical thinkers.
- Many chapters also include a troubleshooting section related to the topics covered. This helps students handle "contextual and evaluation" type problems as well as assist them in troubleshooting circuits in the laboratory.

The main purpose of the lab component is to verify and reinforce concepts and principles learned in the theory section of the course. In this reading-intensive course, students are required to read the lab manual before coming to class. This manual contains 16 detailed experiments and students are required to submit a weekly typed written lab report responding to specific questions at the end of each experiment. Since these questions often require comprehension, analysis, and conceptual skills, it is imperative that the pre- and post-assessment tests given to the students embed the proper blend of the theoretical and lab type questions.

The second goal of the READ program was to train faculty in different reading strategies and implementation. This was accomplished by having EMT faculty attend workshops and conferences with READ faculty from different disciplines and administrators to discuss best practices. It soon became obvious that reading strategies incorporated in the lower-level courses could not all be used in EMT 1255, so faculty selected those strategies which applied to the EMT 1255 course and READ outcomes.

In EMT 1255, highlighting, text annotation, misconception checks, chunking, modeling, brainstorming, and exit slips were all used to help students become better readers. At the beginning of the course EMT faculty explained and distributed an "Active Reading Checklist" and a textbook reading guide to all EMT 1255 students in the READ sections.

The "Active Reading Checklist" provides the instructor immediate feedback on what strategies the students bring into the course, and what strategies are not being used. The textbook reading guide helps students locate, identify, and review materials learned in the lecture. However, the greatest challenge students face in this course is integrating and using concepts learned in other courses in order to analyze and solve problems in this course, which often require step-by-step analysis and critical thinking.

Chunking

To help students build confidence and motivation, a "chunking" strategy was incorporated into the lectures and reading assignments to scaffold problem-solving. "Chunking" can be defined as a breaking down of a difficult text passage or problem into manageable pieces or "chunks" so that the learner or student can rewrite or state the text in his or her own words. The use of chunks explains how greater knowledge can lead to an increased ability to extract information from the environment, in spite of constant cognitive limitations (Gobet et al., 2001). Faculty have found this strategy cut down the number of formulas students must memorize and also provides the student with a pathway to analyze and solve problems.

Chunking facilitates easy retrieval of information since students have only to list the chunks instead of memorizing all the text. Chunking focuses on one concept at a time pertaining to a given topic at a given time and may be implemented using "pictorial schematics" or models, or in some cases index cards. Simply stated, chunking helps learners visualize a given situation, pair phrases, and plan a method to organize and analyze the data in order to find a designed quantity by integrating concepts learned in previous courses.

Steps or chunks in solving most descriptive electronic/electrical problems in a given course:

1. **Read the problem** carefully and identify the goal of the problem. What do you want to find? You may have read the problem again.
2. **List** all known or given **information** stated in the problem.
3. **Draw a neat schematic diagram** of the circuit to be analyzed. From step 1, label the unknown variables on the schematic.
4. **Determine** if the electronic devices and/or passive devices are conducting.
5. **Devise a plan of attack**, how you are going to solve the problem. List methods and theorems to be used.
6. **Solve the problem.**
7. **Verify the solution.** Is it reasonable?

In the following example the solution to the problem is broken down into chunks, and the results are found by integrating knowledge from dc circuits and algebra courses.

Chunking Example

1. Two silicon diodes are connected in series to a 5-volt power supply, and a load resistor of 2 kΩ. Find the current (I) in the circuit and the voltage (V_R) across the resistor.
2. Given information: R = 2000 Ω = 2 kΩ, E = 5 V, V_{Diode} = 0.7 V for each silicon diode when conducting. Find current (I) and voltage (V_R).
3. A schematic diagram of the circuit to be analyzed.

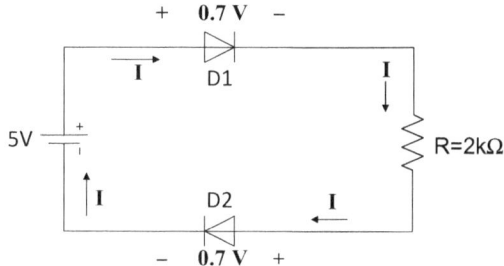

4. All elements are conducting. The voltage across each silicon diode is 0.7 volts from anode to cathode. In a series circuit, if the power supply is greater than 1.4 V (2 × 0.7 V) each diode will conduct.
5. Use: (1) Kirchhoff's Voltage Law (KVL), (2) Ohm's Law
6. 1. V_R = 5 V − 1.4 V = 3.6 V
   2. I_R = I = 3.6 V / 2000 Ω = 1.8 mA
7. It is reasonable. KVL is satisfied.

Modeling

Modeling is another strategy used in EMT 1255 to help students visualize and analyze electronic devices such as diodes and bipolar amplifiers. Figure 7.6a is a common emitter amplifier. To analyze this amplifier students are introduced to the small signal, low frequency "Γ parameter model" in Fig. 7.6b. Using this model, students can find all the ac gains (voltages, current, and power) as well as the input and output impedances of any given amplifier without memorizing the formulas in the text by integrating concepts learned from previous courses.

a

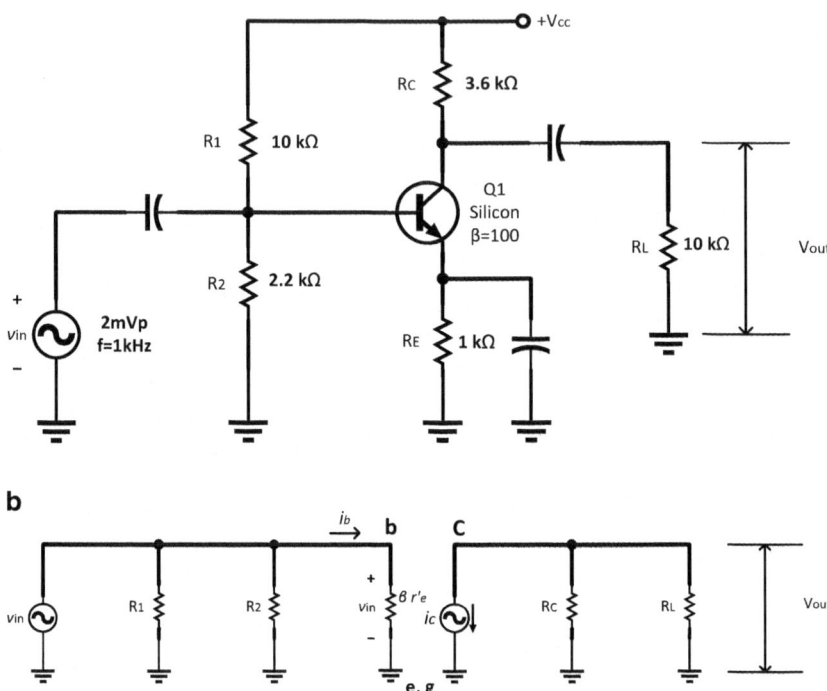

b

Fig. 7.6 (a) Emitter amplifier. (b) Low frequency "Γ parameter model"

Modeling also helps students improve their evaluation skills. Many "what if" type questions can be immediately solved by modifying the standard model accordingly, as specified in a given problem, and then applying Ohm's and Kirchhoff's laws as applicable. This helps build students' confidence and motivation.

Checking Misconceptions

As most engineering students focus on getting the correct answers in the problem-solving process, many of them do not gain a thorough understanding of the theory and concepts that underline the process. Problems are designed to help students identify the misconceptions or insufficient understanding and application of content knowledge while solving problems.

The following example illustrates a common misconception made by many students of electronics.

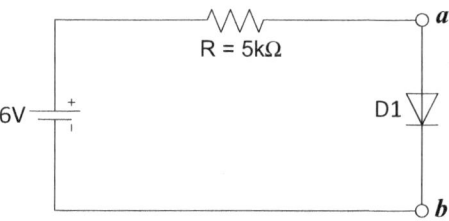

Students are asked to determine the status or state of the diode, and then deduce the voltage drop across the diode from anode pin a to cathode pin b. Most students correctly answer that the diode is reversed bias or non-conducting. However, most students incorrectly answer 0 V across terminals *a-b*. By simply applying KVL around the loop correctly gives −6 V or in general whatever the power supply is set to.

Once the common misconceptions are identified, the errors in the process were evaluated in class discussion. Instead of receiving the answers from their instructor, students were guided to examine the problems and come up with solutions.

Brainstorming

Peer-led team learning was not implemented in EMT 1255. However, small group discussion and learning still took place in the classroom. During brainstorming sessions, students listed sequential steps and then applied different methods to solve a given problem. Brainstorming sessions help to build critical thinking and analytical skills. The interactive class discussion enabled students to think critically and consider diverse perspectives and reasoning in the process of problem-solving. Students were observed to be more engaged during the brainstorming sessions, as compared to solving the problems on their own in class. Students also expressed that they enjoyed their own and others' contributions and could generate more ideas in the discussions. In addition, their ideas were also challenged when they were asked to explain their thoughts, which also promoted deeper understanding and engagement of the content knowledge. Articulating different ways of solving the problems, students were also actively applying the language in the discipline and making it comprehensible to their peers. This is a useful tool in developing disciplinary thinking.

Assessment

Another goal of the READ program was to establish effective assessment metrics to monitor student progress and to share these findings with faculty from other departments at City Tech via workshops and meetings. To this end, three assessment tools were used in EMT 1255. The first was a survey conducted by READ faculty instructors with their students. Students were asked to list whether the course outcomes from the syllabi of EMT 1255 were met, and what READ strategies proved most effective in achieving this goal.

EMT 1255 Assessment Checklist

  I. The course outcomes for EMT 1255 can be summarized as follows: Place a check next to the course outcomes, which you learned from the EMT 1255 course.
   1. Explain and analyze semiconductor devices including diodes, BJTs, FETs, and Op-Amps.
   2. Analyze and design practical electronic circuits consisting of semiconductor devices.
   3. Working in teams, configure, test, and troubleshoot semiconductor devices and circuits in the laboratory.
  II. The formative assessment techniques used in EMT 1255 to learn the course outcomes are the following: Place a check next to the assessment techniques which helped you achieve the course outcomes of part I above.
   1. Lecture presentations and reading assignments/strategies
   2. Homework assignments
   3. Observations
   4. Lab experiments and Lab reports
   5. Solving a given problem using multiple methods
   6. Misconception checks
   7. Brainstorming
   8. Self-assessment
   9. Quizzes/Exams
  III. 1. Can you suggest any additions or improvements to master the course outcomes of part I? Be specific and clear.
   2. List any difficulties you encountered when learning the course outcomes.

During the period of one academic year, the students responded favorably with regard to this survey monitoring course outcomes. Students were also asked to write what READ strategies proved most effective for them. The results are tabulated below.

Chunking/Modeling	85%
Brainstorming	78%
Exit slips	75%
Misconception checks	70%
Tests/Quizzes	65%

Most of the students found chunking and modeling strategies as the most helpful classroom routines. An interesting result of the survey showed brainstorming sessions came in second with a 78% favorable rating, while exit slips and misconception checks were also considered to be useful in helping students to reflect on their learning process and the strategies they used in problem-solving. The results reported by students revealed that conventional assessments such as tests and quizzes were not as effective as the other strategies to drive their learning.

Pre- and Post-READ Assessment on Electronics
In addition, with the help of the READ administrators, faculty developed pre- and post-READ assessments to monitor performance criteria in comprehension, analysis, context, and evaluation. The assessment rubric was similar to the one in Chap. 3.

As college educational demands are constantly changing, ABET, the Accreditation Board of Engineering Technology, has been tasked in finding a new set of guidelines to assess engineering technology programs in the United States. From 2000 to 2017 ABET required college engineering technology programs to adhere to Criterion 3, 11 Student Outcomes (*a-k*) found in TCK 2000. ABET developed a new Criterion 3 with 7 Student Outcomes in effect in the United States in 2019–2020 (see Table 7.1). The new Criterion 3 in Fig. 7.6 reduces and redistributes the 11 Student Outcomes from TCK 2000 to 7 Student Outcomes.

The new Criterion 3 in the 2019–2020 cycle lists the seven skills engineering programs must show in order to achieve accreditation. With the help of the READ administrators, the READ team developed a new Integrated ABET-READ assessment rubric which specifically targeted ABET Student Outcomes 1 and 6 from the new Criterion 3 standard (see Table 7.2) This rubric will be used beginning in the spring semester of 2020. This rubric will

Table 7.1   2019–2020 TAC/ABET Criterion 3 Student Outcomes

1. An ability to identify, formulate, and solve complex engineering problems by applying principles of engineering, science, and mathematics
2. An ability to apply engineering design to produce solutions that meet specified needs with consideration of public health, safety, and welfare, as well as global, cultural, social, environmental, and economic factors
3. An ability to communicate effectively with a range of audiences
4. An ability to recognize ethical and professional responsibilities in engineering situations and make informed judgments, which must consider the impact of engineering solutions in global, economic, environmental, and societal contexts
5. An ability to function effectively on a team whose members together provide leadership, create a collaborative and inclusive environment, establish goals, plan tasks, and meet objectives
6. An ability to develop and conduct appropriate experimentation, analyze and interpret data, and use engineering judgment to draw conclusions
7. An ability to acquire and apply new knowledge as needed, using appropriate learning strategies

Source: *ABET Accreditation*, 2019–2020. Retrieved from www.abet.org

Table 7.2   Integrated ABET-READ assessment rubric

Performance criteria	4	3	2	1
1. An ability to identify, formulate, and solve complex engineering problems by applying principles of engineering, science, and mathematics;	Understands the main ideas and major details of written and graphical data from the text and is able to make logical inferences.	Understands most of the information in the text and is able to make some logical inferences.	Understands some ideas in the text and struggles to make logical inferences.	Unable to understand the main points of the text and make logical inferences.
ABET Outcome (1) maps to Comprehension and Context of the READ rubric.	Able to identify and use all of the concepts and ideas from the text to solve proficiently problems having several unknowns.	Able to identify and use most concepts and ideas from the text to solve problems having several unknowns.	Struggles to identify concepts and ideas from the text needed to solve basic problems.	Unable to identify concepts and ideas from the text needed to solve problems.

(*continued*)

Table 7.2 (continued)

Performance criteria	4	3	2	1
6. An ability to develop and conduct appropriate experimentation, analyze and interpret data, and use engineering judgment to draw conclusions;	Understands and analyzes relationships among ideas, and interprets information in diverse formats and media.	Understands and analyzes some of the relationships among ideas, and interprets information in diverse formats and media.	Has difficulties in identifying relationships among ideas and interpreting information in diverse formats and media.	Unable to identify and analyze the relationships between ideas and interpret information in diverse formats and media.
ABET Outcome (6) maps to Analysis and Evaluation of the READ rubric.	Able to apply and integrate a knowledge of math, science, and technology to evaluate and/or solve engineering technology problems. Responses show critical reasoning and relevance.	Able to apply and integrate most knowledge of math, science, and technology in evaluating and/or solving engineering technology problems. Responses are relevant, but not complete.	Has some difficulties integrating a knowledge of math, science, and technology in evaluating and/or solving engineering technology problems. Responses lack critical reasoning and relevance.	Unable to integrate a knowledge of math, science, and technology, to evaluate and/or solve engineering technology problems. Responses lack critical reasoning and relevance.

4 Full proficiency, *3* Adequate proficiency, *2* Approaching proficiency, *1* Low proficiency

not only verify data presented in the standard READ rubric, but assess the new ABET outcomes 1 and 6, and will be presented in the upcoming 2019–2020 accreditation cycle.

"Outcome 1" focuses on the process of identifying, formulating, and solving problems by applying engineering and mathematics principles. This involves the cognitive process of literal comprehension, and organizing and interpreting data and information. The outcome specifically emphasizes the application of engineering, science, and mathematics principles to achieve problem-solving. The purpose of mapping this outcome to the READ rubric is when developing the assessment, we require students to draw upon their prior knowledge and synthesize it to new knowledge to solve problems. While "Outcome 6" also highlights the role of application, its emphasis is on the strategies and reasoning that students use to achieve the problem-solving objectives. It is particularly vital to developing disciplinary literacy in Engineering.

The READ assessment results consistently revealed that there was a major weakness in students' ability to evaluate problems and information. Students scored above target expectations in comprehension, analysis, and context, but struggled with the evaluation criteria.

To address this concern, faculty have now added more "evaluation type" questions in their presentations, lectures, and READ assignments. To strengthen this area of learning, students are also asked to reflect on their thinking, reasoning, and problem-solving processes instead of simply providing the answers. Reviewing their misconceptions can also help them identify when their reasoning and evaluation fall short.

Before the implementing the additional strategies, the gain in student performance in the READ assessment was 4.9% in the mean rubric scores in the semester before implementation of the new strategies. The improvement in the following semester was 18.7% after the implementation of the additional strategies and indicated a 14.8% increase compared to the previous semester of the academic year.

After Implementation of Strategies	Initial (Pre-)reading Assessment	Mean Rubric Score: 2.45
	Final (Post-)reading Assessment	Mean Rubric Score: 2.91
	Δ MRS = +18.7%	
Before Implementation of Strategies	Initial (Pre-)reading Assessment	Mean Rubric Score: 2.44
	Final (Post-)reading Assessment	Mean Rubric Score: 2.54
	Δ MRS = +4.9%	

7.5   Conclusion

During the past three years, assessment results reflect a marked improvement in discipline literacy and critical thinking due to various READ strategies employed in first-year engineering courses in the CET department.

Disciplinary literacy in today's engineering industry is more broadly defined than having sufficient technical knowledge and skills. It is instead a way of thinking, speaking, and functioning in a dynamic environment where ideas, technologies, knowledge, and teamwork at various levels converge and are actively engaged with one another. To improve specific areas of disciplinary literacy among our students, we implemented formative assessments and strategies that better address their academic needs as well as supporting their preparation sufficiently for a successful engineering career. There is no doubt that in the three courses described discipline literacy improved significantly. This can be shown by the improved scores of the final over the initial assessment reading assignments as well as the overall retention rates. Another benefit of the READ program in collaboration with self-assessment is that student motivation to learn and confidence to participate in communicating engineering concepts and solving engineering problems have been enhanced. When students understand the purpose of a task and participate in establishing meaningful goals using criteria to assess their work, they not only reach new heights but also tend to incorporate learning strategies toward their scholastic and professional goals.

REFERENCES

ABET Criteria For Accrediting Engineering Programs, 2019–2020. [Online]. Available: https://www.abet.org/wp-content/uploads/2018/03/C3_C5_mapping_SEC_1-13-2018.pdf

Bloom, B. S., Krathwohl, D. R., & Masia, B. B. (1956). *Taxonomy of educational objectives: The classification of educational goals handbook I. cognitive domain.* New York: Longman.

But, J. C., Kwon, O., & Laboy, H. (2015). Reading effectively in first year electromechanical engineering courses. *ASEE 7th First Year Engineering Experience Conference*, August 3–4, Roanoke, VA.

Dreyfuss, A. E., & Fraiman, A. (2015). Peer-led team learning: An active learning method for the 21st century. *Proceedings of 8th Annual International Conference of Education, Research and Innovation, 698–706;* Seville, Spain, November 16–18; ISSN: 2340-1095.

Dreyfuss, A. E., Villatoro, M., Loui, M. C., Becvar, J., Saupe, G., & Johnson, W. (2015). Getting past the first year: Retaining engineering majors. *Proceedings of 2015 IEEE Frontiers in Education Conference*, Session S3D; El Paso, Texas, October 21–24.

Floyd, T. L., & Buchla, D. M. (2013). *Analog fundamentals: A systems approach.* Upper Saddle River, NJ: Prentice Hall.

Fowler, B. (2004). Bloom's taxonomy and critical thinking. *Critical Thinking Across the Curriculum Project*, Longview Community College, Missouri. Downloaded on 1/8/2005 from http://www.kcmetro.cc.mo.us/longview/ctac/blooms.htm

Gobet, F., Lane, P. C., Croker, S., Cheng, P. C., Jones, G., Oliver, I., et al. (2001). Chunking mechanisms in human learning. *Trends in Cognitive Sciences, 5*(6), 236–243.

Kwon, O., Xu, C., & But, J. C. (2016). Reading matters in first year electrical circuits course. *ASEE 8th First Year Engineering Experience Conference*, Columbus, OH, August.

Liou-Mark, J., Dreyfuss, A. E., Yuen-Lau, L., Lu, C., Scott, S., Young, J. A., et al. (2013). From peer-assisted learning to peer-led team learning at City Tech: An historical overview. *Conference Proceedings of the Peer-Led Team Learning International Society, May 17–19, 2012*, New York City College of Technology of the City University of New York, www.pltlis.org; ISSN 2329–2113.

Peters, E., Västfjäll, D., Slovic, P., Mertz, C. K., Mazzocco, K., & Dickert, S. (2006). Numeracy and decision making. *Psychological Science, 17*, 407–413.

Pinkhasik, A. (2015). The use of reflective strategies to develop problem-solving, reading, and writing skills in electro-mechanical manufacturing workshop. *2014 Conference Proceedings of the Peer-Led Team Learning International Society, May 29–31, 2014*, California State University at Dominguez Hills, www.pltlis.org; ISSN 2329-2113.

Richard, C. (2012). *Motivation in the workshop: How can leaders use this knowledge? Peer-led team learning: Leader training.* Online at https://pltlis.org/wp-content/uploads/2012/10/Motivation-Richard-Motivation.pdf

Rugarcia, A., Felder, R. M., Woods, D. R., & Stice, J. E. (2000). The future of engineering education I. A vision for a new century. *Chemical Engineering Education, 34*(1), 16–25.

Schemo, D. J. (2006, August 9). It takes more than school to close the gap. *The New York Times*, Web.

Shanahan, T., & Shanahan, C. (2012). What is disciplinary literacy and why does it matter? *Topics in Language Disorders, 32*(1), 7–18.

Vygotsky, L. (1978). *Mind and society.* Cambridge, MA: Harvard University Press.

Wilson, S. B., & Varma-Nelson, P. (2016). Small groups, significant impact: A review of peer-led team learning research with implications for STEM education researchers and faculty. *Journal of Chemical Education, 93*, 1686–1702.

Xu, C., Kwon, O., But, J., Mendoza, B., Liou-Mark, J., & Ostrom, R. (2018). *Peer-led team learning bridges the learning gap in a first-year engineering technology course.* ASEE Mid-Atlantic Section Spring Conference, Washington, District of Columbia https://peer.asee.org/29471

CHAPTER 8

Mathematical Literacy and Critical Thinking

Estela Rojas and Nadia Benakli

> *...Socrates: And it won't be as a result of any teaching that he'll have become knowledgeable: he'll just have been asked questions, and he'll recover the knowledge by himself, from within himself.*
> —Meno dialogue by Plato

8.1 Introduction

When faculty in any discipline start planning their lessons, some of the important questions they might ask include the following: What makes a lesson effective? How can students become empowered through the learning process? In addition to covering content knowledge, college faculty are entrusted with the task of *developing students' abilities to become independent learners.* This potential of preparing students as lifelong learners is crucial. Carnevale and Smith (2013) state that "learning is now a fact of life if workers are going to keep up with the blur of change in modern workplaces. Workers who have 'learned how to learn' can achieve competency

E. Rojas (✉) • N. Benakli
New York City College of Technology, City University of New York, Brooklyn, NY, USA
e-mail: erojas@citytech.cuny.edu

© The Author(s) 2020
J. C. But (ed.), *Teaching College-Level Disciplinary Literacy*,
https://doi.org/10.1007/978-3-030-39804-0_8

in other required workplace skills, but for those who have not, learning is not as rapid, nor as efficient or comprehensive" (p. 4).

Mathematics is more than hard numbers and data; it is a conceptual tool for social change. When integrating mathematics and statistics into world problems, the solid numbers speak not only to logic (*logos*) but also to our emotions (*pathos*). Mathematics, a discipline that has a pervasive presence in everyday life, can be a catalyst for change—both socially and personally. These real-life connections can make a personal difference to math students who would otherwise be bored or unable to relate to the subject. If it is taught right, mathematics can be a great conversation starter, a mirror of facts, supporting great truths, and resolving challenges.

The role of educators is to guide students through their personal and educational journeys, throughout the paths of both their successes and failures. Therefore, gaining a solid knowledge of the student population is key to reaching the widest spread. Each student has various gifts and weaknesses within the discipline, and students come in with their own unique perspective, history, and background knowledge pertaining to the subject. To ensure that teaching and learning is relevant, mathematics educators have to consider these facts, which, for instance, can inform the design or selection of word problems in a mathematics class. Students need to feel some kind of ownership in the investigation process by asking questions and sharing their opinions on the subject in a supportive and safe environment. For novice students, even understanding the problems can be challenging. In mathematics, words can sometimes be misleading, language can be interpreted to the students' natural language, and there are different levels of comprehension intake, or other learning differences, that can alter reading and processing of word problems. In addition, faculty's knowledge of the social culture of the student body can facilitate the process of learning. Students can progress more readily in understanding and problem-solving as faculty frame the word problems in relatable contexts.

8.2   Challenges That Mathematics Instructors May Encounter in Today's Classrooms

Today's society tends to give students the wrong impression that learning should happen in an instant, not knowing that to be engaged in a formal learning process requires time, discipline, responsibility, and to be equipped with several competencies. Therefore, instructors are confronted with several challenges to motivate and immerse students in their learning experience. Some of the challenges are the following:

1. Students come in ill-prepared for higher education. Some are greatly lacking both academic and life skills needed for this transition.
2. Students lack prerequisite knowledge and skills. While each prior school is different, some students enter college without the basic concepts or needed classes to progress in the subject.
3. Selecting material and problems that engage and motivate students to learn mathematics. Material needs to inspire students and create broader-thinking questions that translate into other aspects of life and their world.
4. Many students have inaccurate preconceived ideas about mathematics such as "men are better than women", and "mathematics can only be understood by a selective group of bright people". Mathematics must be made accessible to all students, not just perceived as a selective subject for an astute few.
5. Many college students experience "math anxiety". The social and emotional triggers of math and test performance can be tempered with open conversation and aid from the instructor.

Primarily, in many classrooms, mathematics teachers need to heal students' negative experiences toward math and help them overcome the stigma that they will never amount to being "math people", or those who are born with the "math genes". These myths are some of the issues which can lead to students' resentment against phobia toward mathematics and can cause math anxiety, hindering learning and interfering with performance on tests. To help students develop a positive attitude toward mathematics, instructors need to promote an encouraging and supportive learning environment, which acknowledges individual students' histories and capacities, including both their personal strengths and challenges. Anthony and Walshaw (2009) recognized that "effective teachers take student competencies as starting points for their planning and their moment-by-moment decision making. Existing competencies, including language, reading and listening skills, ability to cope with complexity, and mathematical reasoning, become resources to build upon" (p. 11). Mathematics is not merely a subject to be taken as a rote course of education, but it is crucial to so many diverse career paths and everyday practices. However, sometimes students cannot even pass the roadblocks that bar their access to the vast knowledge of mathematics. In fact, the path to comprehension can be daunting to math students and instructors alike:

Mathematics education is a key to increasing the post-school and citizenship opportunities of young people, but today, as in the past, many students struggle with mathematics and become disaffected as they continually encounter obstacles to engagement. It is imperative, therefore, that we understand what effective mathematics teaching looks like – and what teachers can do to break this pattern. (Anthony & Walshaw, 2009, p. 6)

Mathematics teachers in the U.S. face an additional challenge as students' math skills performance are continuously in decline. Based on the Program for International Student Assessment (PISA) 2015 score results, the U.S. students ranked 40th in mathematics among the 73 countries who participated in the assessment, and the score of the U.S. was lower than the Organization for Economic Cooperation and Development (OECD) average (OECD, 2016). Between the 2009 and 2015 PISA assessments, the average math score of the U.S. fell from 487 in 2009, 481 in 2012 to 470 in 2015.

Many mathematics classes are still taught using the traditional rote memorization approach. This approach hinders students' abilities to make connections and improve their inquiry skills:

Students believed that they were not responsible for mathematical understanding, only for their ability to plug in numbers to the correct algorithms and calculate the answers with accuracy. If they were able to do this, by their way of thinking, they were mathematically proficient. This view resulted in large numbers of students who failed to retain the knowledge of mathematics that they had "learned" and who were also unable to apply what they did know to solving problems in unfamiliar contexts. (Sammons, 2011, p. 252)

There is no meaningful learning when there is no transfer of knowledge. It is not surprising that students' math scores are trending downward. Therefore, it is imperative that we transform the way we teach mathematics and break the traditional teacher-centered pattern. Faculty need to understand how learning happens.

Mathematics teachers should aim to integrate strategies in the lesson plan to engage students in the learning process, nurture a positive attitude toward mathematics, and support the development of students' mathematical thinking and reasoning. At this important juncture, we need to ask ourselves, what entails to think critically and solve problems? How this could be a platform to develop students' mathematical literacy? How do we become actively involved in the process of thinking in Mathematics?

What are the necessary skills needed to go through this process? What are some methodologies that will assist students in understanding their thinking process?

8.3   DEVELOPING MATHEMATICAL LITERACY THROUGH THE THINKING PROCESS

Thinking critically is a conscious act and process that requires very specific actions. Thinking critically begins with the identification of an idea or ideas which arise through the act of observing an object, situation, or a phenomenon. In this process, concentration is essential in order to begin a task, work through its challenges, and ultimately arrive at a conclusion. By understanding the way thinking happens, a student will be better prepared as a professional and as an active contributor to society. Faculty, thus, have a responsibility to help students acquire the necessary skills that support the thinking process.

To help students learn mathematics and become better problem-solvers, faculty can focus on developing their thinking, understanding, and proficiency in the following competencies/skills:

1. Observations through reading (key words, general and specific math vocabulary).
2. Inquiry/Questions (distinction between questions that facilitate/hinder the thinking process).
3. Connections (find answers to their questions, application of concepts).
4. Listening (listen to their own thread of thought and listen to class-mates' ideas).
5. Communication (comprehension of the math concepts in writing or orally).
6. Emotions (distinction of emotions, by self-observation, that could facilitate or impede learning: motivation, attitudes, feelings, curiosity).
7. Collaboration (work and share ideas in partnership in order to find common conclusion/answer to the task).
8. Reflection (assess self-performance/mistakes in the learning process).

The following problem will be used throughout the different components stated above to exemplify each one of the competencies (Table 8.1).

Table 8.1 Trees and the Environment

While we all have a very personal connection to the natural world and our environment, the data collected about the multiple benefits of trees and forests span every aspect of life. Our social and economic well-being depends on the state of our trees. The animal population and the future of the world's climate are directly linked. Our health is the forest's health. Through numerical data and equations, we can establish vital concepts that can aid with saving our precious natural resources, and counter the effects of mankind's impact on the environment

"Forests cover 31% of the land area on our planet. They help people thrive and survive by, for example, purifying water and air and providing people with jobs; some 13.2 million people across the world have a job in the forest sector and another 41 million have a job that is related to the sector. Many animals also rely on forests. Eighty percent of the world's land-based species, such as elephants and rhinos, live in forests. Forests also play a critical role in mitigating climate change because they act as a carbon sink—soaking up carbon dioxide that would otherwise be free in the atmosphere and contribute to ongoing changes in climate patterns." (World Wildlife Fund [WWF], n.d.)

Rachel's car runs on gasoline and has a fuel economy of about 22.0 miles per gallon. Rachel drives around 11,500 miles per year. Given that every gallon of gasoline burned creates about 8887 grams of carbon dioxide

1. *How many metric tons of carbon dioxide did Rachel's car create per year? How much is it in pounds?*
2. *How much carbon dioxide per mile is emitted by Rachel's car?*
3. *A mature tree can absorb as much as 48 pounds of carbon dioxide per year. How many mature trees are necessary to absorb the pollution that Rachel created in a year?*
4. *Esdia town has a 50 acres forest with 400 mature trees per acre. Will this forest be able to absorb their emitted carbon dioxide?*
5. *If there are a million cars circulating in Esdia town, similar to Rachel's, how many mature trees are necessary in order to absorb the carbon dioxide created in a year?*
6. *From your perspective, what could you do in order to contribute to the solution of too much carbon dioxide in the air from cars?*
7. *What other kinds of pollution do cars bring into the environment? How are these pollutants affecting humans?*
8. *Write a one-page reflection about the importance of our forests, the different threats to our forests, and how this is affecting all living beings on our planet. If the trend continues, what will happen in the future?*

8.4   OBSERVATION SKILLS AND CLOSE READING

The act of observing is done by finding elements and characteristics of the situation in question. The recognition of the elements is determined by the observer's own experiences and is limited or expanded by them. Although we all possess an innate ability of observation, it is a skill that can be developed, especially during childhood education. The answer to who is responsible for supporting learners to acquire and develop this skill is simple yet complex at the same time. Observation is the first step in any life process. It is one of the first skills used by babies and children to relate to the world they are now part of. A long way from the challenges of early life, scientists must also engage in this elementary and essential step as the foundation of any theory or experiment they wish to pursue. However, math teachers do not always pay enough attention to this skill when they develop their lesson plans. Also, crucial to note is that telling students to observe is not enough, instructors have to prepare students to develop the skills "through education of the senses" to observe in order to "give them power and the means for this observation" (Montessori & Holmes, 1912, p. 229).

Observing is different from just seeing or noticing something. Unfortunately, most of the time, students do not know how to observe. According to Community College, Massachusetts Institute of Technology (CCMIT) (n.d.), "observation is more than just noticing details to answer questions you already have. It also involves engaging with your environment, deliberately noticing details, and using logic and imagination to visualize possible outcomes". As faculty, we need to explicitly give directions to students, so that they could understand and appreciate the power of observation in the thinking process. In mathematics, students need to observe shapes, math symbols, text, diagrams, data, numbers, and so on. They need to observe with a purpose that includes but is not restricted to understanding a concept, solving a problem, or writing a conclusion, or making connections, or asking questions.

Observation through close reading should be deliberately embedded in activities and examples as a preliminary step to finding solutions to problems and/or to the understanding of mathematical concepts. This can be done in a progressive manner. Before reading words, syntax, and symbols, students could be asked to describe their observations of a picture or painting. Students might be surprised to find out that they could come up with different observations of the same item, as every person observes from the prism of their own prior knowledge and experiences. For instance, the students could see a right triangle drawn on the blackboard, but not necessarily observe where the right angle is located, or notice the other two angles involved, or any other relations that could be perceived in a right triangle. This also takes place when it comes to problems involving symbols. All students can see the same symbol x. However, some students read it as the variable x, others as the product symbol. Alternatively, in the case of $2x$ some students do not notice that there is a multiplication between the number 2 and x. Even a simple confusion about a mathematics symbol, or a misunderstanding of a mathematics expression can lead to a student's frustration, which can impact his/her interest and motivation in the subject.

When unguided, observations are subjective and personal to the observer. But in the learning process, observations should be intentional and guided. How can faculty in general help students develop their observation skills? It can be done by asking specific questions that aid students to consistently make the type of observations that are necessary for understanding the mathematical language and solving a problem.

In particular, in a mathematics class the observations based on the context of the problem are important for the understanding of the problem. As students observe, they need to read the context of the problem carefully. They have to pay attention to the sequence of events, analyze the use of language, and mentally transcribe it into mathematical concepts that they have learned. Subsequently, they have to communicate their observations. Therefore, instructors need to create activities in which students will be able to write or share orally.

To guide students to develop observation skills, the following steps could be implemented:

1. Ask students to:
   • Focus on a particular object.
   • Write a list of what they see (two or three items).
   • Share the list with another student (Think-Pair-Share).
   • Merge their lists.
   • Share with the whole class. The instructor will call several students from the different pairs to write only one observation on the board.
   • Explain and discuss their choice of observations in order to decide which ones will support the purpose of the activity.
2. Guide students to discuss vocabulary in context, embedded in the problem.
   • Find meaning to the words in English and math to distinguish their differences and commonalities.

To do so, the development of students' language skills becomes a key component to successfully accomplish the activities. Specifically building the disciplinary vocabulary and language in the subject matter is fundamental.

Faculty should pay close attention to language issues such as polysemous words that have more than one meaning or definition and have specific mathematical meaning as well as everyday meaning in the English language. For example, the word "average" in mathematics can mean the "mode", the "median" or the "mean", but in English, the words "average" is used to describe something (or someone) that (who) is not excellent but not bad either. The word "volume" in math is the size in a three-dimensional space. In English, the word "volume" is used to describe the intensity of sound. As another example, the word multiply implies that something is increasing, getting larger in the English language; but in mathematics, if the number we are multiplying by is 0.1, then the product is smaller than the original number. In an algebra class, students do not know the difference between the words "equation" and "expression", "term" and "factor", and "simplify" and "evaluate", for example. If a student does not understand or is confused by the meaning of a word in a problem, the student's learning becomes obstructed, and he/she will not be able to move forward with the lesson.

Another hurdle for understanding mathematics for English learners can be linked to their lack of prior knowledge and socio-cultural experience to understand some of the word problems. For English learners who need to translate between English and their mother's tongue, a word could be translated to have a different meaning in addition to the meaning in mathematics. The three different meanings will confuse the student. Faculty should be very sensitive in their selection of word problems in order not to offend students with different social and cultural backgrounds. However, faculty do not always address these problems, because "teachers of mathematics are often unaware of the barriers to understanding that students from a different language and culture must overcome" (Anthony & Walshaw, 2009, p. 13).

Therefore, one very important component of the lesson plan should be explicitly focused on students' understanding of English and mathematics words, and expanding their vocabulary. Instructors could use concept maps, the Frayer Model, and any other pedagogical tool available to build vocabulary in the discipline.

Faculty typically approach students expecting them to already have the reading and observation competencies that are necessary to do two things: to identify the question being asked and to identify the given information that are instrumental to solving the problem. This kind of assumption of

Table 8.2   Trees and the Environment: Observations

Observations:
1. *Trees clean the air for other living species to breathe (context of the problem)*
2. *Key words: mitigating, carbon sink, atmosphere, environment, pollution, carbon dioxide, mature trees, fuel economy, gallon, and metric ton*
3. *We have different units: grams and pounds*
4. *Different quantities: miles per gallon, and miles per year*
5. *One gallon creates 8887 grams of carbon dioxide*
6. *Rachel drives around 11,500 miles per year*
7. *An acre of mature trees absorbs 20,000 pounds of carbon dioxide*

familiarity and proficiency with preliminary thinking and reading skills is deeply problematic and counterproductive.

When making observations and engaging in close reading, students are learning to:

1. Collect evidence.
2. Organize their ideas.
3. Find explanations.
4. Make connections.
5. Make distinctions between facts and judgments.

As students learn to organize their observations through active and close reading, they can start making connections between the objects and key concepts. These connections will often come in the form of a question, which brings us to inquiry skills.

Next, we provide a sample of list of observations for the "Trees and the Environment" problem introduced in Table 8.2.

8.5   INQUIRY/QUESTIONING SKILLS

To develop students' mathematical literacy, it is necessary that faculty engage students in the habit of inquiry. Anthony and Walshaw (2009) remark that "by asking questions, effective teachers require students to participate in mathematical thinking and problem solving" (p. 17). Questions are essential for students to assess and understand contents/problems, connect ideas, and communicate. With this intention, faculty aims to facilitate and support students to build the skills of the art of asking questions. By stimulating students' natural inquisitiveness, better questions arise. As research indicates, creating prompts, taxonomies, and teacher modeling also encourages an educational environment that promotes conversation and interest (Chin & Osborne, 2008). Using a variety of questions of different difficulty levels and asking students to generate questions rather than only to provide answers during the lesson, the faculty can support the students' organization of ideas, assessment of their own thoughts, and growth in their process of thinking. As questions are at the center of the cognitive process, learning how to ask the "good" questions stimulates creativity and leads to deeper understanding. Unfortunately, many instructors do not ask the "good" questions. Instead, they ask ineffective questions that hinder the learning process such as "Do you have any questions?", "So far so good?", or "Do you understand?" These questions are usually followed by silence in the classroom as students worry about showing their ignorance.

To prepare an effective lesson plan, it is important to have in mind in what way we, as faculty, will be impacting students' learning process. To help us accomplish this endeavor, it is necessary to think about two aspects—to promote learning in the cognitive and affective domains. (McComas & Abraham, 2004) developed the following questions to help achieve these goals. They enable instructors to include a more effective process of inquiry when developing their lesson plans:

Cognitive Domain Questions

1. How often do you use questions to establish a foundation for new work?
2. How do your questions help reveal or clear up misconceptions?
3. To what extent do your questions encourage students to listen to each other's responses, opinions?
4. To what extent do your questions verify the degree of comprehension of your students?
5. To what extent do you pre-plan key questions you want to ask during the lesson?
6. To what extent do you consider possible responses to these key questions and strategies to use in the event that something goes astray?
7. Do you ask a variety of questions—recall versus thought questions?
8. To what extent do your questions ask students to interpret, to analyze, to think critically, to see relationships, or to judge?
9. To what extent do your questions call for students to think for themselves?

Affective Domain Questions

1. How often do you challenge students by asking questions that arouse their curiosity? Do you make them want to know more?
2. Does your question asking regime help build class rapport?
3. Do you get all students involved in class discussions?
4. Do you distribute your questions both to students who volunteer to answer and to those who do not?
5. Do you ask questions to discover special interests of your students?
6. Do students speak to each other when responding or only to you?
7. Do you distribute your questions both to students who volunteer to answer and to those who do not?
8. Do you accept student responses in a neutral manner or do you use verbal rewards (Good! Fine idea! Great!) or sanctions (No! Wrong!)?
9. To what extent do your questions promote self-evaluation by your students?
10. Does your question asking regime help students to feel that each one has something positive to contribute to the class?
11. Do you wait a reasonable time for students to think about their responses before calling on them or permitting them to speak?
12. Do you encourage your students to ask questions?

Students learn by asking questions as these lead to information that unlocks the door to learning. Active questioning between the instructor and the class leads to a deeper, more comprehensive dialogue of the subject—it is a two-way street that must involve exchange between both parties. The communication should not be limited merely to calling and responding, but co-creating questions and answers to problems. To accomplish this, faculty need to instigate inquisitiveness in their classes and ask questions that engage students and lead to responsive problem-solving. By merely asking students to repeat procedure and recall formulas, students are kept at a basic level of comprehension. Asking more dynamic questions allows students to assess what they do and do not yet understand, builds connections, and relates to other concepts and ideas from peers. Asking specific questions helps students in breaking down a more complex concept. All of these aspects assist students in advancing from merely searching for quick answers to becoming independent problem-solvers. To gain a deeper understanding of mathematics, students have to learn how to transition from answering simple questions to more sophisticated inquiry (Chin & Osborne, 2008; Sammons, 2011).

The questioning process will not support the learning process without integrating effective and actionable feedback. Instructors need to give constructive and useful feedback that reinforces what students did well and guide them to find and correct their mistakes. To do so, instructors need to understand the types of mistakes their students make, and misconceptions they have:

> Learners make mistakes for many reasons, including insufficient time or care. But errors also arise from consistent, alternative interpretations of mathematical ideas that represent the learner's attempts to create meaning. Rather than dismiss such ideas as "wrong thinking", effective teachers view them as a natural and often necessary stage in a learner's conceptual development. (Anthony & Walshaw, 2009, p. 12)

One very important element of the questioning process is wait-time. This relates to question 11 in the affective domain category. The concept of "wait-time" was first introduced by Mary Budd Rowe (1974). It is important to give students enough time to understand, reflect, and connect the question asked, before needing to elaborate an answer. Research has found that faculty in average wait between 0.7 and 1.4 seconds before moving on and answering their own questions (Stahl, 1994). By giving enough time for students to ponder not only the question itself—but also *question construction*, *goal orientation*, *individual elements* versus *containing context*—instructors create the possibility for students to shift from passive to active learning. In this process, students will unlock an abundance of connections between their observations and their questions. For the wait-time to have an impact on the learning process, students need to feel comfortable to share their ideas. They also need to have enough time to listen to the ideas voiced by their classmates and comment on those.

As Rowe (1974) indicated, "Exploration and inquiry require students to put together ideas in new ways, to try out new thoughts, to take risks. For that they not only need time but they need a sense of being safe" (p. 4).

Metacognition and Bloom's Taxonomy

Our ultimate goal as educators is to prepare our students to become independent learners and thinkers. In this process, it is necessary to get students "thinking about thinking", or bringing them to the level of "metacognition", which is defined as the "awareness or analysis of one's own learning or thinking process". Flavell (1976) was the first to use the word metacognition "metacognition refers to one's knowledge concerning one's own cognitive processes or anything related to them, e.g., the learning-relevant properties of information or data" (p. 232). Furthermore, "metacognitive practices empower students to have an active control by monitoring and assessing their own learning. Metacognition is very useful and proved to be effective with mathematical problem solving" (Lester, 1982; Schneider & Artelt, 2010; Silver, 1982; Verschaffel et al., 1999).

As faculty, it is fundamental to realize that what students consider as learning is commonly the misconception that it is our responsibility to teach them, and that it depends on us if they learn or not. Therefore, our first task is to help students to change their beliefs about what "learning" is, and what steps to take for learning to occur. To accomplish this, our questions should be structured to promote higher order of cognition according to Bloom's Taxonomy as presented below. This way we can help students apply those cognitive processes that enable them to become independent thinkers. Moreover, students should be flexible in their ability to adopt different strategies conducive to learning, and plan and develop their goals as learners. For example, they need to reflect on their goals, whether they are prepared for an exam, and what do they need to change to reach their goals. In addition, students need to be able to self-evaluate and self-question themselves. In other words, they need to practice how to find errors in their work, to which end, they need to develop their observation skills and be able to make connections. Also, they ought to understand that on many occasions, there might be different approaches to a particular situation. Sometimes, because of their partial understanding and limited ideas, it is more productive for students to collaborate with others. Through collaboration, students can learn to listen, to articulate and express their own ideas and compromise, and be able to reach agreements based on facts and evidence. The diverse information and ideas generated in a group setting come from the contributions and observations of each member. An important benefit of collaboration is that the student will develop the capacity to accept the ideas and integrate the contributions of others to solve a problem. In this manner, solutions become the result of group work, and there is no need to become defensive or protective of one's ideas. We must realize that collaboration also motivates students to develop their vocabulary and expand their reasoning capacities as they express their thoughts.

Based on the cognitive categories (knowledge, comprehension, application, analysis, synthesis, and evaluation) of the learning process developed by Bloom (1956), we have a comprehensive overview of how learning happens. We need to connect all the different levels of the categories to understand the progression and relationships between these processes. It becomes even more transparent when these categories are described as actions. Anderson and Krathwohl (2001) developed the revised Bloom's Taxonomy where they replaced each category (nouns) by words that represent action (verbs): Remembering, Understanding, Applying, Analyzing, Evaluating, and Creating.

Specifically, the frameworks of Bloom's Taxonomy help inform instructors how to plan their lessons based on the different levels of cognition. These levels are crucial to developing students' thinking abilities and engaging them in problem-solving activities. Instructors are responsible for planning their lessons by incorporating the cognitive categories into questions. Instructors need to combine open and closed questions in the lesson plan, and include a significant percentage of questions of higher order of cognition. Renaud and Murray (2007) observed that there is a strong relationship between the frequency of Bloom's higher order of cognition and the thinking process. Closed questions mainly consist of recalling information (such as "what is the formula for the quadratic equation?"—this is a lower level of cognition; "based on the given information, are there enough forests to clean the carbon dioxide air from the air?"—higher level). These are restrictive in developing the learning process of the students. On the other hand, open questions promote learning, understanding, ideas, and stimulate creativity. Open questions (such as "what is an example of a proportion?"—lower level of cognition; "what are different ways you might solve the car pollution problem?"—higher level) can foster the use of the higher-level thinking that incites critical thinking and supports deeper learning. As a result, students will be taking ownership of their knowledge and be able to make connections to prior and new knowledge and ideas. As we ask students questions, we do not have to restrict them only to the formats of "Why"; a variety of questions that include the "How", "When", and "What if" are very important contributors to the critical thinking process, and help students develop their own questioning skills. For instance, in the "Trees and the Environment" problem (see Table 8.1), the questions cover two different orders of Bloom's Taxonomy. For example, question 8 requires the processes of evaluating and creating, which are in the higher order of the cognitive domain. On the other hand, questions 2 and 4 fit into the lower order as it requires applying and understanding.

Table 8.3 Trees and the Environment: Questioning

Questions: Ask as many questions possible related to the observations
1. *Do we have more than one system of measurement?*
2. *Is metric tons part of the metric system or English system?*
3. *What is the difference between metric tons and tons?*
4. *How to convert metric tons into pounds?*
5. *What is the relationship between grams and metric tons?*
6. *Should we convert all quantities to metric system or English system?*
7. *How many years does it take for a tree to be considered mature? Is it the same number of years for all trees?*
8. *What mathematical concepts are involved in the problem?*
9. *What is the interpretation of miles per gallon?*

To assess if students understand a lesson, we need to ask them to rephrase or paraphrase the information presented. This strategy will help students to develop their vocabulary, communication skills, and self-assessment, and in essence support their mathematical thinking skills. Anthony and Walshaw express that "high-level mathematical thinking involves making use of formulas, algorithms, and procedures in ways that connect to concepts, understanding, and meanings. Tasks that require students to think deeply about mathematical ideas and connections encourage them to think for themselves instead of always relying on their teacher to lead the way" (Anthony & Walshaw, 2009, p. 13).

As we discussed in this section, questioning is a vital component of problem-solving. Instructors need to promote questioning skills on multiple levels to aid students' self-directed learning and generate their own questions. Both lower order and higher-order questioning skills are needed to make sense of a problem. Table 8.3 shows an example of questions that students can ask themselves to help understand and solve the "Trees and the Environment" problem from Table 8.1.

8.6   MAKING CONNECTIONS

The role of faculty is to guide students on how to make connections between their observations and their prior knowledge by asking relevant questions, listening to others, and communicating their ideas and thoughts. Undergraduate mathematics content should be taught in a relevant and meaningful context, especially in the lower-level math courses, as students can discover links between the new material and everyday life. Chin and Osborne (2008) found that the "guiding assumption of much of the research is that deep thinking and reasoning is fostered through contextualized answering of questions" (p. 3). By doing so, students can incorporate their ideas in context and expand their repertoire, their vision and understanding of the world they are living in. Carnevale and Smith (2013) remark that "in a work environment, mathematical skills need to be contextual and rooted in problem identification, reasoning, estimation, and problem solving" (p. 4).

Instructors aim to design relevant, engaging, and challenging activities to help students develop a deeper understanding of the lesson's concepts, build literacy, and nurture reasoning skills by offering students the necessary tools for problem-solving. Students need to be given the opportunity to explore alternative methods to solving the same problem. As Anthony and Walshaw (2009) indicated, "providing students with multiple representations helps develop both their conceptual understandings and their computational flexibility" (p. 15).

In order to support students' ability to solve problems, mathematics teachers can apply Pólya's principle to guide them. By adopting this approach, students will acquire the necessary strategies to become independent problem-solvers. The following steps are adapted from Pólya's *How to Solve It* (Pólya, 1963). These are suggested steps that a student should take, and questions he/she should ask while solving a problem.

Principles

1. My understanding of the problem

This first principle, understanding the problem, is most of the time overlooked, creating a situation that impedes students from solving the problem, and very often lagging behind on the subject matter. Based on Pólya's suggestions, teachers and/or students should get into the habit of asking questions similar to the following:

- What is the context of the problem?
- What are my observations?
- What are the key words? Do I understand all the words?
- What is the data?
- Can I use a picture, graph, or table to understand/solve the problem?
- What is the problem asking for?
- What connections do I make with the information I gathered?
- Can I estimate the answer to the problem?

2. Devise a plan

Pólya mentions that there are many reasonable ways to solve problems. The skill for choosing an appropriate strategy is best learned by solving many problems. The following is a partial list of the strategies:

- Make the problem simpler.
- Use diagrams or draw a picture.
- Collect data systematically.
- Use variables.
- Find the connection between the data and the unknown.
- Use a formula.
- Solve an equation.
- Work backward.
- Act it out.
- Use cases.
- Use organized lists to find patterns.
- Use graphs.
- Build a model.
- Solve a related problem.
- Estimate.
- Be creative.

3. Carrying out my plan.

This step is usually easier than devising the plan. In general, all you need is care and patience, given that you have the necessary skills. Persist with the plan that you have chosen. If it continues not to work, discard it and choose another. Do not be misled, this is how mathematics is done, even by professionals.

Carrying out my plan of the solution, check each step. Can I see clearly that the step is correct? Can I prove that it is correct? If necessary, devise and use a different plan.

4. Looking back at my work: examine the solution obtained

After I have solved the problem, I think about questions like the following:

- What have I learned?
- What larger generalizations can I make?

Table 8.4 Trees and the Environment: Connections

Connections: Start to answer the questions above and finding how they are related to each other 1. *Connect the metric system and English system: conversion from one system to the other* 2. *Use ratios to solve the problem* 3. *Using scientific notation to write big numbers* 4. *Estimate answers—Round off numbers*

- What insights have I gained into the problem-solving process?
- What related problems can I solve?
- Is there an easier way to solve the problem?
- Can I check the result(s)?
- Are the result(s) making sense in the content of the problem?
- Can I find the solution using a different approach?
- Write in words the solution(s)/conclusion to the problem.

Pólya mentions that much can be gained by taking the time to reflect and look back at what I have done, what worked, and what did not. Doing this will enable me to predict what strategy to use to solve future problems.

Table 8.4 shows an example of connections that students can make based on the observations in Table 8.2 and questions in Table 8.3 to solve the "Trees and the Environment" problem from Table 8.1.

8.7 LISTENING

Little attention has been given to listening as another important component in the learning process, and one of the hardest to acquire. In using lecturing as the dominant model of teaching, the majority of the faculty are expecting students to be proficient in listening skills. While research has shown that we spend 70–80% of our waking hours in some form of communication, 45% of this time is spent listening (Wilt, 1950). Also after a 10-minute oral presentation, the average listener remembers no more than half of what he/she heard, and after 48 hours, this goes down to one-fourth (Lee & Hatesohl 1993). Therefore, the ability for students to remember and be able to apply all the different concepts and ideas discussed in one lecture can be very limited.

Among all the communication skills, listening is at the top of the list. Effective listening improves communication, and this impacts students' performance in their classes and as employees in their jobs. Listening can be described as "Listening is the learned process of receiving, interpreting, recalling, evaluating, and responding to verbal and nonverbal messages" (Jones, 2013; Ridge, 1993). Therefore, there is a need to incorporate strategies and activities in the mathematics content that will explicitly support the growth and expansion of the different stages of this competence. We cannot assume that students will develop this competence by attending hours and hours of presentations; active listening involves more than just hearing. Faculty as well as students need to remain actively aware of the difference between hearing and listening with intention.

8.8   COMMUNICATION

Any activity we are engaged in involves all the different components of the thinking process. Among these components, communication is the one that allows us to deliver our ideas, thoughts, and feelings. We have many ways to engage an audience or ourselves, whether they are by writing, speaking, listening, or reading. Communication is by itself an ability that manifests in a variety of forms, and in order to be as successful as possible, we must develop proficiency in all of these forms. According to Carnevale and Smith (2013), "Communications skills such as reading comprehension, critical thinking, speaking, and active listening are skills that are highly valued in occupations" (p. 10). They also note that "Employers need workers who have mastered reading processes that allow them to locate information and use higher-level thinking strategies to solve problems. Similarly, writing on the job often requires analysis, conceptualization, synthesis and distillation of information and clear articulation of points and proposals" (p. 4).

Our students often find it difficult to express their ideas in any form (orally or in writing) because of their lack of the ability to make connections and ask questions and their limited vocabulary in certain disciplines. Students often complain when asked to write in a mathematics course. There is a false belief that writing only happens in English courses. They are not aware that through writing, they can start organizing their thoughts and learning to realize what they do not understand. Therefore, "Students need to be taught how to communicate mathematically, give sound mathematical explanations, and justify their solutions. Effective teachers encourage their students to communicate their ideas orally, in writing, and by using a variety of representations" (Klerlein & Hervey, 2019).

However, students lack reading comprehension skills, do not read textbooks as much as they used to, and in many instances, they rely on PowerPoint notes, which often consist of formulas and simplified definitions. With this in mind, instructors should aim to create assignments with questions on readings that cover all of the Bloom's Taxonomy cognitive levels (knowledge, comprehension, application, analysis, synthesis, and evaluation), as we discussed in the questioning section, to foster students' comprehension and cognitive skills to mathematical literacy.

8.9   EMOTIONS IN THE LEARNING PROCESS

Emotions play a key role in the learning process, particularly in mathematics. By ignoring the affective domain, there is a high probability that, as teachers, we will not be able to be effective educators. The affective domain is the emotional component of the learning process that has to go together with the cognitive domain, because emotions have a significant impact in the learning process. According to Lawrence and Deepa (2013), "Emotions are the relay stations between sensory input and thinking. When the input is interpreted positively, we are motivated to act and achieve a goal. When the input is interpreted negatively, we do not act and do not learn. Negative emotions can be the cause or the effect of problems with learning". As a result, students need to be aware of their emotions and develop their emotional skills as they are engaging in any learning activity. To become emotionally competent, students need to know how to distinguish their emotional states, through self-observation, and how each state facilitates or impedes actions (learning).

Emotional support is important for students learning mathematics, especially among those who are struggling to understand and apply mathematical concepts to solve problems. Some of the emotional support that faculty can institute to facilitate the development of students' disciplinary literacy include ignoring some errors, providing a safety net to allow for mistakes, and structuring experiences to prevent failure (Bean & Stevens, 2002).

There is a tendency for faculty to ignore students' errors or fail to acknowledge students' contributions when their answers are incorrect in mathematics classes. In a traditional classroom, instructors expect correct responses for the questions they ask. They tend to ignore a student who gives incorrect answers. These students could be placed in two categories: those who do not feel intimidated and have confidence in themselves; and those who feel threatened, embarrassed, and anxious. The students in the second category are more affected by the instructor's attitude. They tend to experience a mixture of emotions such as fear and anger, which will in turn promote a dislike of the subject. A student who experiences these emotions develops a fear of expressing himself/herself publicly, sharing ideas, or answering questions. The student then mistakenly believes that an incorrect answer translates into lack of intelligence.

An important role of instructors as educators is to create a safe classroom environment. Faculty need to promote and incorporate habits of collaboration in the classroom. Students need to learn to respect their peers' opinions and develop constructive criticism. While working in such an environment, students will feel comfortable in analyzing their own errors and verbally share their own ideas. This will provoke a healthy understanding that errors are an important and critical component in any learning environment that will stimulate an inquiry process, giving the opportunity to students to learn through experience. This will eventually encourage students to learn more in depth and engage more in the process of critical thinking in the discipline, and ultimately develop their self-confidence in mathematics.

8.10   Cooperative Learning

Today's world calls for rapid changes and multiple facets of knowledge. Students need to be proficient in a range of knowledge to become successful professionals. The complexity of the modern work environment demands that workers are familiar with the dynamic of working as part of a team, and are able to share that knowledge for a common purpose or goal. We need to stress the importance of supporting students to acquire the skills to cooperate with others. Using different cooperative learning strategies in a mathematics class can improve students learning, indeed "When beginning to work cooperatively, students (and their instructors) are actually learning both to construct mathematical ideas and to cooperate with others in this process. There is an active interplay between the construction of mathematical concepts and the development of cooperative social skills" (Reynolds & Dubinsky, 1995).

To encourage cooperative learning, faculty can introduce diversified methods such as Think-Pair-Share, round table, and many other approaches to support students' ability to work in a team. By working together, students will more likely develop a positive attitude, accountability, ethics, and feedback skills. In addition, they will have the opportunity to actively practice all the skills discussed above. For example, in the think-pair-share activity, students are expected to work in pairs, and each student has to listen when the other is speaking. Students find this activity very difficult as they need to be completely silent while listening to their partner, something we are often not used to doing.

8.11   REFLECTION

A very important component in the thinking process is reflection. It is necessary that faculty support the development of this component, which will teach students to use the higher order of cognition. When engaging in higher-order thinking, students will be able to draw conclusion based on accurate analysis of personal experience and observation, to make decisions and predictions, and to distinguish between right and wrong answers. If students are continuously engaged in reflecting on their individual and cooperative work, this will increase their confidence and help them feel comfortable with applying and practicing the mathematical language.

We can support students to develop their reflection skills by using different strategies. In a math classroom, we should require that every activity includes a reflective component in which students have the opportunity to write, summarize, and share ideas or answers. Other strategies that can be used include journals, learning logs, oral presentations, and discussions within and outside of the classroom.

Sample Lesson Plan/Creating Classroom Routines

We have created a sample lesson plan that starts with a problem that instructors could use to introduce a topic, while following the different ideas introduced and discussed in the chapter. Each idea should be implemented using pedagogical strategies that will allow students to continue developing their communication, listening, and cooperative skills (Table 8.5).

The following are key questions the instructor should reflect on:

1. Do my students possess the necessary skills and knowledge to solve the problem? Do I need to review some material? (Knowing the student population)
2. How do I present this problem to my students?
   For example, start by asking pre-questions:
   - How many plastic bags do you use per week?
   - What do you think happens to your bags when you dispose them?

Table 8.5   Topic: Plastic bags and the Environment

After attending a presentation on the environment, Antonia became curious and interested to know about the world she lives in. She started to research and read about climate change and air and water pollution. She discovered that the 2016 per capita *carbon dioxide emissions from fuel combustion in the U.S. was 15.0 metric tons* (Union of Concerned Scientists [UCS], 2019). *A staggering 20 tons of carbon dioxide is produced each year by the average American* (Jaines, 2018)

Carbon footprint has a harmful effect on the environment, as it impacts global warming. Plastic has a big carbon footprint, as it is just a form of fossil fuel. Our plastic consumption is overwhelming; each year, 100 billion plastic bags are used in the U.S. To produce these, 12 million barrels of oil are utilized (Center for Biological Diversity, n.d.). *In addition to its impact on global warming, plastic pollution is considered one of the most concerning environmental issues. While paper and hard plastics are recycled in the U.S., only 1% of plastic bags are returned for the same purpose* (Center for Biological Diversity, n.d.)

Antonia was then motivated to start a movement. She also actively participated in meetings and conferences to raise awareness about the impact of, and the danger in, continuing with this trend of polluting our planet. In order for Antonia to prepare for her talks and use convincing scientific facts, she raised the following questions and used published data to find possible answers to them:

1. *If each person disposes of two plastics bags per day, how many plastic bags will one person dispose of in a week? A month? A year?*
2. *If a person continues the same trend of plastics bag usage for the next five years, what will be this person's contribution of plastic bags to the landfills over this time?*
3. *What would the yearly percentage decrease of plastic bags be, in the U.S., if instead of using two plastic bags per day, 100,000 people used a tote bag?*
4. *Given that one oil barrel holds 42 liquid gallons, how many gallons of oil are consumed to make the 100 billion plastic bags?*
5. *How many plastic bags* per capita *are disposed of in the U.S., in one year, on average? (U.S. population)*
6. *Why are people still using plastic bags? List three reasons*
7. *What should be my message to invite people to make changes in their lives that will have significant, positive impact on the environment?*

3. Very often, students are stymied when attempting to solve math problems. In the above word problem, what do I think could interfere with students' understanding of the problem?

Table 8.6 can be used by the instructor to organize the different thoughts covering the components of the thinking process: observations, inquiry, and connections. A column is included for the instructor to list misconceptions that he/she foresees students will have. Students will use similar table to work on the problem.

Table 8.6 Organizing my thoughts

List of observations	Vocabulary		Raising questions to make connections	What possible mistakes/misconceptions can students make/have?	Which strategies/action plan will I use to solve the problem?
	English	Math			
1. Fuel combustion is 15.0 metric tons	1. Per capita 2. Carbon dioxide 3. Fossil fuel 4. Global warming 5. Decrease	1. Metric tons 2. Average 3. Percent 4. Liquid gallon 5. Barrel	1. What is the meaning of per capita? 2. What is the population of the country? 3. How many days are in a year? 4. What does the 12 million barrel of oil represent in the problem? 5. How many liquid gallons will be in 2 barrels? In 10 barrels? In 100 barrels? 12 million? 6. What is the impact of my town on the plastic bag pollution? 7. Are there any unknown values? 8. How do I label the unknowns?	1. Confusing 2016 as a value per capita 2. Confusing metric tons and tons 3. Using the wrong unit/ignoring to write the unit in the final answer 4. The place value of a number	1. Write down all my thoughts 2. I break down the problem sentence by sentence 3. Extract from each sentence key word, numerical information or any other observation I feel or think is relevant 4. Start to answer each of the questions I have raised 5. Distinguish "good" and relevant observation/questions for the problem 6. Make connections between the relevant observations/questions and the problem I need to solve 7. Write the mathematical connections using mathematical symbols 8. Use appropriate mathematical concepts to solve the problem 9. Verify if my answers are solutions to the problem 10. Make sure I have included the correct units 11. Write solution/conclusion in the context of the problem
2. Plastic-form of fossil fuel					
3. The number of plastic bags in a year is 100 billion					
4. Twelve million barrels of oil are used to produce 100 billion plastic bags					
5. One percent of plastic bags are returned to be recycled					
6. Two plastic bags per day					
7. One hundred thousand people					
8. One oil barrel holds 42 liquid gallons					

The instructor can ask students the following questions to support them in the process of solving the problem.

4. What is the context of the problem? This is the first observation that the students should make.
    Plastic bags and the environment
5. What mathematical concepts did you use to find the solution to the problem?
    Percent, ratios and proportions, basic operations, tables, unit conversions, scientific notation, place value
6. Are there different ways to answer the questions in the "Plastic bags and the environment" problem?
    In question 1: I can use basic operations, a table, and linear equation (algebraically or graphically).
7. Concept Mapping and Building Vocabulary
    There are different ways to design a diagram to visualize relationship between different concepts. The instructors should give students the freedom to create their own design.
    For the "Plastic bags and the environment" problem, I choose to create a map where the main idea is "metric system" (Fig. 8.1).

The next table is an example of how we can evaluate a concept map using a rubric (Table 8.7).

8.12   CONCLUSION

The approach presented in this chapter is to help mathematics faculty to fulfill the college promise that students will acquire an education that empowers them to be informed citizens and active participants in the process of democracy. The main focus of this approach is "the thinking process", as applied in the discipline and beyond. Mathematics gives us a wonderful opportunity to develop students' abilities in reading comprehension, communication, and collaboration. When faculty frame the math contents in relevant contexts and meaningful ways, they can promote students' active participation in their own learning process and invigorate their development of mathematical literacy. This will also extend students' levels of responsibility, develop their self-confidence, and prepare them to be problem-solvers and decision makers.

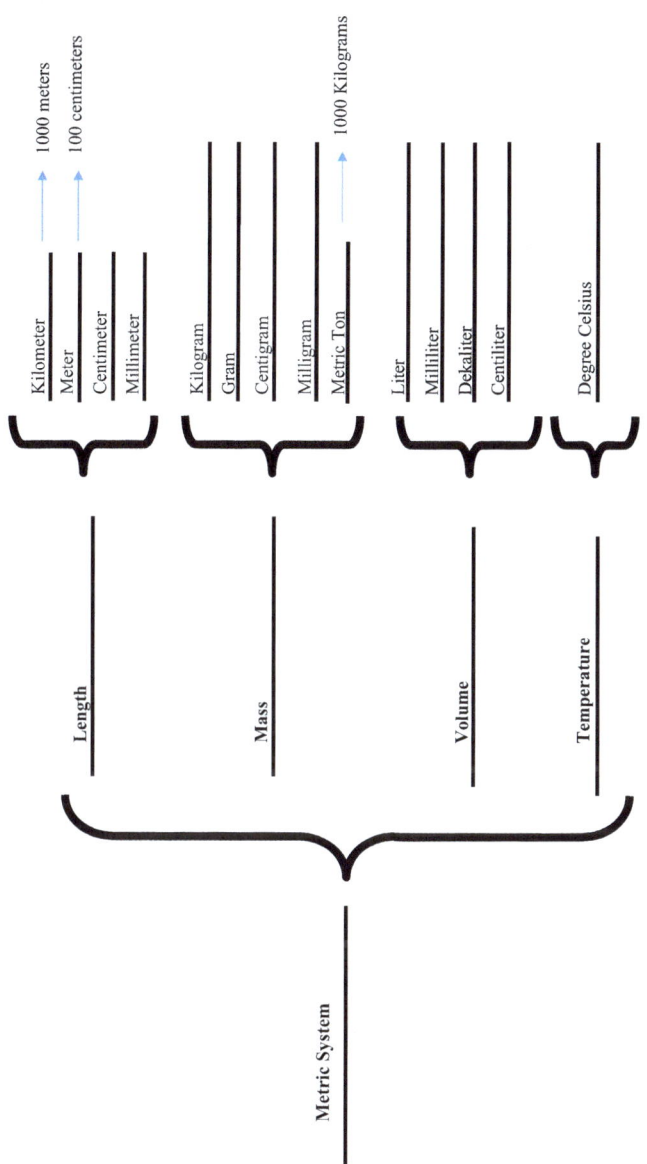

Fig. 8.1 Concept map

Table 8.7   Concept map rubric

Questions	Scores (points)
1. Are the key ideas, concepts, words, processes, algorithms, and theorems included?	25
2. Are all the basic connections drawn?	25
3. Are there sufficient depth and complexity of details?	20
4. Is the concept map presented clearly and creatively?	10
5. Are all the necessary explanations included?	10
6. Are connections to previous concepts included?	10

For faculty to be able to implement this approach to teaching, it is necessary that they actively participate in professional development. To institute a transformation on students' academic and professional performance, instructors need to see their role as educators in a holistic way. Mathematics faculty are not only content experts, but they are also educators who support students' disciplinary literacy development, so that students can be actively and competently partake in the language, thinking, and practices of mathematics. This can be done through pedagogical professional development, which offers faculty the opportunity to engage in a reflective process about their teaching responsibilities and their own professional growth.

REFERENCES

Anderson, L. W., & Krathwohl, D. R. (2001). *A taxonomy for learning, teaching, and assessing* (Abridged ed.). Boston, MA: Allyn and Bacon.

Anthony, G., & Walshaw, M. (2009). *Effective pedagogy in mathematics* (Vol. 19). Belley, France: International Academy of Education.

Bean, T. W., & Stevens, L. P. (2002). Scaffolding reflection for preservice and inservice teachers. *Reflective Practice, 3*(2), 205–218.

Bloom, B. S. (1956). *Taxonomy of educational objectives, handbook I: The cognitive domain.* New York: David McKay Co.

Carnevale, A. P., & Smith, N. (2013). *Workplace basics: The skills employees need and employers want.* Taylor & Francis.

CCMIT. (n.d.). *Improving observation skills.* Retrieved from https://ccmit.mit.edu/observation/

Center for Biological Diversity. (n.d.). *10 facts about single-use plastic bags.* Retrieved from https://www.biologicaldiversity.org/programs/population_and_sustainability/sustainability/plastic_bag_facts.html

Chin, C., & Osborne, J. (2008). Students' questions: A potential resource for teaching and learning science. *Studies in Science Education, 44*(1), 1–39.

Communication in the real world: An introduction to communication. (2016). University of Minnesota Library Publishing. Retrieved from https://open. umn.edu/opentextbooks/textbooks/communication-in-the-real-world-an-introduction-to-communication-studies

Flavell, J. H. (1976). Metacognitive aspects of problem solving. In *The nature of intelligence* (pp. 231–235). Hillsdale, NJ: Lawrence Erlbaum.

Jaines, K. (2018)..*Effects of carbon footprint*. Retrieved from https://sciencing. com/effects-of-carbon-footprint-4984464.html

Jones, R. (2013). *Communication in the real world: An introduction to communication studies*. The Saylor Foundation.

Klerlein, K., & Hervey, S. (2019). *Mathematics as a complex problem-solving activity*. Retrieved from https://www.generationready.com/mathematics-as-a-complex-problem-solving-activity/

Lawrence, A. S., & Deepa, T. (2013). Emotional intelligence and academic achievement of high school students in Kanyakumari District. *Online Submission, 3*(2), 101–107.

Lee, K., & Hateshol, D. (1993). *Listening: Our most used communications skill*. Retrieved from https://extension2.missouri.edu/cm150

Lester, F. K. (1982). Building bridges between psychological and mathematics education research on problem solving. In *Mathematical problem solving* (pp. 55–85). Philadelphia, PA. The Franklin Institute Press.

McComas, W. F., & Abraham, L. (2004). Asking more effective questions. *Rossier School of Education*, 1–16.

Montessori, M., & Holmes, H. W. (1912). *The Montessori method: Scientific pedagogy as applied to child education in "the children's houses"*. New York: Frederick A. Stokes Company.

OECD. (2016). *PISA 2015 results (Volume I): Excellence and equity in education*.

Pólya, G. (1963). *Induction and analogy in mathematics*. Princeton, NJ: Princeton University Press.

Renaud, R. D., & Murray, H. G. (2007). The validity of higher-order questions as a process indicator of educational quality. *Research in Higher Education, 48*(3), 319–351.

Reynolds, S. D. S., & Dubinsky, E. (1995). *A practical guide to cooperative learning in collegiate mathematics*. Mathematical Association of America (MAA).

Ridge, A. (1993). A perspective of listening skills. In *Perspectives on listening* (pp. 1–14). Norwood, NJ: Ablex Publishing.

Rowe, M. B. (1974). Wait-time and rewards as instructional variables, their influence on language, logic, and fate control: Part one-wait-time. *Journal of Research in Science Teaching, 11*(2), 81–94.

Sammons, L. (2011). *Building mathematical comprehension: Using literacy strategies to make meaning* (Teacher created materials). Huntington Beach, CA: Shell Education.

Schneider, W., & Artelt, C. (2010). Metacognition and mathematics education. *ZDM, 42*(2), 149–161.

Silver, E. A. (1982). Knowledge organization and mathematical problem solving. In *Mathematical problem solving: Issues in research* (pp. 15–25). Philadelphia, PA. The Franklin Institute Press.

Stahl, R. J. (1994). *Using "think-time" and "wait-time" skillfully in the classroom.* ERIC Clearinghouse.

Union of Concerned Scientists. (2019). *Each country's share of CO2 emissions.* Retrieved from https://www.ucsusa.org/resources/each-countrys-share-co2-emissions

Verschaffel, L., De Corte, E., Lasure, S., Van Vaerenbergh, G., Bogaerts, H., & Ratinckx, E. (1999). Learning to solve mathematical application problems: A design experiment with fifth graders. *Mathematical Thinking and Learning, 1*(3), 195–229.

Wilt, M. E. (1950). A study of teacher awareness of listening as a factor in elementary education. *The Journal of Educational Research, 43*(8), 626–636.

World Wildlife Fund. (n.d.). *Deforestation and forest degradation.* Retrieved from https://www.worldwildlife.org/threats/deforestation-and-forest-degradation

INDEX

© The Author(s) 2020
J. C. But (ed.), *Teaching College-Level Disciplinary Literacy*,
https://doi.org/10.1007/978-3-030-39804-0

Printed by Printforce, the Netherlands